J. Dudley Haynes

'On an eminence…'

Celebrating 150 years of Framlingham College

'On an eminence...'

CELEBRATING 150 YEARS OF FRAMLINGHAM COLLEGE

Mark Robinson & Michael Cooke

III

THIRD MILLENNIUM
PUBLISHING, LONDON

'On an eminence…': Celebrating 150 years of Framlingham College

© Framlingham College and Third Millennium Publishing Limited 2014

First published in 2014 by Third Millennium Publishing Limited,
a subsidiary of Third Millennium Information Limited.

2–5 Benjamin Street
London
United Kingdom
EC1M 5QL
www.tmiltd.com

ISBN: 978 1 906507 92 3

British Library Cataloguing in Publication Data

A CIP catalogue record for this book is available from the British Library.

Authors	Mark Robinson and Michael Cooke
Project Manager	Neil Burkey
Design	Matthew Wilson
Production	Bonnie Murray
Reprographics	Studio Fasoli, Verona, Italy
Printing	Gorenjski Tisk, Slovenia

CONTENTS

FOREWORD

I am delighted to present this splendid volume to the very many enthusiasts for Framlingham College, be they Governors, staff, parents, former and current pupils or just well informed third parties. All in their way contribute to the pages that follow.

When Prince Albert died in 1861, in a positive spirit London purveyors of GUINNESS® decided their beverage could be mixed with champagne and the resulting concoction, 'Black Velvet' should be drunk in honour of the memory of the Prince Consort. It was good to see the History department of Framlingham College raising a similar toast before the Prince's statue in preparation for their labours in writing and editing this great work. As a long term player in English Heritage I am delighted to see Framlingham Castle maintained so well and, as Chairman of Governors of the College since 2001, I have an even closer interest in the College that faces it across the mere. It is a pleasure to attend occasions great and small there, whether they be rugby games down on Lords, theatrical productions in the fine Headmaster Porter Theatre, or concerts in the wonderful venue of St Michael's parish church. It

may take students some time to appreciate fully the legacy that led to the founding of the school and the glorious surroundings in which it is set, but time and again one meets people who have spent a short or long time here, and they are drawn back by an abiding affection. I warmly commend this book to them as a record both of the founding of the College and a survey particularly of the recent past, and I hope it will give them much pleasure in the reading of it, even more so if they are able to raise their own toast in Black Velvet!

Andrew Fane, Chairman of Governors

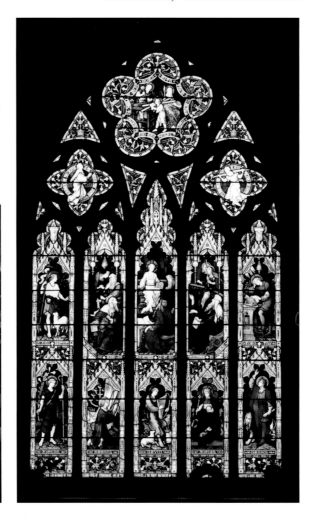

INTRODUCTION

The centenary of the founding of Framlingham was celebrated by the opening of the Athlone Hall by Queen Victoria and Albert's granddaughter, Princess Alice, the 125th saw the opening of Borrett's, and the 150th sees the 'reinvigoration of the heart of the College', with major building work to enhance facilities behind the old mock-Gothic façade. For some reason, histories of Framlingham have come out at sixty-year intervals, with John Booth's definitive record of the first sixty years, and Bob Gillett's characteristically dry take on the second sixty. Brandeston Hall has more recently been covered by Norman Porter and John Maulden has written on the College's late twentieth-century links with the Society of Old Framlinghamians.

However, somewhere between the 120th and the 180th anniversaries it seems fitting to publish a book of a slightly different kind, more on the lines of Sellar & Yeatman's *1066 and All That*, a history of what the authors and more recent generations of Framlinghamians can remember about their time at the College.

Many O.Fs have made remarkable written, photographic and artistic contributions to this book, along with a wealth of fascinating artefacts. As well as the usual suspects, Messrs Porter, Pitcher and Martin, Professor Marsh, and Drs McGuire and Bull were particularly quick to respond to our request for suitable materials, while others were equally prompt to let us know that their memories of their time at the College were too 'scarce and uninteresting' to mention. True

to form some Framlinghamians promised much, but delivered nothing, while others were horribly late with their essays – we might sigh like the Protestant martyr John Bland, who wrote of a former pupil officiating at his trial for heresy in the 1550s: 'though I was never able to do him good, yet once I was his tutor'.

The authors have also struggled with the chaotic state of the College archives – like the Foulstons searching on Southwold beach, turning up small pieces of amber amongst a mass of pebbles, and the O.F. diaspora means that materials are still coming in from all over the world. We hope this book at least stems the tide of loss and provides a fitting record of the College's recent past: perhaps the 150th anniversary will spark a new interest in collating and organising the archives.

Inevitably many people will find themselves omitted from this record and the authors have faced a difficult task of selection and interpretation. When Robinson and Gallagher wrote their seminal history of the British Empire in 1953 they tried to move away from a Eurocentric perspective: Robinson and Cooke have been more narrowly Framlocentric, but we are only too well aware, as Sir Walter Raleigh wrote in the Tower shortly before his execution, that 'whosoever in writing

a modern History, shall follow truth too near the heels, it may haply strike out his teeth'. Even so, we hope most readers will enjoy this history. We have tried to capture the essence of the place, we've tried not to be boring and we trust that the combination of Robinsonian hyperbole and Cookeian litotes has produced a golden mean.

Mark Robinson and **Michael Cooke**

Opposite: The College, 1912.

SECTION I:
MOCK-GOTHIC

PRINCE ALBERT:
MEMORIA DIGNUS

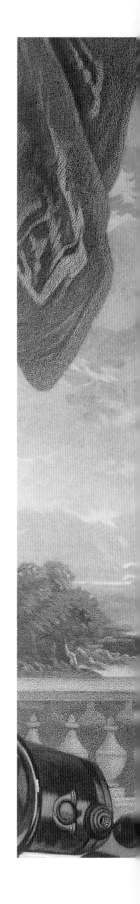

'Beyond all titles, and a household name,
Hereafter, thro' all times, Albert the Good.'

– Alfred, Lord Tennyson

There may be something fortuitously appropriate about the school founded at Framlingham having been called the Albert Memorial College. Those who know little about Framlingham College, as it now is, may be surprised at what they discover beneath the mock-Gothic façade of a minor public school. The same may be true of many who think that Albert, Prince Consort, was merely the father of Victoria's children, the paterfamilias of a rather dull family, a strait-laced German who somehow brought the Christmas tree to England. Albert deserves better than this: perhaps he should be Albert 'the Artichoke', richer and richer as one peels off the layers, and how Sir Robert Peel would have enjoyed any punning association. How the draped Victorian piano legs would have blushed at any such exposure. Indeed, Albert's most recent biographer, Jules Stewart, boldly claims: 'Very few have made such a permanent mark on British Society. If any one person can be credited for laying the foundation of Modern Britain, it is Albert.' He created the modern British monarchy, was a proponent of British science, inspired the Great Exhibition, honoured war heroes while working for peace and was a cultured man, but he could

also play with his children in the nursery and ensure Victoria was amused at night. Often cold-shouldered by the British establishment, he devoted himself utterly to a whole host of genuinely good causes in the vanguard of 'Victorian' social concerns: for the younger son of a broken marriage in a minor German duchy, Albert did pretty well in his 42 years.

EARLY LIFE AND MARRIAGE

'You cannot imagine how delightful it is to be married. I could not have dreamed that anyone could be so happy in this world as I am.'

– Queen Victoria to her cousin
Victoria Augusta Antoinetta

Albert Francis Charles Augustus Emmanuel was born on 26 August 1819, second son of Ernest, Duke of Saxe-Coburg-Gotha. More handsome than his father or elder brother, he was his mother's favourite and also later subject to scurrilous and anti-Semitic suggestions of illegitimacy. The rumour circulated was based on the fact that Albert looked and acted so very differently from his brother, Ernest, and that his mother, Louise,

His Royal Highness Albert, Prince Consort of Great Britain and Knight of the Most Noble Order of the Garter, Duke of Saxony and Prince of Coburg and Gotha, idealised in his uniform as Colonel of the Rifle Brigade in 1859 by Franz Xaver Winterhalter.

later had an affair with a young officer, Alexander von Hanstein, whom she subsequently married after divorcing the philandering old Duke. It was somewhat unkindly speculated, therefore, that this could not have been her first affair and that Albert was really the son of Baron von Mayern, a chamberlain of Jewish origin in the Coburg ducal household. Like the authors of this volume, Edgar Feuchtwanger, in *Albert and Victoria*, suggests otherwise: 'This seems unlikely, for Louise had probably not yet begun to stray when she became pregnant with her second child at the end of 1818.'

Albert's health was always frail, but this did not stop him throwing himself into physical as well as intellectual activity. He was thus to be very different indeed from many of his relatives, as Victoria was from her Hanoverian forebears. Albert was brought up a strict Lutheran, with a strong sense of duty as well as a constant desire to be active. At the age of 11, he wrote in his diary: 'I intend to train myself to be a good and useful man.' He did not know then that Victoria, born on 24 May 1819 and thus also aged 11 in 1830, simply said when she realised that she might be queen: 'I will be good.' Although a number of dynastic planners saw the possibility of a future marriage between them, Albert did not visit England until 1836 when he was 16 and, although deprived of his mother from the age of five (she was much younger than the Duke, and they separated in 1824), he otherwise had a happy childhood in Coburg, always being close to his brother Ernest and loving the Schloss where he was brought up. Privately tutored and then spending short periods at various German universities, Albert acquired a rounded education and the accomplishments of a gentleman, developing a particular love of music. Such was the young man who arrived on his second visit to England in 1839, by which time Victoria had been Queen for two years and was in search of a husband.

The day of 10 October 1839 was a memorable one for Victoria: she awoke to find some windows smashed at Windsor by a madman, but then received a letter saying that Ernest and Albert were arriving that evening; they had had a rough crossing of the Channel, but enough of Albert's good looks survived for Victoria to write in her journal: 'It was with some emotion that I beheld Albert – who is beautiful.' She had a chat with Lord Melbourne, and by 15 October Albert had been summoned to the

'A Cabinet Lecture' – Queen Victoria with that worldly Whig Lord Melbourne, in whose company she allegedly played draughts, while he explained the advantages of a good match and the complexities of the Constitution.

Blue Closet, where he accepted Victoria's proposal. On 10 February 1840 they were married in the Chapel Royal at St James's. After the celebrations, at 4pm they left for Windsor where an exhausted Victoria recorded: 'Albert sat on a footstool by my side, & his excessive love and affection gave me feelings of heavenly love and happiness I never could have hoped to have felt before!' In reality there was nothing buttoned-up or strait-laced about these 'Victorians'.

After the happiness of the wedding, one did not need to be Hogarth to know that there would inevitably be a number of tensions which would prove more or less challenging to resolve. The monarchy had changed significantly since Queen Anne's day, and simply

The Royal Family in 1846, by Franz Xaver Winterhalter.

'HRH Field Marshal Chancellor Prince Albert taking the Pons Asinorum' – Punch in 1848 applauds Albert's achievement in modernising the Cambridge University curriculum.

choosing a title for Albert was an initial problem, while much more significant was the question of what his role in British public life would be. This overlapped with more delicate questions within the Royal Household over whether Queen or father would have the final say in family issues, and over the manner in which Victoria would do business with ministers more privately. The title 'Prince Consort' might be quickly settled, but Albert was determined not to be a mere flunkey in his own house and not to be kept out of a major role in British politics and society; the latter determination in particular would prove to be a long and continual battle.

The battle within the household was won first. Although Victoria was a feisty lady, she was also an admirably practical one. Her love and admiration made it easier for her to work with Albert, and her distaste for politics and paperwork combined with his willingness to take on the burdens soon had the two of them working at adjoining desks, and Albert's role steadily increased. Victoria, who never supported women's suffrage, later remarked simply, and without irony, that women were not meant to govern (a view apparently not shared by the College Governors in 1994). In 1841 began the series of nine babies she bore, and pregnancy, anxieties about births, and post-natal depression all took their toll: although she remained the ceremonial head of the government and her views always mattered, she

steadily took more and more account of dear Albert's opinions. The power that Uncle Leopold, King of the Belgians, and his man of affairs, Baron Stockmar, hoped that Albert would have, he did finally begin to exercise, but only after a fretful period. Victoria's former governess, Baroness Lehzen, was removed from the household, the children would be brought up as Albert and Victoria jointly wished, and such power as remained to the monarchy would in reality be exercised by the 'King without a Crown'. Prime Ministers no doubt had the greatest power, but they, like Whig and Tory governments, would come and go. Here was an opportunity for Albert to play a major role.

A.N. Wilson writes that in 1840 'Prince Albert's arrival in England brought qualities of seriousness and intelligence to public life which are almost without parallel'. He aimed to win the respect and the love of the Queen and of the nation, pursuing an extraordinary social and cultural crusade that has become his greatest legacy.

EQUITY, ENLIGHTENMENT AND EDUCATION

Albert's early actions aimed to detach the monarchy from party politics. Victoria was strongly attached to the Whig Lord Melbourne, but the Tory Sir Robert Peel would come into office in 1841, and whatever the Queen's private views, the impartiality of the Crown's role steadily became clearer, even if later Albert would

'Prince Albert "At Home,"' – Punch in 1847.

work doggedly but discreetly for Peel in what he saw as the national interest during the Corn Law crisis. Meanwhile an assassination attempt when the Queen was in her first pregnancy helped through a measure that would have made Albert regent in the event of the Queen's death. Albert's first public speech in June 1840 was to an anti-slavery society, and his description of the slave trade as 'the blackest stain upon civilized Europe' was an omen of things to come. In every area Albert seems to have supported rational and enlightened programmes, whether sorting out the running of Buckingham Palace or attempting (in vain) to lighten the gloom of the English 'Victorian' Sunday.

Despite the occasional assassination attempts, the Queen and Albert loved to be out and about, and they were generously received on most occasions, even during serious social and Chartist unrest. Apart from a brief visit by George IV, no reigning monarch had been to Scotland since the 17th century, and Victoria and Albert's extensive tour of 1842 was a great success: they would return in 1844, and Balmoral would be purchased in 1847. The couple would have visited Ireland in the 1840s too (potato famine and all) if ministers had not advised against it. In 1843 Osborne House became their home on the Isle of Wight, accessible now by train and steam ferry. Visits to such residences as Balmoral and Osborne cemented royal popularity in the localities, and the Royal Family's links to Scotland in particular remain to the present day, the wrong sort of Salmond's current leapings towards independence notwithstanding.

Albert may have enjoyed all this, though he continued to detest any sea travel involved, but he always yearned to do more, and his role in wider areas of science, culture and educational reform in England also began in the 1840s. Albert's close relationship with Peel, serving a second term as Prime Minister from 1841 to 1846, greatly helped and encouraged him here. Albert became Chairman of the Fine Arts Royal Commission, giving him contact with leading artists and musicians, and in 1847 he was elected Chancellor of Cambridge University, a body narrowly concerned with theology, mathematics and the Classics. Albert played a major role in modernising Cambridge,

THE INDUSTRIOUS BOY.
"Please to Remember the Exposition."

encouraging focus on areas of the sciences and the humanities already studied at German universities. Robert Rhodes James writes that Albert was not only the greatest Chancellor Cambridge ever had, but he was 'a pioneer of the principles of enlightened scholarship and of the love of learning for its own sake'. Cambridge should fit men to play an active role in society, but this meant a broadening and deepening of the education offered there.

Moreover Albert was far from being concerned merely with the elite. He was keen to make art available to all in exhibitions at Kensington Palace and Westminster Hall; he encouraged art colleges, including what became the Royal College of Art; in the age of Chartism he was sympathetic to social reform; and his support of Peel over the Corn Laws reflected his belief that rich landowners should not prosper at the expense of the poor. Many of these strands fed into the Great Exhibition of which Albert was the chief instigator.

'This empty hat my awkward case bespeaks,
These blank subscription-lists explain my fear;
Days follow days, and weeks succeed to weeks,
But very few contributors appear.'

This Punch *cartoon shows Prince Albert raising money for the Great Exhibition in 1850. So determined was he to ensure it was a success that he was more than happy to accept any donation, no matter how small.*

Raising the ribs of the transept roof, Illustrated London News, *14 December 1850.*

THE GREAT EXHIBITION, 1 MAY–11 OCTOBER 1851

'To foster the arts, to promote the extension of industry and commerce, to knit nation and nation in the bonds of universal brotherhood, was a noble object for Prince Albert to engage in.'
– Joseph Paxton

Here Britain and its Empire, along with other nations, could share the latest developments in design and technology with the many. It was Albert who brought the best out of men such as Henry Cole (visionary and innovator, who amongst other things was responsible for introducing a cataloguing system in the Public Record Office, pioneering the Penny Post in 1840 with Rowland Hill and inventing the Christmas card) and Joseph Paxton (working-class genius, friend and landscape-architect of the sixth Duke of Devonshire, who designed the 'Chatsworth Stove' – the largest glass building in the world) and against a background of cynicism and criticism, the Prince Consort and his supporters pressed forward to create the great Crystal Palace.

It was located right in the middle of London in Hyde Park and was built at a total cost of £169,998, which included all manner of internal fittings as well as re-landscaping. Crystal Palace was both a work of art and a technological marvel. It was made of a million square feet of glass covering an area of 19 acres, supported by a series of 72-foot girders in the central aisle, and a succession of vertical columns on both flanks. These columns were hollow to enable them to transport rain water from the roof away from the building, along with any internal condensation. The total length of piping in the building and foundation used for this purpose was 39 miles.

The Exhibition featured a staggering 100,000 exhibits and was visited by six million people in just six months. Twenty-five thousand season tickets were sold in advance at three guineas for men and two guineas for women and, for the first ten days after the opening, tickets were priced at one pound. Thereafter admission was reduced to five shillings and from 24 May visits from Mondays to Thursdays came down to just one shilling and on Fridays and Saturdays to just two-and-six. The result of this was that unlike the Millennium Dome 150 years later, the Great Exhibition made a magnificent profit of £185,437 – money used to buy the Kensington

Left: *Victoria, Albert and family at the opening of the Great Exhibition by H.C. Selous.*

Below: *'The Earth is the Lord's and the fullness thereof' – the Exhibition's motto, chosen by Albert. Coloured lithograph by Augustus Butler.*

lands on which the permanent collections would reside. Its legacy was the Science Museum, the Natural History Museum, the Victoria and Albert Museum, the Royal Geographical Society, the Albert Hall, and the Imperial College of Science and Technology.

Amongst the exhibitors were Garretts of Leiston, Ransome & Parsons of Ipswich and an African elephant apparently from Bury St Edmunds! The clock in Framlingham College's central tower had previously featured at the Exhibition and won a gold medal there for its makers, Cook and Son of York.

Elizabeth Garrett Anderson (1836–1917) and her sister were taken around the Great Exhibition by their uncle, Richard Garrett (the sixth), who not surprisingly made an excellent guide. The experience clearly had a profound and lasting effect on Britain's first female doctor: 'we can picture them,' wrote her daughter Louisa in her biography, 'keen sightseers, full skirts

billowing over crinolines, poke bonnets with lace behind and roses under the brims, shawls draped on their shoulders and each with a dainty parasol in one mittened hand while the other clasped the money. To the end of her life, as she strolled across Hyde Park, Elizabeth would say: "the exhibition buildings came as far as this" or "the glass covered that elm".'

Martin Tupper's 'Hymn of the Crystal Palace' summed it up thus:

> For it is a glorious teaching,
> Albert, thou hast taught mankind,
> Greatly to perfection reaching,
> And enlarging heart and mind;
> Stirring us, and stirring others,
> Thus to do the best we can
> And with all the zeal of brothers
> Help the Family of Man!

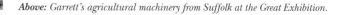
Above: *Garrett's agricultural machinery from Suffolk at the Great Exhibition.*

MILITARY REFORM AND THE VICTORIA CROSS

Albert's international perspective on the 'Family of Man' would also prove a healthy corrective to any incipient jingoism in Victorian England. He would risk unpopularity with the officer class by supporting the abolition of duelling in the Army in 1844, and he would do all he could to prevent troubled relations with Russia declining into the Crimean War in 1854. His only thanks for this was a torrent of abuse from the popular press which portrayed him as a disloyal foreigner involved in a Coburg conspiracy against British interests. Still, once war was declared, Albert proved far more active than most ministers in his concern over the state of the armed forces. He proposed a new medal, open to all ranks, to be awarded for supreme valour in the face of the enemy: this Victoria Cross (VC), later to be won by three Framlinghamians in the Great War, was conceived, instituted and even designed by the Prince Consort himself.

Albert would champion the breech-loading rifle long before it was generally adopted; he would support 'Clemency' Canning against those desiring revenge after the Indian Mutiny of 1857; he would advocate restraint in any support of Napoleon III's military intervention in northern Italy in 1859; and he would inspect new buildings at Sandhurst in November 1861, a month before he died. In his final illness, he defused a serious risk of Britain being drawn in on the Confederate side in the American Civil War: a British ship, the *Trent*, had been boarded by Federal officers, and British reaction endangered relations with the government of the Union states. Nine years later Bismarck would create a war by altering a royal telegram; Albert, by royal amendment of a ministerial protest, prevented one!

The VCs and citations of three Old Framlinghamians at the back of the College Chapel: 'while the light fails on a winter's afternoon, in a secluded chapel history is now and England'.

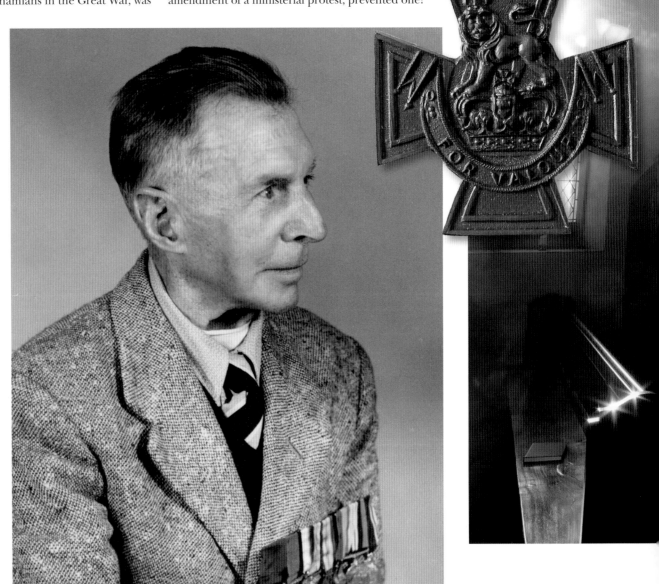

Far right: *The original Royal Warrant for the Victoria Cross stated that the award should be: 'ordained with a view to place all persons on a perfectly equal footing in relation to eligibility for the Decoration, that neither rank, nor long service, nor wounds, nor any other circumstance or condition whatsoever, save the merit of conspicuous bravery shall be held to establish a sufficient claim to the honour'.*

Right: *Major W.H. Hewitt (OF, 1894–1900) after the war with his VC and other medals.*

Black Velvet, made from champagne and GUINNESS®, was first introduced in 1861. In mourning for the death of Prince Albert, husband of Queen Victoria, the barman in Brookes Club, London announced that even the champagne should be put into mourning and added GUINNESS® Extra stout to the champagne.

Far left: 'Anyone for Blackers?' Historians Robinson, Cooke and Marvell in 2011 raise a glass in time-honoured tradition to commemorate the 150th anniversary of the death of Prince Albert 'the Good'.

Left: This photo was taken at the GUINNESS® storehouse in Dublin.

A NATION IN 'BLACK VELVET' AND A FITTING MEMORIAL

Only 40 in 1859, Albert became increasingly ill in the last two years of his life. His favourite daughter, Vicky, had married Prince Frederick of Prussia, and Albert missed her greatly. The strain of his ceaseless round of activities gradually took its toll and Victoria became more and more worried about him – the diary entries about his poor health became almost continuous. Although he was a much more popular figure by now, he seems not to have realised the extent of the change, and he became more melancholic as he grew more ill. After an arduous visit to Ireland in August and September 1861, he had to deal with his eldest son's ill-judged amorous flirtation with an actress called Nellie Clifden, who proved far from discreet. By December he was finally succumbing to illness and exhaustion: the family gathered at Windsor as what at first seemed a severe case of influenza turned out to be typhoid. He died on 14 December 1861, leaving Victoria and her children distraught, and a nation in mourning.

Not always appreciated in life, in death Albert was eulogised partly out of respect for the Queen, who would mourn for another 40 years before she herself was buried beside him at Windsor, and partly because the breadth and visionary nature of his interests encouraged memorials and statues and the dedication of institutions to him. Framlingham is only one of a whole cohort of such institutions, and the statue at the front of the College (made by Joseph Durham – paid for by Sir Thomas Lucas, Governor and Founder, at a cost in excess of £1,000 – representing the Prince in the robes of the Great Master of the Most Honourable Order of the Bath) has its counterparts from Cambridge to Coburg, from Salford to Sydney and from Birkenhead to Bombay.

The Countess of Athlone with Major Podd, R.W. Kirkman and the Earl, 1949.

Left: Prince Edward and the Countess of Wessex visiting the College in 2006.

Right: Statues of Prince Albert in Hyde Park (right) and Framlingham (far right).

Other colleges may have mixed feelings about their founders, but the men who assembled in 1862 to plan a college at Framlingham could hardly have made a more felicitous choice. Albert can look over towards the Castle as he once looked out from the Rosenau in Coburg: he had much to be proud of in his career, but he would have been happy to be associated with the aspirant Middle-Class College, as well as to witness his granddaughter, Princess Alice of Athlone, so graciously visiting Framlingham in 1949, 1964 and 1975, and more recently his great-great-great grandson, Prince Edward, along with the Countess of Wessex, coming to the College in 2006.

In the year in which Karl Marx and Friedrich Engels had launched their *Communist Manifesto* and seen the future as class conflict, Albert had said to the Society for Improving the Condition of the Labouring Classes:

> Depend upon it, the interests of classes too often contrasted are identical, and it is only ignorance which prevents their uniting for each other's advantage. To dispel that ignorance, to show how man can help man, notwithstanding the complicated state of civilised society, ought to be the aim of every philanthropic person.

It is, perhaps, a better vision of the classless society and one which, as the Albert Middle-Class College fades into history, its successor can surely still wholeheartedly embrace.

2

GREAT EXPECTATIONS, 1864–1939

*'The children not yet borne with gladness shall
Thy pious actions into memorye call.'*

The inscription on Sir Robert Hitcham's tomb in the parish church showed remarkable foresight in 1636, as generations of Framlinghamians have benefited from his legacy. Many former pupils and benefactors have also wonderfully supported the College, enabling it to develop into the splendid institution it is today.

THE FOUNDATION

There was a long-term need for better education in Suffolk and the death of the Prince Consort, 'Albert the Good', in 1861 was taken as the opportunity to do something about it. The College was to be the Suffolk memorial to Prince Albert, which was appropriate, as he had once visited Suffolk and had expressed his concern about the lack of educational establishments in agricultural counties. Consequently, when it was founded, the College was known as the Albert Memorial College or the Albert Middle-Class College. *Studio sapientia crescit* (Through zeal wisdom grows) was chosen as the school motto, the original armorial bearings of the school were: 'Sable, a chevron between three crowns Or', and 'The boys [wore] a black School cap, with the arms in gold'.

The individuals most involved in the setting up of the school were Sir Edward Kerrison, Richard Garrett and the Earl of Stradbroke. The land on which the College was to be built was originally part of the Castle estate, left by Sir Robert Hitcham in 1636 to Pembroke Hall, Cambridge, and a charter was granted by Queen Victoria in 1864. The architect was Frederick Peck of Furnival's Inn, London (who just happened to be Richard Garrett's son-in-law!) and the design an interesting example of Victorian mock-Gothic, an engaging contrast with the genuine medieval castle across the mere. Peck's design for Trent College was very similar.

The Albert Middle-Class College in Suffolk.

22

Revd W.W. Bird and College, c.1875.

The Fram Flyer, with the College crest on the front.

FRAMLINGHAM CASTLE

FRAMLINGHAM

IT'S QUICKER BY RAIL

FULL INFORMATION FROM L·N·E·R OFFICES AND AGENCIES

The purpose of the school was quite clearly laid down in Garrett's correspondence: 'The Institution is designed to afford a practical education, at a small cost, adapted to the needs of the middle class, and calculated to be of utmost advantage to Young Men destined for agriculture or business generally. It will be in connection with the Church of England, certain exemptions being made to the children of Dissenters.'

The choice of Framlingham for the site for the College was surely swayed not only by the available land, but by the fortuitous arrival of the railway in 1859. The branch line, which connects with the main line from London to Lowestoft at Wickham Market, meant that prospective pupils could access Framlingham from a much wider hinterland than would otherwise have been the case. The impact of the railway locally was very significant for agriculture and local business, not to mention two fine public houses, the Railway Inn and Station Hotel.

Like the College the railway would evolve: from the East Suffolk Railway through the Great Eastern to the London and North Eastern Railway. In the 20th century this would live up to its sobriquet, the 'Late but Never Early Railway' (LNER), and British Rail would

FRAMLINGHAM CASTLE

Framlingham Castle is one of the finest examples of a medieval 'keepless' castle in England. With its 12th-century curtain wall, magnificent gate-tower and 12 further mural towers, Framlingham was the chief seat of the Earls and Dukes of Norfolk (sic) for well over 400 years. From its formative developments in stone in the early 12th century, through its slighting in 1173–5 and re-development from *c.*1190 into its present form, this imposing edifice reflected its owners' might, enclosing the residential buildings befitting the status of such aristocratic families as the Bigods, the Mowbrays and the Howards. In the late 15th century, 'it could and did act as the political focus for the entire region – a court in miniature' (Roger Virgoe).

As the country moved away from the Wars of the Roses (1455–85) into a period of relative peace and prosperity under the Tudors, the need for such strongholds amongst the once 'over-mighty' nobility was diminished. As a result, from the early 16th century the Howards attempted to bring this emphatically medieval structure up to date with a number of red-brick additions. These included windows, a new causeway, surrounds of the coat-of-arms above the main gateway and, most amusingly, a series of elaborate Tudor chimneys impertinently perched on top of the ancient mural towers.

Framlingham remained the centre of the ducal estates until the Howards, in search of greater comfort and ostentatious display, completed their new palace at Kenninghall in 1525. Even then it was at Framlingham

Tudor chimney.

Castle that Mary Tudor was proclaimed Queen in 1553: 'the only successful rebellion in Tudor England' (C.S.L. Davies). In 1572 Framlingham's decline was accelerated with the execution of Thomas Howard, fourth Duke of Norfolk, for treason, and from the 1580s it was downgraded to a prison for religious recusants.

The Castle was subsequently bought by Sir Robert Hitcham before being bequeathed to Pembroke Hall, Cambridge, in 1636. It was neglected thereafter and most of its interior buildings were pulled down. Fortunately it has since been resurrected to something approaching its former glories and visitors can enjoy the wonderful views from the wall-walk across the mere to the College. Generations of Framlinghamians used to be able to visit the Castle gratis simply by flaunting their College ties, though sadly now the increased efficiency of English Heritage has all but raised the drawbridge on this time-honoured tradition.

View of the Castle from the College over the mere.

COLLEGE FOUNDERS

Sir Edward Clarence Kerrison, Second Baronet (1821–86)
Possibly the most important of the College's founders was Sir Edward Kerrison. He was the eldest son of a general who fought at Waterloo and in 1852 he succeeded his father as MP for Eye, overseeing the creation of a branch railway line to his constituency. Clearly the apophthegm *noblesse oblige* applies to Sir Edward, as he took an active part in many aspects of Suffolk life. Described as 'a great friend of the agricultural labourers', he was a good judge of livestock and a formidable huntsman.

Within weeks of the Prince Consort's death, he and his wife, Lady Caroline, conceived the idea of using the Hitcham bequest to enable the College to be founded in Albert's memory. Sir Edward played a leading part in the campaign to raise money, personally contributing £2,500. This figure was by some distance the largest single sum given towards the cost of the building, showing a generosity later matched in 1886 when Lady Caroline gave a further £500 to help the College out of a financial crisis. He continued to take an active interest in the College as Vice-President of the Corporation for more than 20 years and briefly acting as President of the Corporation before his death in 1886.

Richard Garrett (1807–66)
Richard Garrett (the sixth) inherited the family business at Leiston in 1837. He carried the Long Shop agricultural machinery works to unprecedented heights and 'by 1850 Garrett of Leiston drills and horse-hoes were the best known in England. Steam engines followed traction engines for ploughing, and the steam roller, with the familiar trade-mark of a prancing horse in gleaming brass on its funnel,

appeared. Machinery from the Leiston works … was sold all over Europe' (Jo Manton).

Richard was a major supporter of the Great Exhibition, and sponsored a second exhibition in 1862. He was an early member of the Royal Agricultural Society of England, as well as a member of the Institutes of both Civil and Mechanical Engineers. Both he and his family contributed significantly to the building of the College: he paid for the Lodge and Entrance gates; his wife for the construction of the Chapel nave; his cousin, Abraham Garrett of Glemham Hall, gave £500; and one son-in-law, Frederick Peck, donated the College clock and bell, worth £170, while another also gave generous financial support. The family featured prominently among the first list of College governors and continued to do so well into the 20th century.

Seated
E.H.P. Jolly, C.W. LeMay, C.W. Wallace, E.G. Mawby, V. J.W. Spiers

O.F. cricket, 1905.

Second Earl of Stradbroke (1794–1886)

The Right Honourable Sir John Edward Cornwallis Rous was the first President of the Corporation, holding that office from 1864 until his death. He succeeded to the peerage in 1827 and later held the offices of Lord Lieutenant and Custos Rotulorum of Suffolk, and Vice-Admiral of the Suffolk Coast. In 1857, aged 63, Lord Stradbroke married a lady 36 years his junior, and after his death at the age of 91, Lady Stradbroke continued to visit the College. Their son, the third Earl, became a member of the Corporation in 1886 and was President from 1912 to 1947. The family's connection with the College remained close for many years – the fourth Earl was President of the Corporation from 1950.

The esteem in which the second Earl was held was reflected in the construction of the West window of the nave at a cost of £200. This is a striking piece of stained glass, depicting scenes from the New Testament and figures from the Old. At the window's unveiling, the Archdeacon of Suffolk described the Earl as 'a brave soldier, a fine country gentlemen, and a good churchman and Christian'.

maintain this level of service after nationalisation in 1947. Even so the railway in its early days was a vital lifeline for the College and the arrival and departure of school trains at the beginnings and ends of term could be events in themselves.

EARLY VICISSITUDES, 1865–86

'It is situated on an eminence,' wrote the author of the first College prospectus, 'in a healthy and pleasant position. It is about ten minutes walk from Framlingham Station on the Great Eastern Railway, and is distant 90¼ miles from London. The building is well arranged and thoroughly suited to its purpose. It is built to accommodate 300 boys. EACH BOY HAS A SEPARATE BED, and the dormitories are spacious and airy.'

The College opened its doors to pupils on 10 April 1865 with high hopes and expectations. There were over 200 boy boarders, with 12 assistant masters, and the maximum 300 pupils was soon approached. However, although the College buildings were completed with the finishing of the Chapel, the school was not run successfully in the early years. The Reverend A.C. Daymond, the first Headmaster (1865–71) had only limited teaching experience, and Governors who had played a major part in setting up the school interfered in its management. There were soon complaints that the College failed to represent good value for money, as an indignant letter to the *Suffolk Mercury* in 1870 revealed:

> Is the College getting into debt? Do the Governors honestly believe that £30 per annum is a fair charge for an education which, without extra expense, will not prepare pupils for the preliminary examination required by any of the liberal professions? I am afraid the Governors have most painfully failed in carrying out the trust they accepted from the county, and the expectations they originally held out to their constituents.

Scandals about poor hygiene and unhealthy water did not help either, and pupil numbers had not surprisingly fallen considerably by the time Daymond left. His replacement, the Reverend W.W. Bird (1872–81), revived matters significantly. His photograph portrays a more positive individual, and he fostered good relations with the town, playing cricket locally. One of the Governors described Bird as 'the right man in the right place' and *Lambert's Almanack* noted how 'he throws all his energies into his duties'.

Above: *Junior Dormitory, c.1910.*

Left: *Revd A.C. Daymond.*

Above: Revd W.W. Bird.

Above right: A.H. Scott-White, Headmaster (1881–6), who struggled to rise to a difficult leadership challenge.

Right: *The 'widely esteemed' Revd Dr O.D. Inskip, Headmaster 1887–1913, by Myra Luxmore and (**below**) his bust by E. Whitney Smith.*

However, ill health and bad fortune struck the College again: in 1877 three boys died of scarlatina and many parents removed their sons from the school. The headship of A.H. Scott-White (1881–6) failed to turn things round, and by 1886, as Booth writes, 'the roll contained no more than 65 names. The staff was again and again reduced, until finally there were only four members of it.' The finances were in poor shape, and the College's future hung in the balance.

Inspired Leadership, 1886–1929

Following the death of Stradbroke and Kerrison within a few months of each other, Lord Rendlesham took over as President of the Corporation and an appeal was launched to clear the debt. More importantly an inspirational new headmaster, the Reverend Dr O.D. Inskip (1887–1913) was appointed. Looking back on this, the Earl used to say, 'what was wanted for the School was not only a man of scholarly attainments, but also one who could sympathise with and take part in the pastimes of the boys'. Inskip delivered in spades. He managed to increase numbers and to develop the idea of a school that catered for the whole man, making the College 'one of the best and cheapest schools in England…' (*Lambert's Framlingham,* 1901).

Major Developments

In 1891 a Cricket Pavilion was constructed (not the present one), the artesian well made deeper and the water much improved. More significantly still, the Packard Chemical Laboratory (now English Room 1) was built: 'as fine a laboratory as was then possessed by any school' perhaps, but it was 'remodelled and great additions made' (John Booth) in 1904. In 1898 the Berners Library followed at a cost of £500, paid for by Charles Berners of Woolverstone Park, High Sheriff of Suffolk, High Steward of Harwich and College Governor.

In 1899 a major reconstruction of the Gym was carried out, after which 'it was considered that no school in the country at that time had better accommodation for gymnastics, boxing and single-stick play' (John Booth).

A carpenter's shop followed in the same year. In 1905 the College Museum was started with an enormous donation from Edmund Cavell of some 20,000 fossils, and in 1911 the concreting of sides and bottom of the swimming pool enabled it to become 'the best open air bath in the county' (John Booth). Money for these projects came from individual benefactors and from the Society of Old Framlinghamians (SOF), which became a permanent body in 1900.

As a result of these improvements in facilities and accompanying resurgence in fortunes, by the close of the Victorian period the College was firmly established as part of the leading 'public school' community (see box).

In 1901 'Sets' (Scarlet, Blue, Green and Maroon) were introduced for sporting competitions and a system of Prefects was started to maintain discipline

Above: *The Berners Library opened in 1898.*

FIFTH BARON RENDLESHAM (1840–1911)

Frederick Thellusson was President of the Corporation from 1886 until his death in November 1911. He was an Irish peer and was therefore able to sit in the House of Commons as MP for East Suffolk. He was a great public servant, chairing Quarter Sessions and the County Council. He was also a popular Master of Hounds, and as his obituary in the *East Anglian Daily Times* noted, 'his keenness as a sportsman gave him that all-roundness of disposition which nothing else in the English world seems so completely to confer'.

Despite his heavy public duties, Rendlesham took a keen interest in all aspects of College life, presiding at annual Speech Days, and working effectively with the Governors to support Inskip's remarkable Headmastership. Inskip represented the College at Lord Rendlesham's funeral, 'and among the wreaths sent was a handsome tribute from the boys and masters of the School' (*The Framlinghamian*, December 1911).

SIR ALFRED MUNNINGS KCVO (1878–1959)

Alfred Munnings achieved prominence in the early 20th century as a painter of scenes featuring horses racing, hunting, at horse-fairs or simply grazing. Unable to enlist for the Great War because of blindness in his right eye, he became official war artist with the Canadian Cavalry Brigade in 1917 – from this experience came his painting of the famous Flowerdew cavalry charge. He was President of the Royal Academy from 1944 to 1949, and his outspoken criticisms of 'modern' art made him a controversial figure, and one vulnerable to the charge of being something of a philistine. Like Vaughan Williams, Munnings could easily be set up as a conservative portrayer of rural England and little more; however, both their reputations are now being revived: as a 2012 *Times* article on a Munnings exhibition states in its headline, 'Tradition triumphs as Munnings rides again.' An artist profoundly influenced by Stubbs and Constable, Sir Alfred can now be seen as one of England's greatest 20th-century painters, with some of his landscapes among his finest works along with the equestrian paintings. A boy who daily looked from the Front over to the Castle may well have absorbed a love of landscape from an early age.

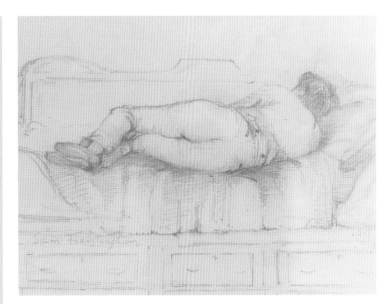

Left: Munnings's drawing of Sam at Framlingham.

Bottom left: Munnings with his dog.

LEADING PUBLIC SCHOOLS BY INTERACTION,* c.1880–1902

GROUP I (22 schools)

Bedford (Grammar), Bradfield, Charterhouse, Cheltenham, Clifton, Dulwich, Eton, Glenalmond, Haileybury, Harrow, Malvern, Marlborough, Repton, Rossall, Rugby, St Paul's, Sherborne, Tonbridge, Uppingham, Wellington, Westminster, Winchester.

GROUP II (8 schools)

Blair Lodge, Eastbourne, Felsted, Highgate, Hurstpierpoint, Lancing, Merchant Taylors', Radley.

GROUP III (20 schools)

Bath College, Bedford Modern, Berkhamsted, Blundell's, Brighton, Cambridge (The Leys), Canterbury (King's Sch.), Cranleigh, Edinburgh Academy, Epsom, Fettes, Forest, Leatherhead (St John's), Loretto, Merchiston, Reading, Shrewsbury, University Coll. Sch., Weymouth, Whitgift.

GROUP IV (14 schools)

Aldenham, Ardingly, Chigwell, City of London, Derby, Dover, Framlingham, Isle of Man (King William's), King's Coll. Sch., Oundle, St Edward's Oxford, South Eastern Coll. (St Lawrence), Ramsgate, United Services Coll. (Westward Ho), Warwick.

*J.R. de S. Honey in his essay entitled 'Tom Brown's Universe: The Nature and Limits of the Victorian Public Schools Community' classifies the above on the basis of 'which schools interacted with each other' and therefore 'accepted each other as members of the public schools community'. This took the form of competition in various forms of examination (university scholarships, Higher Certificate, army and civil service entrance), different types of cadet corps activities, and all manner of 'public school' games competitions (e.g. gymnastics at Aldershot, rifle shooting for the Ashburton Shield at Bisley) and inter-school matches (cricket, rugby and association football, fencing and racquets).

Below: House shields:
Garrett, Kerrison, Rendlesham and Stradbroke.

Above: F.W. Stocks.

Left: College Choir, 1903.

Only Raven, the history master, made our work with him interesting.' Munnings also enjoyed his time with the art master, Bug Lynch, 'a peaceful, fat, curly-headed, middle-aged bachelor', who taught him drawing and painting. This inspired him to make many pictures of Framlingham Castle from the steps of the statue of the Prince Consort. He writes of imagining it as Torquilstone Castle in Sir Walter Scott's *Ivanhoe*. 'We pictured the storming of Torquilstone, seeing Framlingham Castle in our minds.'

with the minimum of punishment. Unfortunately such improvement in civility came too late for the widely acclaimed artist Alfred J. Munnings RA (OF, 1891–2), who in 1950 reflected on 'canings and many unhappy days' at the 'large, ugly Albert Memorial College … What hateful lessons in Euclid and algebra went on there!

Inskip's successor, F.W. Stocks (Headmaster, 1913–29), continued the good work, and numbers returned to around the 300 mark (nearly all boarders), exam results improved and the occasional Oxbridge scholarship was won. The 'Sets' system was further developed in 1914 with the introduction of

Below: Inskip (seated centre) and his Masters, 1903. Bug Lynch is to the right of the Headmaster.

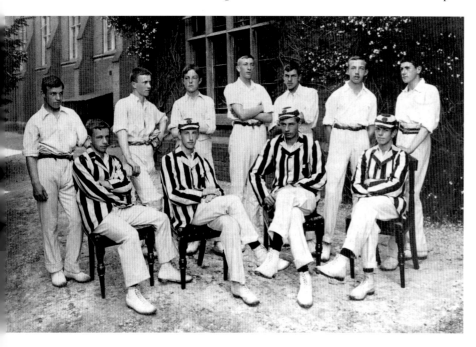

Left: College 1st XI cricket, 1901. Standing, left to right: D. Rutherford, S. Le May, A.S. Leek, A.G. Davey, G.A. Mills, G.J. Willans, R.D. Inskip. Seated, left to right: R.H. Mills, R.S. Le May, N.C. Vidal (Capt.), G.F. Spashett.

'Houses' covering every aspect of College life: Garrett (Green), Kerrison (Blue), Rendlesham (Maroon) and Stradbroke (Scarlet), named after key figures in the early history of the College.

In the same year the Headmaster presented 'The Headmaster's Shield' (later to be known as 'The Stocks Shield') for inter-House sporting competition, which is still eagerly fought for to this day. The sports included in 1914 were cricket, football, hockey, athletics, swimming, boxing, gymnastics, inter-house run, fives and shooting, and the first winners of this illustrious competition were Scarlet.

Stocks died suddenly on 21 May 1929. He had been at net practice with the 1st XI only five days before. The attendance at his funeral in the College Chapel reflected the high esteem in which he was held. He had been a brilliant all-round Headmaster, combining scholarship with excellence on the games field – he had been an Oxford cricket Blue and played county cricket for Leicestershire. Not surprisingly the birth of the prestigious Quilibets CC ('Anyone you please!') was brought about during his time in office. As the Head of History, Winstanley recalled, 'few men can have made a more indelible impression on those with whom he came in contact'.

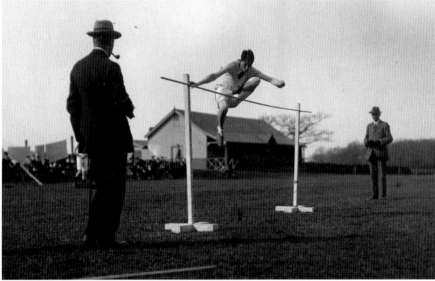

Top: Blue (Mr Barnicott's) with 'The Headmaster's Shield', 1919.

Above: High jump.

Right: The Classroom Block (now Maths and Modern Languages) was built in 1925. Note the electric lights, which replaced the old College gas lamps from 1921. On the dais is Mr Charles 'Squiffy' Thomas.

Captain A.W.S. Agar (OF, 1902–3).

The Great War, 1914–18

Before the Great War the grandeur of human sacrifice would be evoked in the public poetry of the 19th century: from Sir Henry Newbolt's 'play-up, play-up and play the game!' to Alfred Lord Tennyson's 'Charge of the Light Brigade'. The full horror of the First World War soon ripped the romanticism from war poetry, however; it replaced the literary tradition of armchair valour with the cutting commentary of young men of the rank and file sent 'up the line to die' in the most squalid of conditions and on a scale more horrifying than any yet seen in the history of mankind. Three-quarters of a million men from the United Kingdom were killed in this conflict, and the British Empire lost a further 200,000.

In total 957 Old Framlinghamians served 'King and Country' (almost all of them trained in the College OTC founded in 1901), along with 30 College Assistant Masters. 'There was hardly a regiment or a unit in the Army where some Framlinghamian was not to be found; hardly a battlefield or station in any theatre of operations, no matter on what front, or in what part of the world, whether by land, or by sea, or in the air,

CAPTAIN G.M. FLOWERDEW (OF, 1894–9) – 'THE MAN WHO WON THE WAR'

Gordon Muriel Flowerdew was one of ten brothers who all came to the College between 1883 and 1910. His VC citation details an extraordinary act of heroism in which a squadron of Lord Strathcona's horse, part of the Canadian Expeditionary Force, led by Lieutenant Flowerdew, pitted the 19th-century military tactic of the cavalry charge – with plenty of horsepower and sabre rattling – against the new technologies of the German howitzer and machine gun, and won the most improbable of victories, though at the cost of Flowerdew's life at the age of 33. In placing this memorable success in the broader context of the Great War itself, General John Seely maintained that the Flowerdew charge was absolutely pivotal. Writing in 1932 he suggested in his *War Memoirs* that by 30 March 1918 'the German breakthrough had the British army on its knees … [and] the war was effectively lost. That was until the actions of a Norfolk cavalry officer reversed the course of the battle and ultimately led the Allies to victory.' Seely's assessment is supported in a

letter from Marshall Foch, the Allied commander-in-chief in 1918, who credited Flowerdew with 'holding the enemy … and breaking his spirit at last' and by Kaiser Wilhelm II's personal spokesman who, while in exile in 1933, claimed that the failure of the German Command to exploit the supremacy of their position in March 1918 owed much to the 'heroic deed of the British lieutenant'.

Although modern historians have seen an element of exaggeration in all this, Flowerdew's charge still stands as a most remarkable action, the event immortalised in a painting by fellow Old Framlinghamian, Alfred Munnings.

Above: Munnings's painting of the Flowerdew charge.

Below right: Shooting VIII, 1920.

that did not see some son of the School at the post of duty.' Booth goes on to tell the story of Framlingham meetings, sometimes actually in the front line in France and Flanders, where men who perhaps had not seen one another since leaving school met again on the very eve of death to the sound of guns. 'An Old Framlinghamian shot an enemy marksman who had just killed a Framlingham master and another heard the School Song being sung in a trench in France, and while on his way to greet the singer was buried by a shell-burst and never knew who that comrade was.'

There are 138 former College pupils and four Masters who were known to have been killed in action. Their names are listed at the back of the College Chapel on a War Memorial made of five alabaster panels framed in marble. There are also a number of plaques (e.g. memorials to Captain Abbay DSO, Lieutenant Mawby and Commander Henry Tupper, who was awarded the Albert Medal), plus the framed Victoria Crosses and celebrated *London Gazette* citations of Captain G.M. Flowerdew, Major W.H. Hewitt (OF, 1894–1900) and Captain A.W.S. Agar (OF, 1902–3).

Agar's award was for bravery in the Baltic, where the Royal Navy were conducting operations against Bolshevik shipping in August 1919; a successful attack was carried out in heavy seas on the Russian cruiser *Oleg* despite the need for running repairs and a dangerous escape under enemy fire from land and sea. This was

only the start of a distinguished military career which was to include service in the Second World War and a string of further medals. Hewitt was a lieutenant in the South African Infantry who received his VC for 'conspicuous bravery' in an attack on a 'pill-box', where despite being severely wounded he successfully dislodged the enemy with a bomb. He spent his later life in East Africa, where he was also to serve in the Second World War.

The school was obviously badly affected by the war, but under the strong and inspiring leadership of Mr Stocks, the College survived. Not surprisingly the Officers' Training Corps remained a significant feature of College life, and this naturally was associated with success in shooting competitions – from 1905 onwards the Corps appeared regularly at Bisley. In 1920, after distinguished wartime service in the Royal Marines, Sargeant-Major G.R. 'Nips' Vale began 30 years of loyal service at the College. His shooting experience proved invaluable, and much of the success of the School VIIIs at Bisley and elsewhere could be attributed to his help. It may be a true story that when a pupil, purported to be Charles Harvey ('Maroon', 1925–7), climbed to the top of the College above the main entrance and placed a china chamber pot on the lightening conductor, R.S.M. 'Nips' Vale coolly collected a .303 rifle from the armoury and one live round of ammunition and duly cracked the pot. According to David Pitcher (Rendlesham, 1944–51), this feat of marksmanship was repeated in 1950, when the same offending article was shot from the flag pole on top of the clock tower,

having been put there by John Raynham (Rendlesham, 1945–50). 'Nips' was reputed to be the only soldier to have scored a 'possible' standing up at 500 yards using the Lee Enfield .303, so it is entirely credible that this happened more than once and even became something of a party piece!

From Round to Oval Balls, 1924

The two major games played at the College had always been football and cricket. However, it is interesting to note that in the very beginning, 'Framlingham's football was played according to the rules of Rugby' and it was only 'as a result of much violent usage' in a game involving the Headmaster as an active participant that he concluded that 'the rules should be changed forthwith to those of Association'! It is noteworthy that having played this form of football at school, Rear-Admiral Ernest Roberts OBE (OF, 1890–4) went on to captain England at rugby in 1906, winning six international caps, before becoming a member of the England Selection Committee in the early 1920s.

Thereafter 'in the local 'Soccer' world Framlingham soon began to stand for something, and they competed regularly and with some success for the Suffolk County Cup' (E.W. Swanton, 'Great Schools in Sport', *The Illustrated Sporting and Dramatic News*, 29 November 1935). With a team made up of boys and masters, as was common practice in 'schools of higher station' in those days, the College in fact won this Cup on the Portman Road ground in Ipswich in 1891 and 1894, and in 1888 and 1889 lost to the eventual winners, Ipswich Town, no less. Unfortunately as local 'Soccer' fixtures of the requisite standard became more and more difficult to find, Booth noted that 'the Association game was given up and Rugby introduced in its stead, in the Autumn of 1924'.

Bottom left: Norman Borrett in his new study.

Below: College football.

Bottom: College rugby.

BRIAN ALDISS OBE (OF, 1936–9)

Brian Aldiss is a celebrated science fiction author. He left the College in 1939 to serve with the Royal Signals in Burma in the Second World War. Having later become a full-time writer he was voted the Most Promising New Author at the World Science Fiction Convention in 1958, and elected President of the British Science Fiction Association in 1960. Alongside Harry Harrison he started the first ever journal of science fiction criticism, *Science Fiction Horizons*, while at the same time enjoying significant success as an anthologist in the 1960s and 1970s. Aldiss was named a Grand Master by the Science Fiction Writers of America in 2000, and received two Hugo Awards, one Nebula Award, and one John W. Campbell Memorial Award. His short story 'Super-Toys Last All Summer Long' was the primary inspiration for Spielberg's film *AI Artificial Intelligence*. He was elected a Fellow of the Royal Society of Literature in 1990 and was awarded on OBE for services to literature in 2005.

DEPRESSION, 1929–39

The 1930s were difficult times for the new Headmaster, W.H.A. Whitworth (1929–41), as the financial crash had chilling repercussions around the world. In 1930 the College suffered a serious setback when Whitworth's application for membership of the Headmasters' Conference (HMC) was rejected because of poor results in the School Certificate Examination and the paucity of Old Boys at the universities. This was an especially cruel blow as Stocks had only achieved this status for the school in 1926. Fortunately, however, thanks to the good offices of Doctor Rendall, the school's affiliation to the HMC was restored in 1932, and this was maintained despite further fluctuations in the school roll. Pupil numbers were down to 147 in 1934, but because of a surplus in the War Memorial Fund (£3,000) the College was able to survive and even to modernise: extensive new bathrooms were installed and new squash courts were built in memory of Stocks – the stone recording this can still be seen outside what are now modernised PE classrooms.

The science fiction author and OF Brian Aldiss reflected the unease in an article provocatively entitled 'An introduction to subversion' (*The Sunday Times*, 2 September 1990): 'My first public school [was] a barbarous place called Framlingham College, in Suffolk. There were a lot of rules and regs and they were strictly enforced. There was also a ritual whereby new boys had to stand on their beds and tell a story and if it didn't work everyone hurled shoes at them. I didn't have a shoe thrown at me and gradually I became chief story-teller.'

Despite the improvements made during the 1930s, the College continued to struggle on a number of fronts, and there were only 161 boarders in 1938. Concerned Governors discussed desperate measures such as having a qualified person to show visitors around the school, reducing the teaching staff, and installing an automatic stoker to reduce fuel and labour costs. Governors even wondered whether introducing Biology to the curriculum might persuade parents of the practical nature of Framlingham's education in the countryside. Many other schools suffered hardship at this time, the root causes being economic and financial difficulties. In the end, in Britain as in America, these would be resolved in an unlooked-for way by the outbreak of the Second World War.

The Headmaster, W.H.A. Whitworth, at Speech Day in the early 1930s. Note the low height of the wainscot, which was raised in 1937 when the Dining Hall was fully panelled in oak and re-floored, with the coat-of-arms of Rendlesham, Stradbroke, Kerrison and Garrett on the walls, and the busts of 'the widely esteemed' Dr Inskip and 'generous benefactor' Emile Moreau, installed.

3

WAR AND PEACE, 1939–55

'Their swords are in your keeping.'

DUNKIRK, DISMISSAL AND DERBYSHIRE

Despite the fact that in 1936 the Debating Society rejected the motion that 'War is inevitable in the next five years', the Second World War broke out in 1939 with the Nazi invasion of Poland, and shortly thereafter Whitworth's tenure as Headmaster was brought to a mysterious end. He was forced to resign by the Governors for allegedly abandoning his post in 'an extreme error of judgment', having been 'suddenly inspired to take his yacht and sail to Dunkirk' to play a part in the rescue. J.D'E. Firth's version of events in *Rendall of Winchester, Chairman of Governors (1940–6)*, continues: 'Without a moment's delay Rendall was equally inspired to take to his bicycle and pedal vigorously to Framlingham. Assuming for the moment supreme control and undertaking complete responsibility, he restored a position which otherwise might well have collapsed.'

THE GOOSE STEP

"GOOSEY GOOSEY GANDER,
WHITHER DOST THOU WANDER?"
"ONLY THROUGH THE RHINELAND—
PRAY EXCUSE MY BLUNDER!"

P.

It later transpired that this story was totally untrue. Whitworth had not in fact gone AWOL. Rather in response to an impassioned parental request for him to navigate a small boat from the Deben to Dunkirk, he had first sought guidance and then been granted leave of absence by College Governor and Chairman of the Executive Committee, Archibald Rose. Moreover, it was Rose, and not Rendall, who came in to College to hold the fort until the Headmaster returned. Rose came in from Moat Farm on the Badingham Road – just over a mile away, and Rendall didn't come in at all, which is not altogether surprising as his home at Butley Priory is 14 miles away, which is some distance to cycle for a man who was 78 years old at the time. Fortunately, as it happened, Whitworth wasn't gone for very long anyway as he was turned back at Harwich – 'no more boats needed'. Hence this proud patriot (he had been awarded the Military Cross while serving in the Royal Flying Corps and had later lost a leg near Albert

Pupils march out of Framlingham Castle in the 1936 College production of Shakespeare's Julius Caesar, *the same year that the German* Wehrmacht *was goose-stepping (**left**) into the Rhineland.*

Below: The College Arts and Crafts Society pose for the camera in 1939 (with Derek Fowler DFM, behind 'Pop' Haynes's left shoulder), while in the same year Hitler and Stalin carve up Poland.

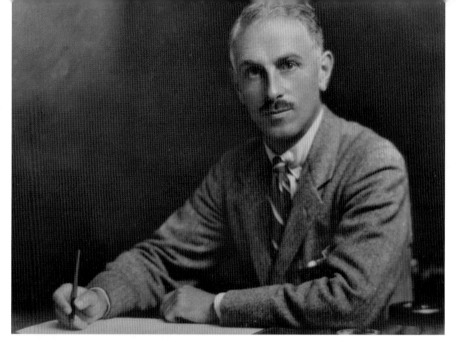

Above: W.H.A. Whitworth, Headmaster (1929–41).

Left: The Colts U15 XV, 1940.

Below: Dr Montague Rendall CMG.

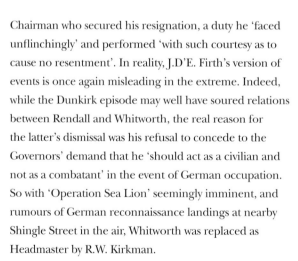

on the Western Front) and expert sailor was unable to play any meaningful part in the famous evacuation. As he lamented thereafter: 'I regret to say that I did not have the honour of being numbered among those who took their small ships to Dunkirk on that occasion … [Moreover] the fact that my Headmastership came to an end … had no more to do with the operations off Dunkirk than with the Battle of Trafalgar' (from a letter written to *The Framlinghamian*, 1955).

So having made detailed provision for College black-outs and shelters, as well as comprehensive arrangements for the evacuation of up to 100 College pupils to the relative safety of Repton School, Derbyshire (where 27 junior boys stayed in Brook House and 72 seniors in Hall House for just five weeks, from 6 August to 10 September in 1940), Hervey Whitworth's Headmastership was over. In *Rendall of Winchester* it states that it was the

Chairman who secured his resignation, a duty he 'faced unflinchingly' and performed 'with such courtesy as to cause no resentment'. In reality, J.D'E. Firth's version of events is once again misleading in the extreme. Indeed, while the Dunkirk episode may well have soured relations between Rendall and Whitworth, the real reason for the latter's dismissal was his refusal to concede to the Governors' demand that he 'should act as a civilian and not as a combatant' in the event of German occupation. So with 'Operation Sea Lion' seemingly imminent, and rumours of German reconnaissance landings at nearby Shingle Street in the air, Whitworth was replaced as Headmaster by R.W. Kirkman.

Orchestrator-in-chief and Second Master, Revd Rupert Kneese (left), in consultation with colleagues W.E. Winstanley (centre) and Junior School Housemaster Quentin Cuckow, during the evacuation to Repton School in 1940.

Market Hill was mostly taken up by a large air raid shelter and a huge, square, chest-high brick water reservoir for use by the fire brigade. The brigade itself was housed in Crown and Anchor Lane, where exit could easily have been blocked. Many homes had either Anderson brick shelters outside, or Morrison shelters inside the house, table height with a strong steel top. Brick walls appeared in front of some windows as protection against bomb blast; many others were criss-crossed with tape for the same reason. There were pill boxes of the type still seen in the countryside at the junction of Fore Street, Station Road and Well Close Square, and that of Well Close Square, College Road and Bridge Street. Pyramidal concrete blocks appeared on both sides of College Road, presumably to impede tanks. Army personnel were billeted with many families and the Royal Engineers commandeered a brick barn in Badingham Road. A crashed German Dornier bomber was put on display on Castle Meadow and a drifting barrage balloon became embarrassingly snarled up in a tree in Station Road. The Blackout was imposed, strictly monitored by ARP wardens, and vehicle headlights were fitted with covers to lessen brightness.

'Tragically the Second World War claimed the lives of four townsfolk. Home Guard member Mr Leeper died in an accident on Castle Meadow while demonstrating a mortar. One Sunday lunchtime in October 1940 a solitary Heinkel 111 dropped a stick of eight high-explosive bombs over Framlingham, one of which hit a house in College Road and killed Miss Harvey, a teacher at the adjacent Sir Robert Hitcham's Primary School. Of the other bombs one fell in the playground behind the school and two others straddled, but mercifully didn't hit, the Hitcham's Almshouses. Miss Harvey is commemorated at the house which bears her name near the school.

'Later in the war a canister of incendiary bombs was dropped during the night in Albert Road, hitting a house integral with the Forresters' Hall (now a Royal British Legion meeting hall) and causing a raging inferno, lighting up the night sky for miles around. The house was gutted and though Percy Stannard and his daughter Gwen survived, his wife Maria and their son perished in the flames.

'After America entered the war the daytime skies over Framlingham were alive with B-17 Flying Fortresses of

IMPACT ON FRAMLINGHAM TOWN

The impact of the war on the quiet, medieval market town of Framlingham is described below by John Maulden (Garrett, 1945–50; later College Chemistry Master and Ziegele Housemaster), who was just six years old in 1939:

'The town was certainly to feel the impact of the war. Precautionary measures were in abundance. The

Above: The College Road house destroyed in 1940.

Right: The pill box in Well Close Square (c.1944).

Below: The Hitcham's Alms Houses suffering the aftershock of a 'near miss' – 6 October 1940. Note the painted white gateposts for enhanced visibility during 'blackout'.

the US 390th Bomber Group, based at nearby Parham, returning from their daylight raids over Germany. They bore a large letter J on their tail fins and many were damaged, with feathered propellers indicating knocked-out engines. Some fired Verey lights signalling casualties on board. Saturday nights saw the town teeming with American servicemen, enjoying the hospitality of the public houses and their specially built club in New Road, or queuing at the nearby Regal cinema (where the College held its Speech Day in Autumn 1946) on a site where Coucy Close now is.

'Near the end of the war townsfolk endured the anxiety of Hitler's last desperate attempt to stave off defeat, his ramjet pilotless V-1, the Doodlebug. Launched from Peenemünde in Germany and aimed at centres of population, it was very inaccurate; one listened in dread if a V-1 passed overhead lest there was a sudden silence as its fuel ran out to signal that it was about to plunge to earth packed with its load of high explosive. Fortunately it didn't happen here.'

FRAMLINGHAMIANS IN THE
SECOND WORLD WAR

The 'total' nature of the Second World War makes it impossible to track the thousands of Old Framlinghamians who saw active service. No doubt

many heroic deeds went unrecorded, and a brief survey can only touch on a few famous names. Some fought in both world wars, such as Brigadier T.P. 'Nobby' Clarke OBE CBE (OF, 1913–16) who served with distinction as a Piffer (Punjab Indian Frontier Force).

Many younger Framlinghamians joined the RAF to fight in the Battle of Britain and in many air operations later in the war. Most spectacular perhaps were the achievements of Group Captain Percy Pickard (Garrett, 1926–32). He was awarded the DFC in 1940 'For gallantry

Shooting Team c.1930, with P.C. Pickard top left.

Queen Elizabeth and King George VI with Percy Pickard (second from left).

In 1949 this wooden War Memorial at the back of the College Chapel was unveiled by Major General The Rt Hon. The Earl of Athlone, to commemorate the 88 Old Boys and one Master killed in the Second World War.

Above: '*Operation Jericho*' *by Graham Coton. This painting was commissioned by Patrick Taylor (O.F.) and presented to the College in 2014.*

Right: *The finishing touches being put to Percy Pickard's portrait by Alex Portner.*

and devotion to duty in the execution of air operations' and thereafter became the first RAF officer to receive the DSO three times in one war. He was also awarded the Czech Grand Cross and starred in the popular wartime film drama documentary, *Target for Tonight*.

Having flown more than 100 missions, Pickard was finally killed in action in 1944 aged 27. He was shot down in his Mosquito while commanding 'Operation Jericho', a bombing attack on a French gaol at Amiens enabling 258 prisoners to escape, including 79 members of the French Resistance, 12 of whom faced imminent execution. This mission was described in *The Times* as 'one of the finest exploits in the history of the Royal Air Force' and it so impressed the French that they later made a film as a tribute to him, *Derrière ces murs*, and added a VC to the decorations listed on Pickard's gravestone in Amiens Cemetery. Official British directives for it to be removed were ignored, and only when Pickard's wife, Dorothy, asked in person was it erased. Pickard himself had always been modest about his extraordinary achievements, and perhaps his Framlingham background played a part in

this: after his hero's death, his old Headmaster, Hervey Whitworth, told a national newspaper, 'he was a nice lad but a great problem. He was always bottom of his form'.

Equally distinguished in a different way was the Whittaker family, who served on land and sea, as well as in the air. Pilot Officer Richard Whittaker (OF, 1931–7), who died in action, was awarded the Distinguished Flying Cross in 1940 for 'great courage and determination, completely disregarding his own personal safety in order to engage and destroy enemy aircraft' (*The London Gazette*). His younger brother, Lieutenant Glyn Whittaker (OF, 1935–42: Head Prefect in 1941–2 when the boys were evacuated to Repton, as well as Captain of Cricket, Football, Hockey and Swimming) of the Royal Marines Commando, died of wounds in the Normandy Landings of 1944.

The eldest brother, Major George Whittaker (OF, 1928–32: Head Prefect in 1931–2 and Public Schools' Rugby and Hockey representative), served in North Africa, where he was awarded the Military Cross for courage in the face of Rommel's tanks at the Battle

JTC (Junior Training Corps)
Inspection by Field Marshal Lord
Ironside in 1941, with Kirkman
and Rendall in attendance.

of the Cauldron in 1942. After being captured by the Germans, he escaped from POW camp in Italy and spent the rest of the war in jungle warfare in India, where he was later appointed MBE for services to the British community in Calcutta.

An even more extraordinary escape story is that featuring Flight Lieutenant Leslie Goldfinch (OF, 1926–32, Garrett), more commonly known as 'Bill'. After enlisting in the RAF in 1939, Goldfinch took part in two epic rescue missions on 25 April 1941, during the evacuation of Greece. The first saw him successfully fly 72 RAF men in his hazardously overloaded Sunderland back to safety in Crete. The second ended in complete disaster. He crashed his plane in the dark, but survived with extensive injuries, only to be captured by the Germans and imprisoned near the Swiss border. Having later tunnelled his way out of Stalag Luft I, he was soon recaptured and sent to the top security prison at Colditz. It was here that the Old Framlinghamian 'designed the glider built in the eaves of Colditz Castle, as part of the most audacious of all the projected escapes from the Second World War's most famous prison camp' (extract from Goldfinch's obituary in *The Telegraph* on 12 October 2007).

The 'Colditz Cock', as Goldfinch's glider with its 33-foot wingspan came to be known, was to be launched from the roof of the medieval Saxon stronghold, before flying over a nearby river and landing on a green field some 500 yards away. Not surprisingly this grand design took some planning, and it was just approaching completion when the prison camp was relieved by the Allies in 1945. As a result it was never tested in practice until a scaled-down version was launched much later, in 1993. When this proved a success, Channel 4 commissioned a full-scale replica 'Colditz Cock' to be constructed to Goldfinch's original specifications. Its spectacular three-minute flight was observed with pride by Goldfinch himself and a dozen or so others that had worked with him on the original, and was broadcast on the 2000 TV series *Escape from Colditz*.

Lt. Col. T.C. Metcalf
(Rendlesham, 1923–7), who
led the British Composite Anti-
aircraft Demonstration Battery,
RA, on a tour to the US in 1943.

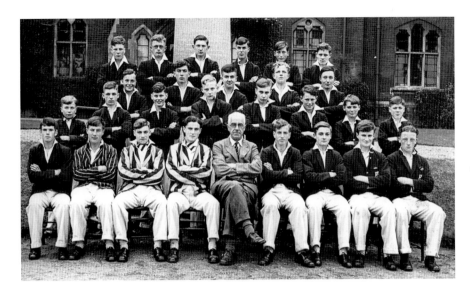

Revd Rupert Kneese with Rendlesham House, 1942.

Right: The Bishop of St Edmundsbury and Ipswich welcoming the Countess of Athlone on 2 July 1949.

Another Framlinghamian inspired by the wartime heroism of his Headmaster, Hervey Whitworth, was Lieutenant Fergus Dempster DSC OBE (OF, 1929–34). Dempster served in the Royal Navy in seemingly unremarkable style. However, it was later revealed shortly before his death that he had in fact been a senior officer in the Secret Intelligence Service (SIS) and had been a leading player in co-ordinating clandestine resistance operations along the coasts of Italy, France and Africa, known as 'The African Coastal Flotilla'. 'For gallantry, enterprise and undaunted devotion to duty in [more than 100] hazardous operations' (*The London Gazette*) during the months leading up to the invasion of the south of France in August 1944, Dempster was awarded the Distinguished Service Cross. He subsequently joined a Special Counter-Intelligence unit tasked with flushing out any remaining German agents from the Antwerp region. In recognition of this, the Belgians later made him a Knight of the Order of the Crown. After the war his career in the SIS flourished. He was made second in command in the Far East, then Head of Station in London and subsequently set up a version of the SIS in Australia, for which he was eventually awarded the OBE.

On a still more secretive note, the quite extraordinary acts of heroism carried out by Prince Constantin Karadja (OF, 1906–8) have only recently been disclosed. After leaving Framlingham College, where his flair for public speaking and persuasion was honed as Honorary Secretary of the Debating Society, the Prince became a barrister and diplomat. During the early stages of the Second World War, when Romania still belonged to the Axis Alliance, Karadja repeatedly exploited his position in the Romanian Ministry of Foreign Affairs to protect Romanian Jews living in occupied territories. Karadja was responsible for saving hundreds of French and German Jews, and over 51,000 Hungarian Jews (the celebrated German industrialist Oskar Schindler is credited with having saved over 1,200 Jews). This was often done against the will and orders of the Romanian dictatorship at great personal risk.

In 2005 Karadja was officially recognised as 'Righteous Among the Nations' by the state of Israel, an award given to those who had put their lives at risk to save Jews from the Holocaust. The concept of the Righteous, as defined by the Yad Vashem Law, has become a revered worldwide term of honour denoting a great form of heroism and of choosing good in the face of evil.

Such may have been the heroism of a few leading lights, but war brought forth many acts of bravery and self-sacrifice from many people, along with the hardships imposed on all. By 1945, the cost of a second victory tempered any sense of celebration. In any case, the victory came in two stages, in Europe on 8 May, and in the Far East on 2 September. Even then, many would remain in uniform for many months until they got their demob suits, rationing and National Service would last for years, and the post-war world was far from stable as the Iron Curtain descended across the Continent. Churchill, broadcasting on 8 May, suggested we might allow ourselves a brief period of rejoicing, and as John Waddell (OF, 1939–46) recalls, even Rupert Kneese was unable (though true to form, he tried!) to continue prep that evening.

The palpable excitement, though, was brief, and the dominant sentiment more sober. When the Bishop of St Edmundsbury and Ipswich dedicated the second memorial at the back of the Chapel on 2 July 1949, Archdeacon Browne in giving the address spoke as a parent to other parents. It is poignant now to see the first name on the list, R.H.P. Browne. Such losses were close to home, and the memorial opposite the south door of St Michael's records those from the parish who gave their lives. Some survivors might talk about their experiences, but most did not. The election of Clement Attlee as Prime Minister of the first Labour government perhaps symbolised the desire to build a better world, and for Framlingham to have Brandeston Hall as its war memorial epitomised that practical search for improvement. The war was not forgotten, but it would not dominate the world that came after, except that the character of so many men was deeply altered by it. Men who had fought through the war were not going to be fazed by the challenge of teaching boys; nor would they put up with any nonsense from above: even before the College went independent, there was a sturdy independence in the men who came to teach here, and with their passing something was lost.

WARTIME LEADERSHIP AND LEGACY

The Headmaster, Reginald Kirkman (1941–55), was ably assisted in leading the College through these difficult war years by his Second Master, the Reverend Rupert Kneese. After just 18 months of his Headmastership numbers had increased to 150 boarders and 40 day boys, and by 1945 the number of boarders had risen to 250. Concessions inevitably had to be made to the extraordinary demands of wartime –

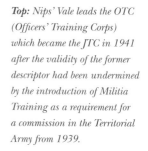

some 'OF Gatherings' were suspended, Annual General Meetings re-scheduled to lunchtimes to avoid blackout, regular sizeable Chapel collections were made for the POW Games and Book Fund, the Red Cross, East Suffolk Hospital, Ex-Services Welfare, Aid for Russia and so on – but the basic order of the day was to 'keep calm and carry on'. As a result games fixtures continued, albeit somewhat restricted in the hockey season of 1941 by 'sanitary and meteorological misfortunes' and in the cricket term by the scarcity of suitable opposition, which necessitated playing against an Army XI on five separate occasions. Not surprisingly the boys found it more difficult to compete against Service opposition in the rugby season! The Debating Society remained

Top: Nips' Vale leads the OTC (Officers' Training Corps) which became the JTC in 1941 after the validity of the former descriptor had been undermined by the introduction of Militia Training as a requirement for a commission in the Territorial Army from 1939.

Inset: College JTC cap badge.

Far left: Reginald Kirkman, Headmaster 1941–55.

Left: Hazardously Adventurous Training.

vibrant, the Play-Reading Society was revived and the JTC and ATC became increasingly focussed on preparing pupils for active service.

On the back of this remarkable recovery in the College's fortunes two further crucial developments took place under Kirkman's headship. The first was the opening of Brandeston Hall by Princess Alice, Countess of Athlone, in July 1949.

The Hall had been purchased and restored by the OFs as a memorial to those of their number who 'in two Great Wars gave their lives for the freedom of the world'. It was to be the College junior school, catering for boys from ten to 13 years of age. In the short term, this investment would significantly reduce the strain on senior school facilities caused by the steep increase in post-war pupil numbers. Originally ideas had been floated of major new buildings around the College Front, which might have created an attractive complex rather like an Oxbridge College surrounding a lawn.

However, the opportunity to purchase an even more attractive building at Brandeston was seized with excellent results for the long-term development of the College, which is so fortunate to have a sister prep school to provide a steady stream of pupils. As Norman Porter has recently illustrated, Brandeston Hall was soon to establish a fine reputation and tradition of its own.

Secondly, and of major importance, was the acceptance of Direct Grant status by the College as a result of the 1944 Education Act. This allowed local boys who had passed their 11+ to attend the College at the State's expense – a system that was to last until 1974. Hence, local grammar school boys came to the College, while their female counterparts went to the Mills Grammar School for Girls.

This was a great fillip for the College during the post-war years, cementing ties with the local community and sharpening the school's academic profile. The 11+ as an examination clearly had its limitations, but as a blunt instrument it served a purpose at the time, and the support of government money kept the College on a secure foundation. However, in the longer term restrictions on financial independence played a part in the lack of capital projects that contributed to the outdated nature of many of the College facilities by the 1960s.

Above: Princess Alice, Countess of Athlone, with College Headmaster R.W. Kirkman and David Kittermaster, first Headmaster of the junior school at Brandeston Hall.

Right: An artistic impression by T. Harvey of the new buildings proposed for the College Front in 1946, prior to Brandeston Hall's appearance on the market. The Junior House which would have accommodated boys from ten to 13 is on the left, the Speech Room occupies the foreground and the Pavilion is seen beyond the main buildings.

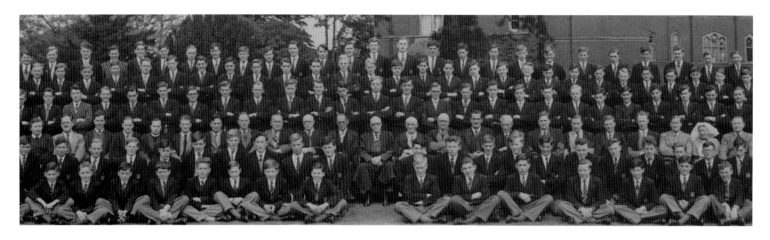

Staff and boys in Kirkman's last year, 1955.

POST-WAR COMMON ROOM

Common Room itself was inevitably affected by the different wartime experiences of its members. Older men, such as Kneese and Winstanley, who had carried on teaching through the war, were joined by others whose young manhood was all but shaped by their experience of active service. However, if there were tensions between colleagues, this did not prevent many from remaining at Framlingham for incredibly long stints, and in time this no doubt contributed to the conservative ethos of the College in the 1950s and 1960s. Messrs Hague, Clarke, Melsom, Gillett, Baly and Borrett all taught for over 30 years from the early 1950s through to the early 1980s. Such men were characters in their own right, and they ran a boys' boarding school on traditional lines, with the Headmaster as an over-all manager and virtually no other interference at all. Boarding meant boarding then, seven days a week for a full term; bachelor Housemasters living in one room in College got to know their boys well and took part in a whole range of activities with them, from early prep and breakfast to dormitory duty with Prefects in the evenings.

Not surprisingly, as the recollections of various Old Framlinghamians illustrate, some of their students have vivid memories of these characters and various related escapades. One of these is Tony Martin (Garrett, 1947–55), who writes that:

THE REVEREND R.H. KNEESE (1889–1957)

'All embracing, unbounded enthusiasm. He had it himself and he demanded it in others.' Rupert Kneese was educated at Cranleigh and Trinity College, Cambridge. He served as a Chaplain to the Forces at the end of the First World War before joining the College staff in 1920. He took over as Housemaster of Rendlesham ('Maroon') two years later, before becoming Chaplain in 1923 and Second Master in 1930. These roles he performed unsparingly and with tireless efficiency until his retirement in 1953. His influence, however, permeated so many other walks of College life. He founded the Scout Troop and led them on holiday parties on the Continent. He coached in his time every game going, including the Shooting VIII, and it was Kneese who formed the Quilibets CC in the late 1920s. He was also an accomplished teacher of modern languages and though his general methods were often eccentric, he was always insistent on standards of behaviour befitting a Christian gentlemen. His extraordinary contribution to College life was put into perspective at his Memorial Service on 29 June 1957: 'we must be grateful to the point almost of joyousness, at the thought of the work done, under God's guidance, by Rupert Kneese.'

The Church Militant in action with the CCF.

Left: Scout Camp – but where's Rupert?   *Below: The Berners Library in 1950.*

'I appreciated what I saw as the continuing steady presence of Kirkman at the top, but we soon became aware of other, newer faces. Winstanley, who looked a bit frightening, Norman Borrett, who definitely was not to be trifled with, H.J. Hague, the gentle Peter Clarke, Hugh Baly and "Pop" Haynes, a hopeless disciplinarian whose lessons were always subject to ill-behaviour. But I have kindly memories of "Joe" Melsom, who taught us biology. "Bertie" Manthorp, who had come over to Brandeston to teach Art and Architecture was a familiar face, as was Tom Fleming, rather a cold disciplinarian to whom I am still grateful for instilling in me at an early age care and perseverance in working with my hands. Lesser souls included a bad-tempered man called Rogers, who looked to be on a perpetual point of explosion and was a dreadful teacher of Physics and Chemistry. A man called Harre was equally ineffectual. I believe Leslie Gillett was a good teacher of English and I remember being attracted to the "colour" of Chaucer's England, although to this day I find Shakespeare completely unintelligible. I think in many of the cases there was a fault with the syllabus and the methods of teaching in those days which failed to provide me with the education for which my Father had

paid. I quite enjoyed Latin and I think Hugh Baly was a good teacher of it. Unfortunately we soon "gave it up", and I regret this when I try to interpret the memorials in churches now.

'Jim Hague was an interesting History master and I was interested in what I was told. But I think he knew he was dealing with barren ground, for he would sometimes digress from the proper path and read us passages from the West Country books of John Moore. I still read *Brensham Village* and *Portrait of Elmbury* and I am ever grateful for Hague's introducing me to this writer. Sometimes Hague would digress into a long, rambling, never-finished story about the Bishop of Cairo's daughter, derived, I think, from his distinguished experience in the war with Montgomery at Alamein.

'I enjoyed our once-a-week lesson on English architecture with Bertie Manthorpe using the Batsford book as our guide. I never see Woolpit church with its crockets and flying buttresses without thinking of Bertie. He meant well despite a propensity to hurl a heavy bunch of keys aimed accurately at the head of a dreaming boy. In winter time he managed to hold a Vick inhaler in one nostril with his tongue and thus cleared congestion. I attended his funeral and was sad at his passing.

'Peter Clarke did give me extra maths lessons, but I never grasped the principles or the point of things like simultaneous equations and so I inevitably failed the subject in School Certificate. I thought I became better in French after an exchange visit with a French schoolboy during a summer holiday, but the towering Martin Irving realised I was not really very good and announced one day to some of Form 5D: "You lot will never learn French: keep quiet and read a book."

'Having an interest in natural things, I enjoyed Biology with Joe Melsom. But we must have annoyed him one day because he lost his temper and told us: "Look! I don't give a damn if you learn anything or not, because I still get paid." It was during Biology one day that a boy who had committed suicide by shooting was carried past our window. I do not remember much discussion about this within the school, although his brother left and returned the following term. Certainly nobody seemed "traumatised" or was offered "counselling" or placed flowers in sensitive places as would no doubt happen today.

'Somehow we progressed, or moved according to our advancing years from the lower forms to one of the Fourths: Lower and Upper Four "B" and Lower and Upper Four "A". There were then three Fifth Forms: 5A, 5B and 5C. However, when many of us were deemed too old to stay in the Fourths and not bright enough for the scholastic heights of 5C, 5D was formed especially for us and became colloquially known as "The Farming Fifth". Several prominent figures in today's Suffolk agriculture and the higher echelons of the county's social and economic structure resided in this illustrious form until we left after fairly dismal results in our School Cert. Exams. My sole achievement was a pass in English Language. I have often wondered whether I was totally thick or just bone lazy …'

John Stevens (Stradbroke, 1951–2) writes that 'On the last day of Summer Term 1952, about eight of us from the Sixth Form got up and dressed very early on a halcyon morning. Our plan was to carry the Austin 7 belonging to John Melsom, the Biology Lecturer, from its parking lot and plant it onto the oak table in the front hall. Many hands made light work of the job, and we were entirely successful. We were happily returning to our beds when Rupert Kneese appeared. At that stage he did not know what we had done; he was NOT amused and caught three or four of us before we made it to our beds. The

car remained on the table until after breakfast, when we carefully removed it and returned it to its park, much to the amusement of the whole school. Later in the morning the culprits were interviewed by the Headmaster, Mr Kirkman, who made some gruff noises of general admonition, but finished up by wishing us well for the holidays. Michael Orvis (1946–52) and Brian Lee (1946–52) from Stradbroke are the only other names among the miscreants that I can remember. *Sic transit gloria mundi.*'

There are other versions of such stories – David Pitcher (Rendlesham, 1944–51) recalls John Melsom's car being taken to the Fives Courts rather than the front hall, where it was parked sideways so that it would have to be physically picked up to get it out again, while Chris Sneath MBE (Kerrison, 1951–6) believes it to have been Martin Irving's car that was removed from the front drive to the entrance hall … or perhaps such carjackings were regular occurrences? There were certainly repeat performances in the late 1980s when Biology teacher and Ziegele tutor Howard Robinson's brown Mini was removed to the Dining Hall and such high jinks appear to have fuelled 'copycat' misdemeanours further afield. As fellow historian Marcus Marvell discovered, in 1989 for instance, a group of Prefects at Ellesmere College began planning their leaving present to the school inspired by events at Fram. Nick Bews (Stradbroke, 1955–63) had often entertained his young son, James, with memories of his days at Framlingham College and in particular a daring stunt involving placing one of the teacher's cars in the school Dining Hall. So a copycat plan was subsequently hatched and executed, which involved manoeuvring a teacher's Fiat Panda along the school's main corridor, up a flight of steps and into the dining room where it remained in place until after breakfast the following day.

Above: Tony Martin (Garrett, 1947–55) on National Service, 1956.

Chris Sneath and Dr John Rankin (Kerrison, 1947–56) remember another incident, when the firing of a Verey pistol on a CCF Corps day mysteriously led to a fire in a haystack. After fire engines had dealt with this, a local police constable entered the dining hall demanding to know who the culprits were. However, the resourceful Messrs Sneath and Rankin were able to persuade him that the stack fire must have been caused by internal combustion!

The End of the Line

As Kirkman's time was ending, so was the longer era of the Framlingham railway. Competition from the motor car and the omnibus was rendering rail transport uneconomic, and rural lines were being closed even before Dr Beeching's swingeing cuts of the 1960s. Framlingham again led the way and the branch line was closed to passenger transport in 1952, although a few Fram specials ran till 1954.

David Pitcher (OF, 1944–52, and later parent, Governor and Rector of Framlingham) recalls the last Fram express and high jinks on the trains:

'*The Framlinghamian* magazine had a very impressive photograph and key of the last steam engine which failed to leave on time at the end of the Spring Term in 1954. The photograph shows the engine swarming with boys all over it under the indulgent eyes of a youthful Mr Martin Irving and an already grey-haired Mr Hugh Baly.

'Ian Allen, the College Doctor, tells the two-fold story of how it came about that the running of the College specials came to an end, up a siding without a carriage. British Railways' version is that the Stationmaster at Ipswich had become increasingly disenchanted by the condition of the carriages when they were returned to the Ipswich sidings after use as a College special. It was, he claimed, frequently found that leather straps for opening windows were missing; with other signs of careless use adding to his indignation he decided that it was no longer worth the trouble of assembling a rake of carriages from various parts of the Eastern Region, storing them in the little space available at Ipswich, and then letting energetic schoolboys do their worst.

'On receiving this decision the College Bursar's version was that on the previous occasion when the boys marched down College Road en route to the station, it was found that the engine had not been fired long enough to build up sufficient steam pressure for the train to leave on time. The Bursar was infuriated, as were many boys and many parents, because subsequent connections with main-line trains at Wickham Market were missed and school holidays up and down the country had a disastrous start. Either way it was a sad end to 100 years of "bonkers" on the branch line!'

By the early 1950s Kirkman was considering retirement and, having suffered a minor heart attack in early 1954, he decided to leave in the summer of the following year. At his final Speech Day the Earl of Stradbroke presented him with a Georgian silver salver, 'a token of appreciation for his 15 years of service to Framlingham'. Only history, the Earl said, could put Kirkman's unremitting efforts and the success of those years in their proper perspective. To enable the College to survive the war and all the difficulties of the post-war years was a major achievement, and to leave the College with a record number on the school roll (425) was to bequeath a rich legacy and a major challenge to his successor.

Below: The last 'Fram Express', 1954.

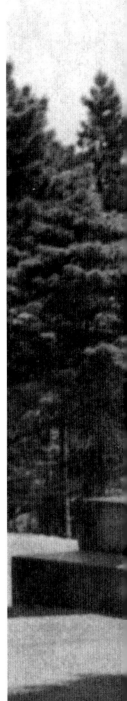

4

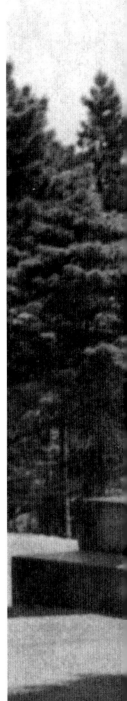

'Oh, Mr Porter!', 1955–71

Kirkman was replaced as Headmaster in 1955 by W.S. Porter (1955–71), a scholarly man who maintained the College's reputation and oversaw some notable building projects. Even though Framlingham avoided some of the more foolish educational fads of the Swinging Sixties, the restrictions of the Direct Grant system and the conservatism of the Headmaster and senior staff meant that Framlingham remained very much an old-fashioned school. The ethos is summed up well by Norman Porter (Kerrison, 1951–7; current Governor and Hon. Sec. SOF):

'In the 1950s we had already moved from preparing young men for running the Empire to the preparation of young men to face National Service and post-war austerity. So what evokes the College of the 1950s?

'The 11+; selection interviews at County Hall; Direct Grant status; few day boys, often scorned; just four houses (boys only) based on four enormous, freezing cold dormitories full of iron-framed beds and four "set rooms" for day-time relaxation and prep; memories of Glenn Miller, Chris Barber, Slim Whitman and Al Jolson played by Prefects with sole control of the house record player; two study corridors for about 20 lucky sixth formers, and 6A where the Prefects gathered; communal eating by houses, service provided by "shacks" scuttling to and fro, carrying as many plates at a time as was possible; basic fare – food rationing finally ended in 1953 – tapioca (frog spawn) and semolina probably the least palatable desserts; a top table, where

sat the staff – often with more than a hint of sherry on the breath at lunchtime; an almost entirely male-dominated environment; dance lessons – the challenge was to avoid being the "girl" in the partnership – preparations for occasional tentative dances with (as it was then) the girls of Mills Grammar School; CCF parades twice weekly – compulsory participation – boots spat upon and polished, gaiters blancoed – Field Days – one included a route march to Brandeston and back; chapel once a day – three times on a Sunday if you chose to go to early morning communion – over 50 per cent did get confirmed mostly in the second year; occasional BBC schools broadcasts, but the timetable had to fit, because there were no tape recorders; black

Stuart Brenan's iconic image of the view from Albert in the late 1950s.

chalkboards, chalk dust, board dusters (occasionally hurled as missiles), dreary un-illustrated text books; boot rooms, ostensibly associated with shoes and boots, but mostly memorable for BRAs – "Boot Room Afterwards" – dread words implying an imminent "tanning"; tuck box courtyard, for breaktime treats; frequent roll calls – before breakfast, most boys still dishevelled – and before chapel, parading along past the elephant tusks and between the glass cases of the Museum while prefects inspected shoes for shininess; herring bone suits (maroon blazers in the summer); detachable collars, with unmanageable collar stud, maroon caps; casual clothes? What did that mean? Cold swims in the murky, occasionally slimy outside pool – avoidable if you could develop an attack of foot-rot, or become a decent cricketer; occasional half-holidays granted off the cuff – if someone made Oxbridge, or as requested on Speech Day; a day off for the Suffolk Show; three exeats a term, necessarily squeezed between matins and evensong; no half-term holidays; a school that was self-contained and inward looking – one heard about Suez but only because it meant a change of location of the Summer CCF camp; Ashburton success; the Asian flu epidemic of 1957; communications mostly by eagerly awaited post – few telephoning opportunities. And so much more… It was a very different world, but Fram was just like other comparable schools.'

CRIME AND PUNISHMENT

'Logs dished out as punishment: who can forget writing out the first page of Godfrey and Siddon's *Four-Figure Tables*: the first numbers 7404, 7482 …'

As House Punishment Books testify, during the 1950s these pages of 'Logs' were given out by Prefects and Sub-Prefects like confetti, often for the most trivial of offences: for 'buttons & pockets' x 3, 'illegal use of

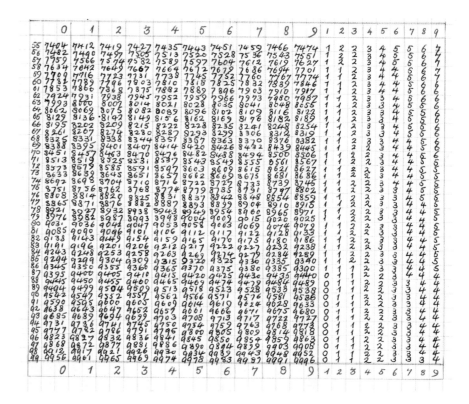

band jams' x 2, 'wearing slippers for chapel' x 3 and 'failure to scavenge' x 4; for 'moving cutlery before Grace' x 2, 'spitting plum stones into the water jug' x 6, 'combing hair in dining room' x 3 and 'arriving at school without a cap' x 2. All such entries were signed by the Prefect concerned and counter-signed and dated by his Housemaster.

In 1961 writing out pages of logarithms gave way to writing out pages of 'Fact Sheets': '1840 – Penny postage instituted'; '1879 – Tay Bridge destroyed …' This remained the standard punishment for minor offences to the end of Stanley Porter's Headmastership in 1971. To add insult to injury, offenders remained obliged to purchase their own special paper for the task, as well as the prescribed fact sheet. As illustrated by the Garrett House Punishment Book for 1969/70, the form of these entries remained largely unchanged: Gardner. S. x 3 – C.H.H. (Prefect's initials) for 'gluttony at tea' in w/b 16th November, 1969 – PdeW (Housemaster's initials), as did the character of the offences, e.g. x 3 for 'drinking (coca-cola) in dorm', x 3 for 'pillow fighting after lights out' and x 4 for 'jacking shack job'.

It should be noted that 'jacking shack job' refers to a junior pupil's failure to fulfil any number of menial tasks prescribed by the Prefects in his House. 'Shacking'

Above: Punishment log.

Below left: Alan Smallwood (Stradbroke, 1953–62) in 1956 wearing his College cap with crest.

was a long-standing tradition in public schools, more commonly known as 'fagging', but Framlingham had its own argot. As Sub-Editor of *The Framlinghamian* in 1964, College Head Prefect Mark Hedley defended the tradition, suggesting it inculcated 'an idea of service and discipline' and was 'part of that process of character-building with which the Public Schools are entrusted'.

Tony Martin (Garrett, 1947–55) recalls his personal experience of some of these 'shack jobs' at meal times: 'We lower orders took it in turn to be "Jam Shacks" who entered the dining hall before meals and our job was to place each boy's jam or cornflakes on the table exactly where he sat. This resulted in a sort of Pelmanism at which I usually failed. More than a foot of deviation resulted in punishment. Junior boys also had to fetch

the food put on plates at the serving stations and I think I could still carry eight or nine plates at a time if I tried. Success in this field meant that only two journeys to the stations were necessary and thus one got to eat one's own food quicker.'

Other less formalised punishments for minor misdemeanours included 'Walking up and Down' on the Front in break, getting changed into games kit at awkward times, running to 'Denny Bridge' and being forced out of bed horribly early in the mornings.

The consequences for more serious offences, however, were altogether more harrowing. Sir Alfred Munnings may have moaned in *An Artist's Life* about having to 'bend over a chair, receiving, in spite of all my "Please Sirs", six vicious cuts with [the Headmaster's] cane', but what is more disturbing is that such 'villainous treatment' was still being routinely administered by Prefects in Boot Rooms into the mid 1960s. The seriousness of the sample of offences below may be varied, but the order of punishment in almost every instance seems pretty savage. I know that one is obliged to view the past through the eyes of a far more sensitive and liberally minded present, but in studying these Punishment Books it is difficult not to notice the prevalence of the names of particular Prefects. In turn, it is also difficult not to suspect that some of their number might have derived some small measure of sadistic satisfaction from their task; for bringing discipline down upon the unruly bottom of the younger years with a Flashmanesque finesse that was institutionally condoned with the counter-signature of the relevant Housemaster: six strokes for 'Jacking match, disregarding authority of a Prefect and late for school and being down town illegally on Sat afternoon'; six strokes for 'Using a master's name in vain as a false excuse to avoid punishment'; four strokes for 'Jacking House Cricket and Deceit'; four strokes for 'Jacking Chapel'; six strokes for 'Borrowing without permission, attempting to rise early at unauthorised time and without permission'; three strokes for being caught 'In possession of cutlery'; four strokes for being 'In possession of drink' and being 'In possession of fireworks'; six strokes for 'Lying, deceit and jacking shack job'.

And one has to remember that this is just a taste of the order of Prefectorial punishments that was formally recorded. God only knows what brutalities were being inflicted by these authoritarian enforcers of College discipline off the record! No doubt such abuse of power was very much the exception rather than the rule, and by the late 1960s most Housemasters only rarely, if ever, gave permission for their Prefects to resort to canings. Nevertheless, it is difficult in light of the evidence to agree with the contention that this peculiar practice 'was dropped' completely during Porter's Headmastership. Enlightened abolitionists would have to wait to the 1970s for complete change here.

PHYSICAL DEVELOPMENTS

Major Chapel renovations were completed in 1956, including the addition of a false ceiling to conceal the rafters, a re-laid stone floor, modernised lighting, new oak

pews (some with House insignia) and a magnificent pair of entrance doors given with characteristic generosity by James Mason Martin – 'J.M.M.' (OF, 1888–94 and College Governor). It was fitting that the former Headmaster Reginald Kirkman was invited back to witness the Bishop's blessing of the completed works that he had masterminded: 'the climax to two years of patient work and generous donations by many friends of the School'.

In 1957 the new cricket pavilion was opened by His Grace the Duke of Norfolk on Speech Day, who spoke of his pleasure at returning to Framlingham, the home of his ancestors four centuries earlier (no mention of the fact that their tenure there had ended with the execution of Thomas Howard, fourth Duke of Norfolk, on a charge of High Treason in

Top: The original Chapel.

Above: The Chapel after renovation in 1956.

THREE INTERNATIONALS AND A PROFESSOR

John Iliffe (Garrett, 1952–7)

John Iliffe was Captain of 1st XI cricket and 1st XI hockey goalkeeper. He was also Head of School, Chapel Sacristan, recipient of the Arts Cup for Acting and a staunch supporter of the Literary and Debating Societies. Having won a History Scholarship to Peterhouse College, Cambridge, he went on to develop a distinguished career as an academic. His book *The African Poor: A History* was awarded the Herskovits Prize in 1988, and he was made Professor of African History at St John's College, Cambridge, in 1990. Since then his most notable works include *Africans: The History of a Continent* (1995) and *Honour in African History* (2005). Iliffe is presently researching and writing a history of the African AIDS epidemic.

1st XI cricket, 1957: top (left to right): David MacMillan, Robin Anderton, David Turnbull, Peter Raynham, Norman Porter and Nick Hancock; bottom (left to right): David Larter, Andrew Wright, John Iliffe (Capt.), Andrew Hancock and Michael Spencer.

A.W. Hancock (Stradbroke, 1952–7)

Andrew Hancock won the first of his three England international rugby caps in 1965 in a home win against France. His last came a year later against the same opposition. However, what singles him out came in between: 'Hancock's 90 yard run to immortality' (*Daily Mirror*) in the 1965 Calcutta Cup match against Scotland. His try subsequently featured first in the celebrated BBC Classic 1990s video '101 Best Tries' and more recently in the 2009 *Telegraph* feature on the greatest tries ever scored at Twickenham, in which it was described as follows: 'The most dramatic of Boy's Own scores and possibly the longest run for a try at Twickenham, being at least 100 yards. England were trailing 3–0 on a quagmire of a pitch … It was do or die. Hancock first dismissed a couple of straggling Scotland forwards with an outside swerve, then cut in to dismiss Stuart Wilson before he gathered himself for the lung-bursting final sprint, just holding off chasing centre Iain Laugland. Extraordinary stuff.'

N.H. Porter (Kerrison, 1950–7)

Norman Porter was a beneficiary of the Direct Grant Scheme and was ultimately to become Head Prefect. He learned his hockey under Norman Borrett on the Back, before going on to captain St Andrew's to victory in the Scottish Universities Championship and to represent Scottish Universities. He won selection for the first of his dozen international hockey caps for Scotland against Holland in Amsterdam with the newspaper headline: 'Two new Scottish Caps and they're both English!' His later career saw him excel as a schoolmaster, teaching modern languages and coaching hockey at Loretto, Dulwich, Wellington College and Woodbridge.

J.D.F. Larter (Rendlesham, 1951–7)

As a Colt David Larter was recognised as 'a very promising fast bowler whose batting can only be described as feeble and his fielding even worse'. He went on to open the bowling for Northamptonshire CCC from 1960 and, as Colin Bateman observes, 'when the mood took him and his 6ft 7in physique was in perfect working order, he was a frighteningly good fast bowler, as a career record of 666 wickets at 19 apiece suggests!' His batting remained notoriously 'feeble', however, though he did manage to hit an unlikely half-century at Trent Bridge in 1962. Larter took nine wickets on his Test debut in 1962. Unfortunately his promising Test career was hampered by a succession of injuries, the last of which was picked up on the 1965/6 tour of Australia and brought about his premature retirement at 29. He played ten Tests for England and took 37 wickets at 25.43.

*His Grace the Duke of Norfolk (**left**) opening the new pavilion (**below left**).*

Above: Spectators on the new Pavilion roof in 1959. Front three: H.F. Burbidge, W.E. Winstanley, L.M. Liell.

Although sport was evidently a central part of College life, there were some students, as ever, not wholly sold on the idea that a straight bat mattered more than anything. Indeed, some Framlinghamians were interested in other types of bats altogether!

1572, one suspects!). This development coincided happily with a star-studded cricket XI and the official story is that the Duke graciously sent a bat to stylish opening batsman A.G. Wright, who averaged 15.27, and a ball to the frighteningly fast J.D.F. Larter for their achievements by the end of the season. The unfortunate truth is that Andrew Wright never received this bat. More unfortunate still perhaps, even with three future international sportsmen in their ranks, captained by a future Cambridge University History Professor, the XI according to Gillett only managed 'a balanced, if not sparkling season': won six; drawn two; lost five – this despite Larter's 52 wickets at 9.50 and Turnbull's 41 at 13.0!

Avoiding Cricket with the Natural History Society
by Neville Marsh (Stradbroke, 1953–61)

Being unashamedly a less-than-average sports player, the opportunities offered by the Natural History Society seemed too good to pass by. Members were able to use bicycles for *bona fide* outings (a privilege not available to the rest of the school) allowing us to ride to seemingly exotic locations. In addition, we were excused the 'tyranny of league cricket', which was disbanded in 1956, and so avoided having to play summer sport. Looking back, I count myself very fortunate in living on nature's doorstep. Within a few yards of the school gate lay the meres, surely one of the richest sites in the county for studying flora and fauna; we were

Above: The meres in Marsh's time.

Below: Lord Cranbrook's pheasants awaiting consumption at the first (and only?) meeting of the Fine Dining Club held in a Stradbroke study c.1961. From left to right: Peter Gooding (Kerrison, 1953–62), David Ballard (Kerrison, 1955–62), Richard Hunt (Stradbroke, 1957–62), Nicholas Whiting (Kerrison, 1955–62) and Neville Marsh (Stradbroke, 1953–61).

surrounded by rolling meadows filled with butterflies and insects of all kinds and a little way beyond, the most wonderful birdwatching opportunities were to be had at Minsmere whilst Coralline Crag pits with their rich supply of fossils lay within easy cycling reach.

I was inspired by two stand-out lecturers. Peter Harold Tremair Hartley was, unbeknownst to us, a larger-than-life character in the ornithology world. In addition to keeping down his job as Rector of Badingham and subsequently, Archdeacon of Suffolk and Royal Army Chaplain, he was Council Chairman of the RSPB and author of several bird books. His lectures covered an enormous range from avian evolution to bird migration. A real joy was to be chosen by him for a field trip to Minsmere Bird Sanctuary.

The other inspirational lecturer was the fourth Earl of Cranbrook. John David Gathorne-Hardy lived at nearby Great Glemham Hall. He was a Governor of the College from 1934 to 1974 and was highly regarded in zoological circles, being Vice-President of the Linnean Society and a British Museum Trustee. It was an unexpected delight when, after a Council meeting, he asked me if I would like to go back to Great Glemham for a session of bat-hunting. Needless to say, this was an opportunity to skip evening 'prep' and get back to the College well after 'lights out'. We erected long nets strung between sets of bamboo poles and awaited the arrival of our prey at dusk. Invariably, noctule and pipestrelle bats would oblige and we would soon be busy examining our catches, measuring and ringing before release. The evening would be capped off by a cup of coffee back at the house with time to review the evening's work and enjoy conversation with the Earl and his colleagues from the British Museum or London Zoo. At one of these evenings, I must have expressed a preference for pheasants and so I was somewhat surprised when a brace of birds appeared at school soon after. These were duly plucked and cooked by the kitchen staff and enjoyed by a select group of us.

In addition to lectures, film and outings, Society members filled in with their own 'lecturettes' and were actively engaged in field work and lab work. We 'acquired' the Old Physics Lab and furnished it with obsolete Middle School lockers, thus enabling both lab work and animal breeding to take place. Mike Hodges (Garrett, 1953–61), the Secretary in 1960, gave the first short talk on 'Serious Bird Watching' in our splendid room. We received a regular supply of gorgeous Burmese and Indian butterflies from Arthur Best (Kerrison, 1921–6) in Queensland. These we religiously pinned out for display, and it was a happy occasion many years later when I met the donor in Toowoomba near my home city of Brisbane. We undertook to survey the mere using plane tabling at a scale of 100 feet to the inch and this revealed all manner of amazing birds such as reed buntings, little grebes, long-tailed tits and the uncommon lesser spotted woodpecker and gadwall duck. We also mapped the wild flowers in the parish for the County Flora Scheme. I undertook this mammoth task with Allan Brown (Stradbroke, 1957–62) and we visited every corner of the district looking for flowers.

Our returns must have been slightly suspect as quite often we incorrectly recorded cultivated flowers and thus were told that these were 'garden escapes'!

My other great joy was collecting fossils from the clay pits around Framlingham. One of these was on the other side of the town and as Sunday afternoon was the best opportunity for collecting, we walked along Saxtead Road and around the town via New Road and Apsey Green. This enabled us to get to the pit 30 minutes earlier than waiting for the 2pm town curfew to pass. It was worth the walk to get just a few fractured belemnites.

The momentum we generated in the 1950s enabled the Society to go from strength to strength. Much of this was due to Bill Donson, who became President in 1967: it was thanks to his leadership that the Society had 'the most active term for at least three years'. Outings continued, though *The Framlinghamian* noted that at the Tollemache and Cobbold Brewery in Ipswich, 'unfortunately brewing was not in progress at the time but this did nothing to detract from the merits of the finished product, kindly supplied by the management at the end of the tour'.

There was a visit to London Zoo led by the fabled identical twin schoolmaster brothers, John and George Newmark, who took the boys behind the scenes and 'those who were courageous, were able to pet a pair of tigers' or 'go into the cage of Rabin the Cheetah'! Rabbits were kept but despite looking 'very contented', were eventually turned loose to fend for themselves and 'made a home under the Chapel near Mr Hague's treasured garden'. Some chickens were bought by Michael Watts (Stradbroke, 1966–71) for 16 shillings with the intention of eventually having them cooked but he could not get his Housemaster's permission. 'Thus they have been a rather low source of income … they sold eggs for four (old) pence each to the domestic staff.' After eviction from the Old Physics Lab, the Society finally took over the Grey Hut behind the CCF Stores: electrical supply was fitted and running water provided 'by siphoning the water through a pipe from the tanks creating a supply for the princely sum of just under £2'.

I hope that something of this natural history rubbed off on me providing a basis for my zoology degree and that I did not succumb to nefarious activities recorded in the summer of 1956 when there was 'a very marked lack of conscientious field work' and that 'some members have used our privilege of not having to play cricket for sun baking on the back'! When I left Fram, the magazine generously recorded that my 'attractive posters which had for so long adorned the School Notice board will be sadly missed', so perhaps I had left a small mark as a non-cricketer.

OTHER DEVELOPMENTS

Neville Marsh's preference for Natural Science over cricket is perhaps not entirely surprising in view of other developments during his time at the College. New science laboratories were opened in 1958 by the eminent physicist Sir Lawrence Bragg. These comprised

Below: The new science laboratories opened in 1958.

Bottom: Speech Day, 1959: awaiting the arrival of Air Chief Marshal Sir Dermot Boyle's helicopter.

The opening of the new squash courts, 1969: N.A. Bellamy and Charles Pryor.

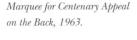

Marquee for Centenary Appeal on the Back, 1963.

the first two storeys of the current Science block and greatly enhanced the possibilities for the teaching of Physics and Chemistry. It also freed up space for a separate Biology laboratory in the old Packard building. This must have given particular pleasure to the Headmaster, Stanley Porter, who had studied Physics at Cambridge and been Head of Science at Felsted and Radley. A strong team of Science masters would teach in these areas over the next 30 years: Mike Robinson and John Maulden taught Chemistry, Philip de Whalley and Tony Coggins Physics, and Joe Melsom covered Biology. The standard of the teaching was generally high and discipline could be strict – despite the fine view across the mere to the Castle from Mike Robinson's Chemistry lab, woe betide the boy who looked out of the window during his lesson! Perhaps this is something of a contrast to earlier days recalled by Tony Martin (Garrett, 1947–55), who remembers his Science teacher in the early 1950s being so ineffective that pupils on the back row in his lessons would regularly heat up cans of baked beans with their Bunsen burners, before consuming them with a fork straight from the tin!

In 1959 Moreau House was built as a boarding house for 40 junior boys during their first year at the College, before being allocated to the other four houses. Bob Gillett ran this house very successfully for over a decade.

This eased pressure elsewhere – containing over 400 boys in the main block must have created very cramped conditions, even by the standards of the 1950s.

This building programme also included the opening of the Clarke-Martin Reading Room (now the Board Room) in 1959 and the construction of the new squash courts ten years later. However, not surprisingly the climax of Stanley Porter's planned developments would be the new Speech Hall, the central project of the College centenary year, 1964. This had been first envisaged back in 1946 and by the early 1960s a major Centenary Appeal Fund was under way run by General R.D. Inskip and W.E. Winstanley. A series of events was held with a splendid Fête on 27 July 1963, which lasted from 2.30pm to midnight and included a Piano Busting Competition ('two teams of four, armed with hammers and crowbars … reducing the instrument to fragments small enough to pass through an aperture six inches square'), a Procession of Cars in Concours d'Elégance (judged by Miss P. Ozanne, the celebrated Monte Carlo Rally driver), Tossing the Sheaf, the sounds of the Stringbusters Hillbilly Western Band and Tractor Backing. Admission was one-and-six for adults, nine pence for children (6–14) and Old Age Pensioners, and free for children under six.

Colonel Clark, Commander of the 81st Tactical Fighter Wing, USAF Bentwaters, allowed many of

W.E. WINSTANLEY MA CANTAB: 'A LIFETIME OF SERVICE TO THE SCHOOL'

'Winstan' joined the College staff in 1925 and retired in 1967. He was meticulous in his use of language and displayed a scholarly appreciation of English literature, as well as a genuine flair for History which he happily shared with his students. He was Editor of *The Framlinghamian* magazine for more than 25 years, Housemaster of Kerrison ('Blue') for 40 years and from 1953 he was Second Master. 'Guide and philosopher' to generations of Framlinghamians, Winstan was 'tolerant and urbane, cheerful and interested', hugely popular with parents and 'hospitable in the extreme'. He was devoted to school cricket and was a pillar of the redoubtable Quilibets CC. His main relaxation, however, was golf, and he was Suffolk County Captain from 1949 to 1959 and President from 1960 to 1965.

Top left: *USAF flipping burgers on the Front.*

Left: *The skeleton of the roofing steelwork for the new Hall can be seen in the background of this Sports Day scene on Dickson's in June 1963, in which Head Boy Michael McGuire (OF, 1954–63), brought the baton home for Kerrison in the senior relay in record time.*

Far left: *Headmaster W.S. Porter, Archdeacon Browne and Bursar T.L. Farthing in August, 1963.*

Below: *OF cricket on the Back in 1959, viewed from 'Foof' Winstanley's favoured perch.*

his men to demonstrate baseball, run a 'real ox and chicken barbecue' for over a thousand people ('Meat, pimento beans, cabbage and roll – 5/-'), set up a Red Indian Camp Fire and provide a jazz band for the dance on the Front. Mrs Clark had opened the Fête and clearly the very special Anglo-American relationship remained in good heart, a century after Prince Albert had kept Britain neutral in the American Civil War.

CENTENARY CELEBRATIONS

The years of fund-raising and months of planning were rewarded with a magnificent day for the opening of the Athlone Hall on 26 June 1964. The College Visitor, Princess Alice, Countess of Athlone, accompanied by the Earl of Stradbroke, arrived at noon to be greeted by the Headmaster, Stanley Porter, and a Guard of Honour from the CCF.

After lunch and a thanksgiving service, Colonel Percy Clarke, Chairman of Governors, formally received HRH at the Centenary Hall, recalling that his father had been amongst the first pupils to enter the school, and he himself, having joined in 1890, had observed the growth of the College for upwards of three-quarters of a century. Princess Alice expressed her pleasure at returning to the College founded in memory of her grandfather 100 years before. While 'not trying to puff an ancestor', she praised the individuality and values that the College fostered and hoped that new Framlinghamians would 'grow up into rational human beings' rather than conformist 'sheep', and 'be equal in every way to [their predecessors] who [had] set such a fine standard for their school'. She was thanked by the Head Prefect, Mark Hedley, and presented with a bouquet by Jane Robinson. Deryck Cox then conducted a splendid concert, including Britten's arrangement of

Top: The Centenary Hall, 1964.

Above: A car fit for a Princess, on the Front.

Above right: Princess Alice with Headmaster Stanley Porter.

the National Anthem and the specially commissioned *Suffolk Suite* by Doreen Carwithen. After tea a dramatic Retrospect written by Bob Gillett traced the College's history. The evening was rounded off in spectacular style, with a firework display and a Ball in the great marquee on the Front.

The final building project of Porter's Headmastership may have been the construction of the new squash courts in 1969, but it was the Athlone Hall that remained the most dramatic …

Far right: Dramatic Retrospect, 1864–1964, being filmed by a BBC cameraman.

Below right: An artist's impression of the Athlone Hall.

Right: Jane Robinson presenting the Princess with a bouquet of flowers.

King Henry V,
*1934 (**left**) and*
The Tempest,
*1928 (**below**), in*
Framlingham Castle.

Below left: *The*
groundlings and
the players in
Framlingham's Globe.

Cultural Impact

Before the College had its own Hall major cultural events often took place off campus, either in the town Assembly Hall opposite St Michael's or *al fresco* in the Castle, where Shakespeare plays were put on regularly in the 1920s and 1930s, such as *Richard II* in 1930, *Julius Caesar* in 1936 or Mr Alfred Lugg's memorable production of *Twelfth Night* of 1938. Dr Michael McGuire (Kerrison, 1954–63) provides some interesting insights into the trials and tribulations of putting on dramatic productions in the late 1950s and early 1960s. He recalls a Kerrison House

performance of *Twelfth Night c.*1958 and remembers that for the female role of Olivia he was allowed to grow his hair long without being told to 'get your hair cut, boy!'

Director of Music Deryck Cox's Gilbert and Sullivan and other productions also had to take place in the town Assembly Hall. *The Mikado* was staged there in 1961 and *HMS Pinafore* in 1962, with Michael McGuire as Captain Corcoran – a role he was forced to play with his arm in a sling owing to a broken collarbone sustained in a 1st XV rugby match.

Below: HMS Pinafore, *1962, in the Framlingham Town Assembly Hall on Church Street.*

Below: A scene from The Netherby Flier – *the first school production to be staged in the new Athlone Centenary Hall. The opening performance was on Thursday, 10 December 1964, and featured B.R. Goodfellow (Garrett, 1961–6) as Henry Clamps (Stationmaster and proprietor of the 'Railway Inn') and R.G.S. Bumstead (1961–8) as his daughter, Clara Clamps.*

A Beggars Opera, 1960, with Tom Otho-Briggs centre stage as MacHeath.

Musicians must have been desperately short of venues for performances before 1964, and Framlinghamians seemed to have been willing to play instruments almost anywhere. There is a delightful informality about the photograph showing members of the Jazz Band (Stephen Llewellyn on clarinet – 1957–64, Robert Goodale on trombone – 1958–66, and David Newson on trumpet – 1954–63), in an impromptu jam session during the tea interval at the Whit Monday cricket match in June 1963.

Clearly the tradition of sacred music sung in Chapel remained unbroken, and the year before the Athlone Hall was opened, Sumsion's *Magnificat* and *Nunc Dimittis*, Handel's *Zadok the Priest* and Purcell's *Thou Knowest, Lord* were all Choir staples. The annual music competition saw a plethora of entries for the Copperwheat Plaque, which Stradbroke won by a mile on this occasion. This plaque was named after Cox's predecessor as Director of Music, Eric Copperwheat;

the high point of his tenure was when the Recorder Group under Mrs Gillett took part in the first performance of Benjamin Britten's *Noyes Fludde* at Orford in 1958, and thereafter in the recording made at Southwark Cathedral.

The pride in the new Athlone Hall is almost palpable in *The Framlinghamian* of 1964 reports of the Centenary Concert and the Hall very quickly became part of the everyday cultural life of the College. In the days before television was commonly available to students, the new facility allowed films to be viewed by the whole school in one showing. Films for the Autumn term 1964, for example, included *Dr No*, *Carry on Teacher*, *North-West Frontier* and *The Loneliness of the Long Distance Runner*.

The Hall could also be used by the Ipswich Gilbert and Sullivan Society for a College audience, as well as for school productions. The first of the latter was a double bill, a homegrown production, *The Netherby Flier*, by L. Gillett and D.H. Cox, followed by Menotti's *Amahl and the Night Visitors*.

Visiting recitalists could also give concerts to town and gown, and large audiences could listen to such celebrated musicians as the great bass Owen Brannigan, leading percussionist James Blades (1965), the London Mozart Players (1967) and the most famous accompanist of his day, Gerald Moore (1968).

CCF IN THE PORTER YEARS

In society at large during the 1950s, the Armed Forces became less fashionable: the age of angry young men

Jamming outside Rendlesham, 1963.

as Neville Marsh went on gliding courses, visits to the many American bases in Suffolk and arduous training in the Cambrian Mountains: by the time Marsh was a Warrant officer, the Air Section was enjoying an annual camp at Cranwell and contained several young men with great RAF careers ahead of them, Group Captain Peter Gooding, Wing Commander Mike Allport and Air Commander Jon Ford among them. Pictures from the College's Centenary Year bear witness to the continuing role the CCF played in the lives of Framlinghamians at school and in the wider world.

THE COLLEGE MUSEUM, 1905–73
by Neville Marsh (Stradbroke, 1953–61)

No young teenage boy could fail to be mesmerised by the array of magnificent and mysterious objects displayed in the College Museum. It was a quintessentially Victorian phenomenon conceived when explorers and adventurers would collect all manner of animals, vegetable and mineral specimens without the slightest regard for conservation or the environment. As Leslie Gillett records in *The Second Sixty Years*, the 'terrifying spider crab' guarded the door to the library; this and Dr Inskip's awesome pike 'never failed to catch the eye and draw attention to other wonders'. These exhibits and many others would offer 'to the curious mind material to browse over for five minutes or to excite the imagination for twice that number of years'. And so in my case, as a natural historian in the making, it seemed inevitable that I would become Curator one day.

The Museum had been established by Edward Walter Lynch (1859–1913), a 'remarkable assistant master … willing to assist in or take over almost any School activity'. The Museum was started by an enormous donation in 1905 from Edmund Cavell, a solicitor from Saxmundham. Cavell, a distant relative of the martyred nurse Edith Cavell, was not a pupil of the college but must have considered Framlingham a suitable repository for his collection. Cavell donated his collection of 20,000 fossils and other specimens. 'Practically every boy … gazed in awe or fascination at the displays' which included, reputedly, a lock of black hair belonging to the beheaded Henry, Earl of Surrey, who is buried in the parish church.

The fortunes of the Museum waxed and waned over the years depending on the supply of dedicated

and teenagers led on to the 'Peace' of the 1960s. However, no one told Framlingham, where the CCF continued to flourish, partly perhaps because many sons of the Forces enjoyed the stability a boarding education here could provide. Nick Vincent (Rendlesham, 1953–8) recalls Field Days at Sizewell in the 1950s in its pre-nuclear days, with a special train on the Framlingham and Aldeburgh branch lines, and in his last year fitting in a few pints at Tunstall's Green Man before discovery, though OC Major Percy Podd was unruffled by such an incident and *The Framlinghamian* wrily commended 'unsuspected initiative in a night exercise'.

By the 1960s the CCF was more seriously threatened by cuts in government expenditure linked with the ending of National Service which finally came in 1964. Nevertheless ways were found of maintaining a CCF some 300 strong, with, from 1959, the additional attraction of an Air Section under Flying Officer Maulden; fly-pasts became a feature of annual inspections, and cadets such

Left: CCF Annual Inspection in 1964, conducted by distinguished OF Maj. Gen. R.D. Inskip CB CIE DSO MC, with Lt Col Podd, Flt/Lt Maulden and the Headmaster in attendance.

Above and below: The Museum in the 1960s in the corridor to the Chapel, featuring Inskip's 'awesome pike'.

curators from amongst the College student population. In 1928, Francis Stocks, the Headmaster, rescued the Museum from a 'state of disrepair and neglect' by setting aside funds for improvements. Enthusiastic curators would set about cleaning and cataloguing after a period of disuse and over the years Old Boys added to the collection by providing specimens often brought back from travels overseas. Donations included a stone from the top of the Tasman Glacier, a section of the Dover–Calais submarine cable from 1850 and flags captured from Arab chiefs in central Africa.

The magnificent pair of elephant tusks, which countless generations of boys will remember at the foot of the main staircase, started life in the Museum. The tusks were lent by Hugh Le May (1893–96), who had obtained them from an animal shot in Portuguese East Africa. The Hon. Andrew Vanneck, a long-time Governor, donated a 'magnificent' case of 56 stuffed birds originally from Lord Huntingfield dated 1862: 'a very notable addition to our collection of taxidermy'. Weapons came from far and wide: a tomahawk from an American Indian, a Nepalese kukri, a Tongan battle club, an elephant gun, a midshipman's dirk and a 'fuzzy-wuzzy' sword from Papua New Guinea.

In the 1950s the Museum had become neglected and new life (and money) was put into the project by Headmaster W.S. Porter. Allan Brown (Stradbroke, 1957–62) and myself were appointed Curators and started the 'immense task of reconstruction from the deplorably decrepit state into which the Museum had been allowed to fall over the past five years or so'. Michael Robinson was the Superintendent Master. There were no records of specimens and the original Cavell collection of 20,000 specimens had been reduced to around 3,000.

We enlisted the assistance of Mr Harold Spencer, Assistant Curator at Ipswich Museum, who came once a fortnight to help catalogue specimens. Spencer weeded out many specimens and we showed some early entrepreneurial spirit by auctioning them off to the boys, thereby raising invaluable funds for the Museum! Importantly, Mr Spencer found two type specimens of fossils and these were taken away to Ipswich for safe keeping. One of these, *Natica cavellii*, was dedicated 'to the memory of its discoverer, (Edmund Cavell) an enthusiastic collector of Crag fossils'. Three mammoth teeth donated from the Harrison and Gibson building site at Ilford also went off to Ipswich museum where they still reside.

We found that a great many exhibits were in store – in perhaps the worst possible spot, the school's universal dumping-place – under the Chapel. Many a long day was spent in this Aladdin's Cave rescuing exhibits. The magnificent albatross with its out-stretched wings found rotting away was retrieved, and the storehouse yielded up other curious things, such as a Sati immolation memorial stone and a Gallo-Roman sculpture from a pagan funerary chapel. Other new specimens were elicited from College boys, for example, Philip Hkio (Rendlesham, 1960–5) persuaded his father to lend a Burmese ceremonial sword. We reported proudly in the magazine that 'in short, the Museum while not pretending to be much more than an array of interesting … and valuable objects, was being run to an orderly plan'. One fascinating object was a miniature reproduction of the Parthenon frieze. Such was my zeal over restoring this exhibit that I organised a book on the subject as the Howard Smith Art prize at the princely sum of five shillings!

Fortunately, constructional work on the exhibit cases was undertaken by the School Carpenter, Mr Marjoram, 'a craftsman of great skill and a man of sterling worth'. However, this did not prevent the occasional disaster coming from the hands of unskilled boys. I had spent many hours wiring up a large show case next to the Berners Library. Alas, my electrical skills were sadly lacking, and upon completing the circuitry I managed to fuse the lights in the entire Library block, much to the anger of the readers!

In the 1960s, the Museum's fortunes continued to fluctuate, and Curators battled against the tide of dust penetrating the cases and the damage frequently done by boys leaning on the glass tops. The Museum was reconstituted in 1969 by Peter Randell (Rendlesham, 1965–9): 'the electrical system, which is dangerous in many places' (!) was replaced and Peter showed 'great administrative ability'. However, after Peter left, 'the affairs of the Museum (were) somewhat in the melting pot' and through a combination of circumstances, the demise of the eclectic collection was swift. One of the economies of the new Headmaster, Laurie Rimmer, was to close the Museum, to the 'dismay of those with long memories and to curious boys, the contents, after return to their donors … were auctioned by agents in Woodbridge'. So ended a fascinating chapter in the history of Framlingham College: a museum collection which excited the imagination of countless boys and remains in the memories of many more.

Far left: Henry Howard, 'the Poet Earl' of Surrey's tomb at St Michael's church in Framlingham. A lock of his black hair was reputedly featured in the College Museum. The Earl's coronet lies at his feet rather than on his head because of his disgrace and execution in 1547. He was found guilty of treason for quartering the family coat-of-arms with those of King Edward 'the Confessor' (1042–66).

Left: Elephant tusks sent by Hugh Le May, from an animal shot in Portuguese East Africa.

Opposite: The Annual Society Dinner of 1903 was held at the Trocadero Restaurant on Shaftesbury Avenue, London.

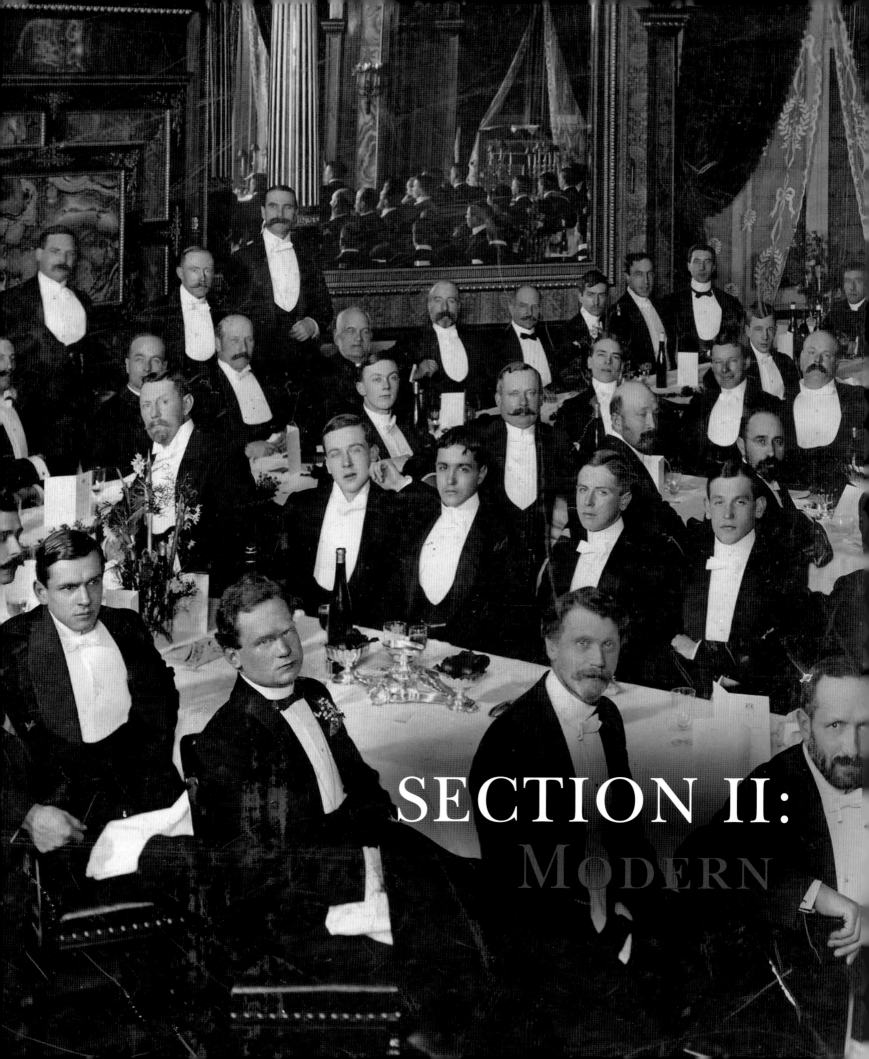

SECTION II:
MODERN

5

'KING RIM' AND REVOLUTION

'THE OLD GUARD'

Framlingham College was a strange, small world in 1971. The men who had won the war 'retired' to teach, to ease out their days quietly in a school untroubled by the social changes of the 20th century. Boys (females of any kind were rare, and even then a moustache was a desirable qualification) were dressed uniformly in green serge, a material of which, it was rumoured, in the distant past there had been a surplus of some kind, and the school mysteriously continued to use it. 'Home clothes' were unknown, exeats rare and limited, and life was simple. The Prefects ran the school, with a nudge now and then from Housemasters. Perhaps the Head of House would be invited in for a sherry on Sunday to discuss any serious misdemeanours, and a quick three across settled it: no long conversations, no children's rights, no filing cabinets full of files, no computers – it was nearly a paperless society (and Jim Hague in the Book Cupboard, now the Maths store, would make you account for the use of every sheet!).

Of course in some ways the continuity was an illusion. In the 1940s things had changed significantly, and the acceptance of Direct Grant status linked the College more closely with day students, funded by the State, until the Labour Government of the 1970s abolished this status and the fees went up to make it harder for the unmoneyed to send their sons. Also in 1949 Brandeston Hall had opened, so the younger pupils had a separate campus: it is hard to imagine Framlingham without

Brandeston today. But perhaps up to that point things had ossified. Direct Grant status limited the financial independence of the school – the State's money was welcome, but regulation less so. The buildings and the campus changed little, there was no money after the war, and only the centenary saw the Athlone Hall built and opened by a granddaughter of Queen Victoria, Princess Alice, Countess of Athlone, wife of the erstwhile Governor General of Canada. Any grander building schemes were put on hold, and the 1960s passed Framlingham by, not in a daze of drugs, but in a Suffolk haze. The Castle hadn't been tidied up (though the view was lovely anyway) and it was a pity both that the trains no longer ran to Framlingham and that the cinemas had closed, but the pace of life was even and there was time to pop to the Railway Inn at lunchtime ('going to the bank') or later to the Hare and Hounds on Double Street, where Jim Finbow would mysteriously provide a spirited chaser to the beer at the evening's close.

In the modern world it could not last, but Common Room, like the Bourbons, was unlikely to see the revolution coming. Mr Porter was a scholarly, gentle Headmaster, and much administration was left to the Housemasters. Borrett (it was an age of surnames) was undoubtedly an active Second Master on the games field, but he was conservative in his approach to boys and teaching. It was pretty simple: don't let them misbehave, and they won't – and generally they didn't! Four boys' houses were crammed into the one

Laurie Rimmer with Norman Borrett at the opening of Borrett's; Brian Underwood, Master i/c Hockey, is on the left.

Far left: Norman Borrett, Second Master and sporting colossus.

Left: Artie Hall became an Honorary OF in 1983.

main building still, with set rooms the only living space for juniors, Garrett and Stradbroke at the west end, Rendlesham and Kerrison to the east. Housemasters had their single rooms (they were single men) and shared a bathroom with an amazing geyser – it was a simple life.

Consolations there were. College servants were College servants, and men such as Artie Hall served Common Room man and boy. It was an age when coal fires and chimneys actually worked. If the food was simple, it was at least served. Common Room was what Palmerston called the old House of Commons, an assembly of gentlemen. When one looks at their modern epigones, one can only lament their passing: *o tempora, o mores!* Borrett never needed a tracksuit to win his myriad national titles – what would he make of the shell-suited lycra-clad wonder-boys of today? It was an incident if a master was seen without jacket and tie. Gowns were worn to chapel and to lessons, where the master was on the dais to view his classes, rather larger than today. The amply flowing gown billowing down the corridor is a vision lost, and the corridor itself is vandalised by fire-doors (we were almost proud of being the greatest fire-risk in Suffolk) – how would the old Chemistry master 'Squiffy' Thomas have made it home today, bouncing as he did (tradition has it) from wall to wall? Even the old Otis lift is gone. Ah, Ichabod!

So this was the world of Hague and Clarke, of de Whalley and Coggins, of Maulden and Robinson, of Melsom and Gillett. Some kept their ranks (Colonel Courtice, Commander Coggins), others not – though three used to meet for dinner at the Crown on Alamein day. Tom Fleming did the woodwork, Martin Irving did the Modern Languages, Bill Baly taught Latin and Sgt Major Howard the P.E. … and no doubt a few juniors came and went. But it was a small world, self-contained and safe, untroubled by aspiration, but respectable at upper-middle-class dinner tables, and a few chaps went on to Oxford and Cambridge and the professions.

Indeed, it could not last. When Porter resigned, even the Governors, in one of those fits of feeling the need for change emerging from their genuinely smoke-filled room, appointed L.I. Rimmer Headmaster (1971–89), and the old age was gone. (It was like 1936, when a new monarch landed hatless from the air.) Balls would still be struck across the Back, Albert would still look out over the mere, but the Lancastrians had come south and the Suffolk idyll was to be rudely interrupted.

The Old Guard stands firm: James Hague disciplines errant M.A. Child (Rendlesham, 1952–6). Child had put a pencil up the breech of his rifle and fired a blank which drove the pencil into a tree. 'Dibber' saw this, took Child's rifle from him and said, 'GO, BOY!' It is not known where Child went.

INDEPENDENCE AND CO-EDUCATION

Laurie Rimmer was educated at Birkenhead School and as a young man did National Service in Cyprus, where he held a commission in the Intelligence Corps, before going up to Corpus Christi, Oxford, to read Geography. He was 'outstanding in all ball games' (Leslie Gillett), but excelled most spectacularly at rugby, in which he won an Oxford Blue, captained Bath RUFC and played for England. He won the first of his five international caps at Twickenham against South Africa in 1961.

After Oxford, Laurie became Senior Geography Master at Dauntsey's School and Housemaster and Master i/c Rugby at the Royal Grammar School, Lancaster, where his bold, swashbuckling approach to life was soon imaginatively translated into the world of education. As friend and former colleague Nick Ward recalled at his Memorial Service:

Laurie Rimmer.

As Head of Geography in a department of one [at Dauntsey's], Laurie operated under his own system of rules. He acquired an out-of-the-way classroom in which he always taught with the window open to enable him to easily flick the ash from his cigarette, which he habitually smoked when teaching. It also enabled the quick disposal of evidence should the Headmaster be on the prowl. He was described as the antithesis of a shrinking violet, well-liked by colleagues and idolised by the boys.

As an international flanker, Rimmer thought nothing of ruffling a few feathers on the pitch before smoothing them in the bar afterwards, and one suspects that it was this combination of tenacity, charm and supreme self-confidence that encouraged the Governors to appoint the young 35-year-old Headmaster. Rimmer was certainly the man to make the radical changes deemed necessary to bring the College into line with late-20th-century expectations. Some long-serving staff not surprisingly found the break with tradition painful, but the College needed to move with the times. Hence, the almost immediate abolition of the time-honoured tradition of 'shacking' (i.e. fagging) at meal times, along with the freedom for Prefects to administer corporal punishment and the requirement of boys to wear the traditional black College caps and blazers. It was no longer

*The new Dining Hall cafeteria experience (**left**) brought about an immediate end to 'shacking' at meal times. It was introduced by the Bursar, Major Farthing (aka 'Penny' Farthing – pictured above with Stanley Porter in 1963), not for economy reasons he claimed, but to offer greater choice and a better dining experience. The 1971 Framlinghamian commented that 'long periods of waiting idle at meals will be no more and here the Bursar hoped to save on bent cutlery'! It's interesting to note the paintings of the third Earl of Stradbroke and Viscount Ullswater, 'Speaker Lowther', hanging at the other end of the Dining Hall.*

obligatory for masters to wear gowns in class and, with his Housemaster's permission, a boy might be granted licence to put on a suitably sober sweater in the evenings. The introduction of a cafeteria system also brought a welcome change to the culinary fare served up in the Dining Hall, as unappetising old school standards such as 'yellow peril', 'Caesar's bricks' and 'dinosaurs' were replaced with a more rich and varied menu.

It is difficult to write the history of a revolution. The new man had brought his lieutenants with him. Hugh Kennon would take over as Housemaster of Garrett and Stuart Westley (after a confusing interlude) would take on Rendlesham. Ruby Graham would take over as Domestic Bursar, a role she would fulfil for the next 16 years. The Old Guard had to take cover. Broad went from Brandeston (where the 'Headmaster' became the 'Master' only), Carruthers went from Rendlesham, taking the last Classics with him to Fettes. Bill Baly would have to settle for other subjects. The rest hunkered down, as Borrett did his best to limit the damage.

The changes came. 'Pryor House' was built in 1972, whose architecture eludes my pen. It was named after Major Charles Selwyn Pryor, Chairman of the Governors (1964–72) and Deputy Lieutenant of Suffolk. As a keen ornithologist, Laurie Rimmer was only too pleased to take advantage of the views of the wildlife across the mere to Framlingham Castle, but the new Head's house freed up accommodation for Housemasters with wives in the main school, and women had a foot in the door.

In 1974 the accursed comprehensivisation of English education faced the school with a stark choice. As Harold Wilson forged ahead into the white heat of the technological revolution, Framlingham turned its back on him and went fully independent. This had two immediate effects: fees rose sharply and the intellectual quality of the intake suffered from the loss of state-funded 11+ pupils. Change had to come, albeit slowly at first.

However, Rimmer and the Governors were able to make bold financial and educational decisions, welcoming girls into Brandeston Hall and the College in 1976–7, while launching a major building programme.

Hugh Kennon with Garrett House, c.1975.

Right: Headmaster Laurie Rimmer and Governors in 1975. MJC's beloved blue Morris Traveller is parked close by. Sadly a later version would be crushed by a fir tree while parked on Pembroke Road in the storms of October 1987 (**below right**). The silver lining in the storm clouds was the fortnight half-term, which we have enjoyed ever since.

BURN BEFORE READING

PRIVATE & CONFIDENTIAL

Bursar

THOUGHTS ON INDEPENDENCE

There can be little doubt that the College is bound to be under politico-economic pressure over the next few years. East Suffolk have ceased to take up places with us, sending 11+ boys (the selective examination continues) to the Mills Grammar School in town. It is difficult to forecast how near the 25% free place requirement we will be but it will become increasingly difficult for this figure to be maintained as fewer and fewer Local Authorities continue to help parents. Numberous meetings which I have attended dealing with the Direct Grant cause, the arguments for boarding "need", the need for variety in education have seldom been helpful and never conclusive. Each Direct Grant School is unique - it's local problems prohibiting a general pattern to emerge. In my view the Direct Grant system is doomed. We must face this fact and realise it is a question of time before Direct Grant ceases to be a viable status. It is important to recognize that this view would not change even if the Government changed - a different Government might mean a postponement of the end.

Above: Rimmer's private thoughts on independence.

In September 1976 expanding numbers (337 boarders and 90 day-boys) encouraged the setting up of a day house for boys – Ziegele House. Its 87 members were based in what is the current IT Suite (on the site of Janet Rutterford's former School Shop), and alongside its fair share of 'smart alecs' included the first three girls to be admitted to the College Sixth Form: Penny Hinves, Rosemary Little and Carol Machen. As a result, as the first Ziegele Housemaster, John Maulden, wittily observed some years later, 'I became Housemaster and Housemistress in one go'.

Was it educational vision, economic savvy, or a sense of humour that led to the introduction of co-education? Probably all three. But the subsequent move from one moustachioed matron to a bevy of female teachers and an increasing number of girls with their white socks about the place would change the ethos of the College for ever.

Right: Girls: viewed with suspicion in 1976 (Penny Hinves, Rosemary Little and Carol Machen: Ziegele, 1976–8), but by the early 1980s happily settled.

Far right: Pembroke Girls: Katherine Ogilvie (1982–5) and Louise Rogers (1982–7).

By September 1979 there were significant numbers of day girls at the College from 13+ and while in the immediate term they continued to be referred to as 'Ziegele House Girls', they at least now had their own accommodation. 'The new house is well suited to the girls' requirements and it offers good comfortable surroundings for study and relaxation and also changing facilities for games' afternoons.' (*The Framlinghamian*, Autumn 1979). Moreover, with the arrival of Mrs Valerie Bidwell in 1979 as Senior Mistress, they also had an able ally to champion their cause. As a result by the Spring Term they were no longer referred to as 'Ziegele House Girls', but as 'Girls House' and by 'the Summer Term, Pembroke House had established a stable position within the College' (*The Framlinghamian*, Summer 1980). When Mrs Bidwell left to become Headmistress of Norwich High School in 1985, Pembroke had become a flourishing unit of 78 boarding and day girls. 'Much of the credit for the smooth integration of girls in what had been an all-male community is hers' (*The Framlinghamian*, Summer 1985).

Philippa Cartmell (née Watts; Ziegele, 1979–80; Pembroke, 1980–4) provides personal insight into the difficulties girls experienced in a traditionally all-male environment:

'Until 1979, there had been a Grammar School in Framlingham so I had spent from 11 to 13 there, as had

Philippa Cartmell.

FRANCIS OTTO ZIEGELE (1900–78)

Ziegele joined Blue Set (later to become Kerrison House) at the College in 1910 at just ten years old and left in 1917. He served in the Royal Warwickshire Regiment during the final years of the First World War before emigrating to Singapore, where he became an East India Merchant Manager in 1920 and Honorary Secretary of the Singapore branch of the SOF in 1937. He was a civilian POW between 1942 and 1945 following Japanese occupation and thereafter remained the most extraordinarily generous of College benefactors until his death in 1978.

most of my friends, in the belief that boys and girls had pretty much the same sort of school lives. When that school closed, my parents were left with the dilemma of the Comprehensive system, which was untried at that time, or the College, who had then decided to accept girls from 13. My brother (and several male cousins) had all been at Framlingham in the preceding years and like many farmers' sons in the area had whiled out their days happily there until they could return to the fishing rod, the guns and the tractors.

'I wasn't enamoured of my parents' choice, since I'd enjoyed the Mills Grammar School, but we did a tour of other schools in the area and eventually I agreed with my mother that Woodbridge was far too far to drive to every day and that Framlingham would be fine. The first term was a shock for us all. Several male members of the College staff had decided to leave when the girls were allowed all the way through the school (girls had been allowed in the Sixth Form before 1979). Many of the boys had come from all-male preparatory schools and had never encountered female classmates. The real problem was, though, that there were so few of us in the early years and that while some issues had been thought through, many others had, I suspect, been understandably left until there were enough of us to warrant the necessary changes.

'Academic life was of course totally unproblematic. The girls were naturally more conscientious than the boys and had mostly come from a Grammar School background, and I felt that the remaining staff seemed happy to have us to enliven the academic performance. Music and Drama were also enhanced, as were all things classroom-related.

'Sporting life, however, was more of a challenge. In the winter months there really weren't enough of

us that first year to make up a hockey team, although tennis and netball were possible, providing every girl played at every opportunity. And as I suspect had been the case in most co-educational schools at that time, only a handful of the girls in that first year actually loved sport. The rest, like me, tolerated the endless afternoon training sessions and wondered why we couldn't be back in the classroom. The summer months were even more difficult. The College hadn't realised that there were different "standards" (an athletics term which gives a minimum level of achievement to be attained in each discipline) for boys and girls, so we were forced to use the boys' standards for that whole first year. Needless to say, we never achieved any standards at all and languished at the bottom of those lovely water meadows with few sporting ambitions realised. Swimming was made even more complicated by the fact that the outdoor pool at that time had a changing area around the pool with wooden slatted swing-doors which started at knee height and finished mid-chest. This clearly wasn't going to work for the girls so we were asked to change in the maintenance shed in the corner, which was excellent, apart from being totally dark when the full-height door was closed. It was also full of paint pots and brooms and we therefore dressed and undressed very slowly and carefully.

'And finally pastoral and extra-curricular life was I suppose a blend of everything. "Fagging" was still unofficially in operation, although it was very quickly stopped when staff realised what the adverse repercussions might be. But again the girls didn't think it particularly odd and we went along with such arcane practices because every new experience at school was just that, and we took everything at face value. We were asked to join the CCF, and the Navy was considered a suitable home for us but of course the uniforms didn't fit too well and the tutor felt the only naval subject girls could possibly be interested in was knot-tying (which he felt was like knitting), so that didn't impress us and we left quite quickly.

'The school discos were the real revelation though. Before girls had been admitted to the College the school had always invited girls from all-girls schools to the end-of-term discos, and this convention carried on despite our arrival. Once the poor girls were herded in, it was up to us to help the boys decide who and how to ask the "outsiders" to dance. It was in these small ways, we gradually gained acceptance although the school retained its status as a boys' school (with a few girls) for several years thereafter.'

The contrast with previous arrangements is highlighted by Keith Isaac's (Moreau, 1972–7) account of the pre-co-education situation: 'Sixth Form dances', he writes, 'remain in the memory. These were not so much "with" the neighbouring girls' schools but "against" them. The Athlone Hall was transformed into a darkened harem of a disco with chairs stacked to the level of the balcony and blankets garnered from all the boarding houses thrown onto the floors. There was no light in these areas. Doubtless Fram has since been civilised by the admission of girls.'

Eventually a girls' boarding house followed in 1985, and was named after Queen Victoria, while Pembroke became the exclusive preserve of day girls. Girls' inter-House sporting competition for the Douglas Shield began. This sporting equivalent of the boys' Stocks Shield was named after Elizabeth Douglas (OF, 1979–86), who had been Head of Pembroke immediately prior to the division of the houses.

Co-education: Upper Sixth, 1988.

For a time the magnitude of such dramatic changes would be hidden by apparent outward continuities. The Old Guard would linger on into the 1980s, some of them always regretting a bygone age. There was enough of the traditional schoolmaster in Rimmer to smooth the change on the wider front. Perhaps the conservatives knew in their hearts that after *Lady Chatterley* and the Beatles' first LP, they would have to change their ways. Like Dr Johnson, they would try to uphold the best of the conservative tradition, but they would face increasing challenges as the 20th century drew towards its close.

PHYSICAL CHANGES

During this time there was a great deal of building, some of it more functional than aesthetically pleasing. In 1973 a new Kerrison boarding house for 70 boys was built on the other side of College Road. Looking at its strong, straight cuboid lines today, it could have been designed on a child's Etch A Sketch (and from an aesthetic perspective, one can quite believe that it probably was!), but it has certainly served its purpose. £60,000 towards the cost of what John Maulden describes as a 'state-of-the-art paradise of luxury accommodation' was generously donated by Francis Otto Ziegele.

For the moment Stradbroke would retain its magnificent 50-bed dormitory above the Dining Hall, later divided firstly into classrooms and most recently into single study-bedrooms. The long line of basins in the upstairs corridor, with two solitary lavatories were the hygiene, though the first floor kept baths awhile,

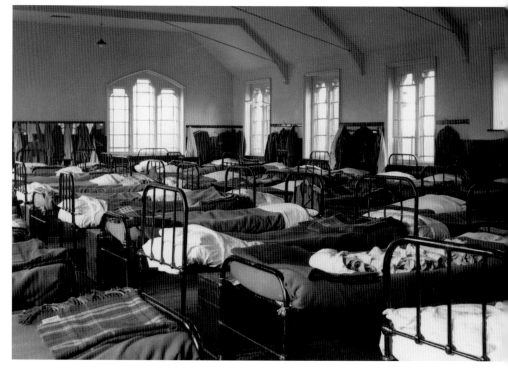

Stradbroke dormitory.

until the second flood into the Head's secretary's office led to their disappearance.

Rimmer himself did not need much study space – the Head's study was in Pryor House. Only later would an SMT (Senior Management Team) be invented and they and their secretaries would multiply along the front rooms on the ground floor.

Netherby became the Sanatorium in 1974 and the old Sanatorium was converted to an annexe for Moreau House – 'Moreau B'. Moreau's numbers

Debra Hardman and Moreau girls, 2014, with the sequicentennial bottle of port.

KERRISON HOUSE

Above: *Framlingham's quintessence of Bauhaus: the new Kerrison, 1973.*

EMILE EDOUARD MOREAU CBE (1856–1937)

The bronze bust of Emile Moreau by E. Whitney Smith in the Dining Hall was commissioned by the SOF and unveiled in 1936. It stands as a fitting tribute to his unstinting service and generosity to his old school (OF, 1871–3). Emile Moreau came to the College aged 15 as a Pembroke Scholar and played for the 1st cricket XI in 1872. After leaving he made his money as a merchant in India (principally in rubber and oil), but before doing so he found time to become Rudyard Kipling's first publisher in 1889 – *Soldiers Three* was the first of seven books he had published through A.H. Wheeler & Co.'s Indian Library, priced at the princely sum of a single rupee. He served with distinction in Munitions and then Propaganda Distribution in India during the Great War and was awarded a CBE in 1919. In the same year he became President of the SOF, and from 1920 he served as a College Trustee and Governor until his death in 1937, aged 80.

His affection for the College was such that he gave all manner of generous donations, from cups for Gymnastics, science equipment and reference books for the library, to large lump sums of money for major building projects and the establishment of a very significant Moreau Scholarship fund for high-flying College leavers, as well as a Benevolent Fund for Old Boys 'who have fallen on evil days and are deserving of assistance'.

A new Garrett House, 1979.

were now made comparable to the four existing senior boys' houses through a sometimes painful process of enforced transfer. Keith Isaac (Moreau, 1972–7), who was transferred from Stradbroke to Moreau in 1974 suggests that 'the Housemasters of the other Houses appeared to bin all their undesirables into it, so a few dozen of us ended up there. None of us was much good at sport as far as I recall.' Later in 1983 an adjoining house for the Moreau Housemaster was added and the Moreau boarding facilities were significantly refurbished. The first Housemaster of this reconstituted senior boys' Moreau House was Barry Pritchard. He took over from Bob Gillett who, along with his charming wife Margery, had been sympathetically running Moreau as a junior feeder house for 13-year-old entrants to the College, prior to their transfer to the main school. Such was Bob Gillett's sense of occasion and style that he sought to preserve the memory of the members of Moreau House in the College's centenary year, by laying down a signed bottle of port to be consumed during its sesquicentennial celebration. The inscription on the bottle reads as follows:

To the Master of Moreau House, June 26th, AD 2014. Sir, We the Master, boys and entire household of Moreau House, invite you to uncork and enjoy this bottle of port wine, laid down on June 26th, 1964, the day of the School's Centenary celebrations. Some of us hope to be with you when you do this. For those who cannot be present, we ask you to drink the toast of absent friends. We ask, moreover, that the boys of your house should on this day receive from you some special mark of favour. Good health sir – and prosperity to Moreau House.

Clearly Bob Gillett wasn't anticipating Moreau becoming a girls' house run by a Housemistress, Debra Hardman, by 2014. A lovely thought all the same. Cheers!

Further pastoral improvements followed in 1979, when a new Garrett boarding house for 70 boys was built on the other side of Dennington Road and new English classrooms were created above the Dining Hall in the former Stradbroke junior dormitory. The area in the west wing vacated by Garrett was cleverly exploited by putting in an extra floor; even though this meant some strange divisions of the ancient windows, it created much more space for Stradbroke boys.

The final Rimmerian pastoral development was the reallocation of space in Moreau B to set up Victoria House for girls' boarding in 1985. This involved adapting an existing building, adding the rotunda as well as Housemaster's accommodation, to provide accommodation for up to 60 girl boarders. It also provided a natural division within the old Pembroke

House between boarding and day girls. Under the sympathetic leadership of Charlie and Caroline Baggs, Victoria started with 23 girls in the Summer Term and by the beginning of its second year numbers had risen to 50.

There was also significant investment in College sports facilities. The old Gym, on the site of the current piazza, was in a very dilapidated condition and so in 1975 a new Sports Hall was opened by HRH Princess Alice. Although at that point 94 years old, the Countess delivered a characteristically direct and engaging speech on a windswept day outside the hall, and then had tea with the boys in the Dining Hall. Its initial cost of some £41,000 was supplemented in 1978 by a further £10,000 investment in a new beech strip floor designed to help facilitate multi-purpose usage as an exam hall and Speech Day venue.

Victoria in the sunshine in the 1990s with the rotunda on the left.

Top: *Princess Alice opening the new Sports Hall in 1975.*

Above: *Pam Rogers, Head of Girls' Games, with the new Sports Hall in the background.*

QUEEN VICTORIA (1837–1901)

On 30 July 1864, Queen Victoria granted the Royal Charter which founded and constituted 'The Albert Middle-Class College in Suffolk'. This was at a time when memorials to Prince Albert were springing up everywhere and the Queen, although something of a recluse after 1861, was more than willing to support projects which perpetuated her husband's name. In many ways, therefore, it was appropriate that the first girls' boarding house was named after her.

Victoria is the longest reigning British monarch. She ruled an Empire on which 'the sun never set', administered by young men from the new public schools such as Framlingham, and the SOF continues to have branches from South Africa to Australia, and from Hong Kong to Canada. She travelled widely on the railways, one of whose humble branch lines brought the first Framlinghamians to the College in 1864. Related to nearly all the crowned heads of Europe she is a singularly suitable patron of a House that now contains many girls from Europe and the wider world.

Victoria was conscientiously devoted to her duties throughout her reign and, surviving five assassination attempts, won public respect for being extremely cool under fire. Her tastes and outlook were closely in tune with those of the middle classes of her time. She disliked the emerging styles of modern art and music. She eschewed the company of those she described as 'fashionable and fast people'. She would probably be amused by much of what goes on today in the house that bears her name.

Above: College 1st XV v OFs on Lords, 1978.

Below: V.G. Bromage pictured goalkeeping in his College Colours blazer in the 1960 OF match on the Back.

Below right: Christine Janes (mother of Nigel Janes, Kerrison, 1984–89) who returned to open the new floodlit Astroturf in 1990.

In 1979 the Bromage Pool was officially declared open at Speech Day by Mrs Carmen Bromage. This was preceded by an address from Mr Jim Smith (OF), who 'spoke of the excellence of the new Olympic standard pool' and how it was named 'as a memorial to Ventura George "Brom" Bromage, "Brom" (OF, 1947–54), Captain of Swimming in his day, and, of course, subsequently a Governor and Chairman of the College Executive Committee and Secretary of the SOF' (*The Framlinghamian*, Summer Term, 1979).

A new all-weather hockey pitch was opened by Grand Slam Singles and Doubles Tennis Champion Christine Truman Janes in 1980. It was named 'Borrett's'

after the retiring College Second Master, former Great Britain Hockey Captain and Olympic Silver Medallist (1948) Norman Francis Borrett (Stradbroke, 1931–6). Borrett was also five times British Amateur Squash Champion and played cricket for Essex and Devon. He was described in his obituary in *The Times* as 'arguably Britain's most talented post-war all-round amateur sportsman', but as a schoolmaster he is perhaps best captured by the Headmaster in his Speech Day address: 'His eyes smile as his voice cuts across the Back. He is a legend in his own time – there cannot be another living man who has an entry in the *Guinness Book of Records* and a Hockey ground named after him. His contribution to this College has been enormous.'

Two other areas of College life cried out for new facilities. In 1981 the Music School was built, mimicking the style in miniature of the Athlone Hall. This provided a Recital Hall along with teaching and practice rooms for the first time, at a cost of £84,363. It is amazing to think that for many years before this, Music teaching and practice took place in all sorts of nooks and crannies around the College, including the lavatories at the back of the Athlone. This new facility meant that under the leadership of the recently appointed Director of Music, John Cooper Green, Music at the College soon began to flourish.

A still more ambitious project was the design and erection of the Technology and Activities Centre (TAC) to the east of the Back. Since this affected the view from the Castle, getting planning permission was a challenge,

and the building that emerged reminds one of the perils of modern design. This was opened in 1985 by Sir Richard Cave (Chairman of Vickers and Deputy Chairman of British Rail) and designed by the College Surveyor, Dick Hollins FRICS.

'The Centre has three floors, and there are 16,000 square feet of floor space: the top floor is devoted to art, the middle floor to a huge workshop with auxiliary rooms for technical drawing, design and computing; and the basement has another workshop, plus a mass of

smaller rooms for activities such as cooking, printing, sewing, hobbies, photography, pottery etc. The CCF also has its headquarters there'. (*The Framlinghamian*, 1985/6). This distinctive Toblerone-like structure certainly wasn't to everyone's liking, and the timing of its official opening on 14 October (Battle of Hastings day) may have even appeared somewhat Freudian to some: another one in the eye for the aesthetes and all that! However, there can be absolutely no doubt that it has served its purpose.

If the TAC could be built on a slope, even Rimmer couldn't expand the Chapel to the south, but increasing pupil numbers made some sort of extension necessary if the whole College was going to be accommodated. It is to the Headmaster's credit that in an increasingly secular age he should prioritise what was a costly and difficult build. In 1986 the Chapel extension and refurbishment was completed, where after over a year of 'holding makeshift services in the Athlone Hall, with play scenery and the guts, veins and arteries of the old organ as the visual uplift … it is a delight to listen to the word of God' (*The Framlinghamian*, 1986/7). As well as the much-needed increase in physical space provided (an additional 300 could now be seated in the

Left: Nick Ward, Director of the new Technology and Activities Centre, with the Headmaster, Laurie Rimmer, and Sir Richard Cave. Nick was appointed in 1982 and after five years as Stradbroke Housemaster was made College Bursar in 1988. He subsequently became Headmaster of RHS, Holbrook.

Below left: Art on the top floor.

Below: The TAC in more sympathetic surroundings in the 1990s.

Bottom: Photography on the bottom floor.

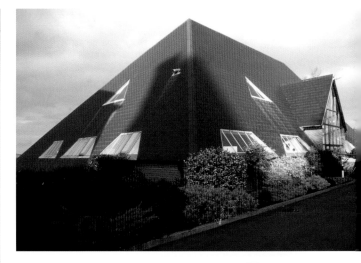

The Chapel extension – Carol Service, 2012.

extension), the Osmond pipe organ installed in 1967 (by this point 'unmatched anywhere else in the world for stodginess', one contemporary critic observed) was replaced by a fine new three-manual electronic organ built by Compton Makin. Tiered choir stalls were set up in the apse. This extension was later consecrated in February 1987 by the Rt Reverend John Dennis, Bishop of St Edmundsbury and Ipswich (with 700 in attendance!), shortly before the October storms almost blew the Chapel spire off. Its repair and replacement was followed by the internal addition of Robert Royston's commissioned crucifix in 1988. The funding for most of these grand designs was managed by the Finance and General Purposes Committee ('F & GP').

Thus the College that Rimmer left in 1989 looked very different from the institution he had come to 18 years earlier, and it had changed in many other ways too. When he walked out of the front door for the last time at the end of the Summer Term in 1989, a banner of three bedsheets was dramatically unfurled from an upstairs window in his honour. It read: 'Bye Bye King Rim, love Fram'.

Left: The Chapel spire, 1987. Andrew Morgan and Stuart Cartwright (Garrett 1986–91) recall the storm sending little Johnny Cooper flying horizontally across the Front like Peter Pan!

Below left: The Finance and General Purposes Committee, 1981, Saxtead. From left to right: Jim Smith, Roger Paul, Ken Knight, General Jack Dye, Iain Ferguson, Headmaster – Laurie Rimmer, Harry Townshend, Bursar – Commander Fawcett.

Below: Laurie's final day – the Headmaster celebrating with Second Master John Whipp.

6

FUN, 'FRIZZ' AND FROLICS

eading the interminable games reports in *The Framlinghamian*, the historian might wonder whether anything academic ever happened at the College at all – and in the case of some pupils, this might well be disturbingly close to the truth. However, Framlingham has always actually had a range of pupils and a number have gone on to good university degrees and careers in which their academic achievements have played a major part. Equally, as the 20th century came to an end, pressures increased on all schools to improve their measurable academic performance, and the College gradually had to respond.

CLASSROOM CULTURE IN THE 1970S AND 1980S

Things were simpler in those days. There were no computers. Some unlikely chap like Mike Robinson did the timetable; the staff grumbled and then got on with it. Gowns were worn to chapel, and many wore them to class. There was none of this early start nonsense: chapel was at 8.45am, had a hymn and a prayer, and started and finished on time. The boys sang, and then all fanned out for lessons, down the corridor of the 'new' classroom block (1925), or to the Science block, or various supplementary pre-fabs. There were no classrooms upstairs in the main block, as these rooms were still dormitories.

A man was alone with his boys in his classroom, for better or worse; he may or may not have been trained. The elder ones had lived through the war, so 20 to 30 boys were relatively small fry. Some younger men, brought up in the 1960s, might have some confusion or some difficulties, but generally order was maintained.

Certainly the older men believed in discipline: Bill Baly was feared; one didn't look out of the window in

Top: Pre-fabs on the Front in 1979.

Above: Mike Robinson in the Chemistry lab.

1st XV rugby, 1974, with N.D. Robinson (Captain) and R.S. Overbury (Secretary).

Far left: *Philip de Whalley in the SDT (Science Demonstration Theatre).*

Left: *Brian Underwood teaching English.*

Mike Robinson's Chemistry lesson; Peter Clarke's pencils were all in place; and Norman Borrett could always, *in extremis*, send for 'Willy', the hockey stick which he could still wield with fearsome force. Tom Fleming could use tools to good effect, many cricketers could aim a wooden board rubber, and Chris Carruthers was not to be messed with. Younger staff such as Stuart Westley (who went on to become Headmaster of Haileybury) took no prisoners either – the maxim was passed down: 'Never trust a boy!' No doubt there were more relaxed and eccentric areas, but at least one of a departmental team would be a no-nonsense disciplinarian. Nearly half the small Common Room were Housemasters or ex-Housemasters. They were used to being obeyed, as was true in John Whipp's German classes.

Was some of it boring? Probably by today's standards, and there were some to whom exam results and the classroom were merely incidental. There wasn't much lesson preparation or marking. Some colleagues might not finish a syllabus. O Level and A Level

seemed permanent and immutable, and paper was not wasted ('Dibber' Hague ran the Book Cupboard with an admirable eye for economy – and no separate stationery staff were required – Jim did 'eight sloggers and the Book Cupboard'). His dictated notes, like those of many others, did not change (though the gold share values recorded at the back might), the original manuscripts only gradually yellowing with age. The advent of GCSE hastened his retirement. Children learnt a broad range of History from the Renaissance to Bismarck, and red herrings on the Desert War could bring things more or less up to date. The question papers for exams were tiny and pupils could fail (and some did!). Internal exam questions could be thought up while walking down the corridor and be chalked onto the wall (painting the uneven wall black was fine, and the gown kept chalk off the old sports jacket). At the end of the lesson, Bill Baly would be tapping his cigarette on the desk, and Tony Coggins would slip out for a gasper. Meanwhile in break the day-boy lavatories could be raided by keen staff to limit student nicotine intake – a two-pronged attack might be needed to be decisive: there were no notices about the government forbidding smoking!

The range of what went on is remembered by Keith Isaac (Moreau, 1972–7):

Right: *John Maulden and Mike Robinson in the 'Stinks' department in the early 1990s.*

'One memory that remains strong is of the school debating society, re-invigorated by the Sixth Form in our last year. One gathering in a packed library on a Sunday evening debated whether "This House regrets the discovery of America", a topic that had been debated years before according to the Minutes filed in the library. At one point the proposer produced a half-bottle of whisky to illustrate what the UK had produced instead of the fizzy drinks made "over there". The then Head Boy was most interested but the proposer politely said the bottle contained only cold tea. (The whisky had been drunk long before.) A riotous evening concluded in defeat when the opponent, Andy Claibourne, an American, told the most obscene joke of the evening!

'I remember a mix of teachers from the early years. Some presented the same stuff from dog-eaten sheets of paper from one year to the next; some had joined after the war and remarkably were still there; others were genuinely keen on teaching. While Laurie Rimmer had been appointed to modernise the school, the task of modernising the staffroom took longer.

'In the days before word processors staff had to handwrite each school report for each candidate without today's luxury of cutting and pasting. My mother kept all my school reports and handed them on to me a few years ago where they have lain in a cupboard largely untouched. Here is a selection of comments:

MJC by Chris Lenton.

- Lower 4th A, English, Easter 1973: 'Poor. He ought to be producing better work.'
- 5th Form Physics, Summer 1975: 'Somewhat erratic work. He is not a strong candidate'. [This was not a great piece of deduction as I believe my mock O Level mark had been around 20 per cent. This was multiple choice and the proverbial monkey writing 'a' to each answer would have scored as well.]
- 5th Form German, Lent 1975: 'Good/excellent when he emerges from his torpor and really bothers.'
- Upper 6th Form History, Spring 1977: 'he goes through flaccid periods'.

'The Head, who had many more of these documents to annotate, rarely got beyond "Coming on well" or "Good", so probably was not paying too much attention.

'That I went on to Selwyn College, Cambridge, was due largely to the inspiring teaching of my two History masters, Jim Hague and Michael Cooke, of John Whipp who taught German, and the support of the Headmaster. I was the only OF there, but a couple of contemporaries had gone to Oxford. Selwyn offered the chance of less work (one essay a week and one hour's one-to-one supervision), and more alcohol and socialising. I also learnt to row, racing at Henley and to taste wine. Thereafter I became a Master of Wine in 1989 and still work in the industry today.'

In the 1980s the science side was still full of characters of considerable eccentricity, but nonetheless effective for that. As author and broadcaster Dr David Bull (Ziegele, 1982–7) writes:

'It's not often that I am asked to write about events that happened some 30 years ago. Most memories of that time have faded. And yet my memories of the classrooms of Framlingham are as clear as ever. That is, in no small part, due to the extraordinary bunch that taught us. You couldn't find a more eclectic cast in a West End revival of a British Farce. Knowledgeable – yes; passionate – yes; good communicators – not many; stylish – ummmn, no. Bonkers – absolutely. Two things fascinate me to this day. Firstly I seem to have retained a huge amount of knowledge from those heady days and secondly, I can visualise the teachers in those classrooms as though it was yesterday.

'Chemistry was a subject I hated with a passion. It made no sense, was intensely boring and deeply complicated. The only reason I did it was because I had to have an A Level in it to get into medical school. But despite rote learning and hours of study, it remained the biggest enigma on the planet. It was taught by two men who had clearly spent far too long in a dark laboratory on their own. Mike Robinson used to leap around the room, holding onto his extraordinary hairstyle, getting overly excited over the most mundane details of organic chemistry such as double carbon bonds, whilst John Maulden harboured an unhealthy obsession with the periodic table – a chart which had clearly been drawn up by wizards. The only way I could learn it was thanks to a Tom Lehrer song: "There's antimony, arsenic, aluminium, selenium", which I changed to "There's hydrogen and helium, lithium and beryllium". And yet with hindsight I now realise how important and fascinating Chemistry really is. Once you understand that everything we do, touch, buy and wear is affected by its chemistry, it suddenly takes on new importance. So why didn't they tell us? For me as a doctor, the chemical reactions that happen inside a person's body and the way drugs affect us are of paramount importance. But that revelation was to elude me for some years.

'The most exciting thing that ever happened in Chemistry was trying to make various powders and potions explode for no apparent reason. I remember super-heating a Pyrex beaker to such high temperatures that it exploded into a bazillion pieces, showering my classmates with boiling chunks of glass and strange fluorescent stains. Light relief was always afforded by trying to set each other's jackets on fire with Bunsen burners when Mr Michael Robinson, or Bin as he was affectionately known, wasn't looking. We learnt very quickly that the green jackets were highly flammable, and let off extraordinary noxious chemicals when presented with naked flame.

'Physics wasn't much better. Philip de Whalley entertained us by embodying the persona of a mad scientist. He would leap around the classroom whilst clearly having a severe episode of mania. He would demonstrate the concepts of potential and kinetic energy by throwing wooden carts attached with ticker tape off the top of two upturned tables. As they hurtled towards the floor at breakneck speed, he would shout "wooooooo! She's a blowin'!" This clinical diagnosis

of mania was further confirmed by his extraordinary choices of clothing.

'Of all the sciences, Biology was the one I liked most. But the teachers were just as insane. Howard Robinson, or Zowie, instilled his infectious appetite for the subject. I can remember to this day him running around the lab holding a large glass beaker full to the brim of water. He was demonstrating how oxygen is transported around the human body. The glass jug represented haemoglobin and the water was oxygen. As he careered around the bemused students holding the perilously full glass beaker with out-stretched arms, he explained the oxygen dissociation curve and how oxygen binds to haemoglobin so it can be carried to the tissues. Once this explanation was complete it was time to explain how oxygen was then released from the blood. This was done by him coming to a complete standstill from a running trot. The beaker, or haemoglobin, stayed in his hands; the water, or oxygen, did not. It sailed over our heads in a mighty fine wave until the laws of gravity took over and dumped the whole lot on one of my colleagues sitting at the front. He was wet, we were convulsed and I have never forgotten it.

'But the subject I loved was English and Drama, taught by the most passionate thespian himself, Tony Lawrence. Tony cast me as a lead in a number of plays and musicals over the years and I really think I have him to thank for changing a shy retiring boy from Framlingham into this confident show-off that I have become.

'It's very telling that my experience at Fram has moulded my career. I have managed to combine the two subjects I loved the most at school – Biology and Drama – into a single career that has afforded me the most extraordinary experiences. I'm writing this from Los Angeles, where I now live. In fact, it gets better. I'm actually in my dressing room in the LA Center Studios where I am hosting a huge prime-time show for a US television network. I have to pinch myself sometimes. I may physically be thousands of miles away, but Framlingham is part of my soul and will always be with me.'

Technology in the Classroom

Very gradually Framlingham began to move away from straight chalk and talk. If the BBC had been making educational programmes for some decades, they had

Howard Robinson by Chris Lenton.

Doctor David Bull.

made little impact here, and on adventurous days staff could play an audio-tape or even LPs, for instance of Churchill's speeches. By the end of Rimmer's time television and video were just beginning to be used, though classes generally still had to be marched off to the OLT (Old Lecture Theatre) or the SDT – only gradually would TV and video facilities become more widely available in the classroom in the 1990s.

Meanwhile the duplicated sheet was starting to replace the dictated note. Hugh Kennon loved his Banda machine and the strong odour of its fluid served as an opiate for many an economist. The key to a legible Banda sheet – and many exam papers were scarcely possible to decipher – was clear and firm calligraphy. Others preferred the Gestetner with its rich, inky aroma, and typing the waxed skins on the manual Remington or Olivetti was part of the craft of lesson preparation. The OHP (Over Head Projector) was also employed by some, either using individual acetates or an entire roll of handwritten transparencies, which would allow a class to copy down notes almost ad infinitum. Ultimately the photocopier would become available, and the rain forests suffered accordingly … ten years on and recycling would have to be reinvented. A lady in a white coat would be employed to fulfil staff duplicating orders, as well as to record radio and TV programmes as departments required. The age of *Blackadder* had arrived.

Most significant of all in the long term was the coming of computers: the idiosyncratic Ben Falat was the computer enthusiast, and in the winter 1980 *Framlinghamian* he wrote excitedly about the new computer centre: 'Can you imagine electronics in the bathroom? The new computer centre has been set up in what is now officially "room 18" – to some OFs better known as the bathroom, or later as the dormitory, with the frosted windows above the main entrance. Three microcomputers purchased from "Sharp" and "Nascom" were in continuous use by pupils who could play "space-invaders", as well as making up and running their own programmes.' By 1985 the TAC had its own designated Computer Room, with a 'network of 16 BBC Model B computers using a 10-Megabite Winchester hard disc file system'. This advance was overseen by Nick Ward, Director of Technology and Activities, until 1989, when he handed this position over to David Morgan. The following year, larger-than-life Dave Fuller would arrive to give computing a further shot in the arm. By now no student could be unaware of the significance of 'lego-bits' or the need to 'Get that certificate'! So eccentric a man soon had to be promoted to Oundle in 1996.

BBC Computing on the middle floor of the TAC, c.1985 (below) … and ten years later (right).

A further advance followed in 2002, by which time the Deputy Head Academic, Clive Norton, was driving the IT revolution: a new suite of rooms was opened in the former College Shop area, with 40 computers (running Windows 2000 machines and Office XP) connected to the College network and Internet access. In 2007 the new College website and e-portal would be launched with potential still being developed in 2014.

However, for many years classrooms themselves were still innocent of computers, though other incremental changes were seeping in. Blackboards were turning white, though with typical Framlingham economy, at first the adhesion of a strip of white plastic to the wall was deemed sufficient and some staff had problems with indelible marker pens. The décor was enhanced by industrial carpet squares and blinds replaced the old Second World

War black-out curtains. The carpeting spelt the end of the old Master's dais, which had raised him nine inches above his class, but whether authority suffered is a moot point. Classrooms were less reverberative and perhaps friendlier places, and boards for subject specific displays that changed occasionally were a further enhancement. Heating also evolved from the old iron radiators to modern electrical fan heaters, so noisy that they had to be turned off while teaching; when there was no independent switch, the canny schoolmaster learned to bring his own screw-driver to remove the fuse.

Nowadays computers with Internet access, speakers, projectors, interactive Smartboards and printers are standard equipment in all classrooms, and the modern teacher and pupil would struggle to operate without them. Many students use their own laptops and the future is 'virtual'.

Above left: David Fuller – 'Get that Certificate!'

Left: The School Shop in 1995, run for many years by Janet Rutterford, later transformed into computer rooms.

Above: Jon Slay taking advantage of the new technology in the teaching of Year 9 Geography in 2013.

Right: Dr Ian Baird in characteristic pose.

THE WINDS OF CHANGE

Annabel Cody (née Cole; Pembroke, 1988–90) remembers the school as Laurie Rimmer handed over to James Miller:

'By the time that I arrived at the College in 1988 for the Sixth Form, I knew a fair amount about what schools have the potential to offer. Framlingham was my fifth school. My father's career had seen us move frequently within Britain and, by the age of 16, I possessed a wardrobe of uniforms in a variety of colours and a far greater stock of experiences and adventures at some of the country's more highly regarded institutions of learning.

'Aged nine, I had struggled to find my place in a sea of regimented girls in mushy-pea-green tunics and formal classrooms; two years in Edinburgh had been vibrant, engaging and culturally eye-opening. The bulk of my secondary education had been spent in an all-girls day school which was then, and is now, one of the UK's top-performing independent schools.

'It cannot be denied that this school got results – but at a significant price. Pressure was intense, building to a frenzy at exam times with extra-curricular activities – even for 11-year-olds – frowned upon unless they would enhance a university application. I left with an armful of GCSEs but wondering if the experience could possibly be classed as an education.

'When we moved to Suffolk, we looked at several schools but the College was the only real contender. I remember going to visit for the first time and being surprised to find that, despite its imposing appearance, the school's approach was extremely down-to-earth. Furthermore, it was a place where the pupils seemed to be the focus, rather than the grades.

'Laurie Rimmer was the Head at the time and any doubts we had as to whether this might be the right school were put to rest as soon as we met him. Our tour of the school was carried out in his typically relaxed and flamboyant style. He was a man very much at home in the College and obviously cared enormously about the pupils and their education. When he told my parents that he did the job because he just "cared about the children", they grabbed the nearest pen and signed me up.

'When I eventually started at the College, it did not disappoint. I was a day girl in Pembroke, under the watchful eye of Mrs Nesling, and soon found myself with a group of friends far more diverse and engaging than I had found in other schools. What struck me most clearly, however, was that at my last school, the pupils had often seemed burdened by their education and were certainly reduced by the pressure put upon them. At Framlingham, my peers were far less afraid and as a consequence, more open to ideas.

'As far as the teaching goes, it would not be an exaggeration to say that it was a revelation. Learning was made easier because the approach was less formal than I had been used to – my teachers had natural enthusiasm for their subjects which was not limited to within the formal timetable. Play readings were conducted over tea at our English teacher's house (Dr Ian Baird) and extra poetry lessons fitted in at weekends. Having come from a background of day schools, I found the boarding element remarkable. The school had a family atmosphere and I quickly got to know teachers who did not teach my subjects. Indeed, I am still in touch with one or two.

'The outstanding thing about the College was that it gave me chances that my other schools had not. I felt the school cared about me, not as a statistic in the league tables, but as a person. As a consequence I gained confidence which I believe enabled me to do far better in my A Levels than I would have done had I remained at my previous school. Laurie Rimmer retired after my first year at the College. This was certainly a

Informal fizz in the English department in 1990.

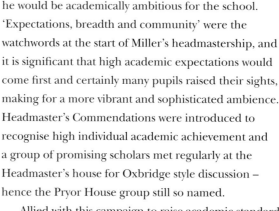

loss but I am enduringly grateful that he introduced me to Framlingham – and turned my expectations of education on their head.'

'EXPECTATIONS, BREADTH AND COMMUNITY'

After 18 years as Headmaster Rimmer retired in 1989. He was succeeded by another man still in his thirties at the time of his appointment, James F.X. Miller (1989–94), whose son Tom would attend the College as had the Rimmer boys, Shane, Drummond, Daniel and Arran. James's wife, Ruth, would also play a full part in College life, including tutoring in Pembroke House. In many ways James brought a breath of fresh air, having a strong academic background from his time at Oxford where he read PPE and 17 years teaching Classics and Economics at Winchester. James's initial reaction to Framlingham was very positive, but early on he made it very clear that

he would be academically ambitious for the school. 'Expectations, breadth and community' were the watchwords at the start of Miller's headmastership, and it is significant that high academic expectations would come first and certainly many pupils raised their sights, making for a more vibrant and sophisticated ambience. Headmaster's Commendations were introduced to recognise high individual academic achievement and a group of promising scholars met regularly at the Headmaster's house for Oxbridge style discussion – hence the Pryor House group still so named.

Allied with this campaign to raise academic standards was the desire to attract more able students from local preparatory schools, and Miller worked hard to show what Framlingham had to offer at events such as the annual Prep Schools' Challenge, orchestrated in the early years by Brian Smallcombe. This has since grown into a series of annual events, some with an academic twist such as the Geography-History-Environmental Science days run by David Barker, and Ken Hoyle's Maths Challenges; Stewart Reeve hosted OBH students for silversmithing in the TAC; and a whole range of sports tournaments take place throughout the year.

Above: Second Master, Tony Lawrence, addresses the congregation in 1993.

Below: Miller at the Prep Schools' Challenge presenting prizes.

Bottom: Mrs Randall in her study with German scholar Julia Sassen in 1998.

Below: Speech Day, 1991 – Katie Norton and James Fingland (Head Boy) welcome the visiting speaker, with James Miller and Sir Patrick Howard-Dobson in attendance.

He also strengthened the academic Sixth Form by inviting able students from Germany, an initiative that was to blossom and flourish under his successor, Mrs Randall, whose fluent German was a further encouragement to students from Prince Albert's homeland to stay for two years and to study at English universities. A brilliant example of this interchange was Felicitas Köhnen, who read English at Magdalene College, Cambridge.

Miller also began to exploit the HMC Eastern European Scheme to bring in exceptionally talented students from Central and Eastern Europe, a practice that continues to the present day. From Estonia came Maria Haal, who won a place at Girton to read Economics. From the Far East, Erica Zhang was one of many very capable mathematicians who excelled in a succession of Maths competitions, such as the UK Mathematical Challenge, the British Olympiad and the European Kangaroo. The universal language of mathematics was more accessible to these students than many other subjects in the curriculum, and some found full integration difficult, but over recent decades, helped by a supportive ESL department, they have become a vibrant part of the College community, making a particularly noteworthy contribution in art and music.

Not surprisingly, Miller's emphasis on academic excellence was a useful preparation for the age of league tables, and his speeches were notable for their citation of percentage pass-rates which, even allowing for grade inflation, improved markedly over his tenure at A Level and the new GCSE. Miller constantly reviewed the whole curriculum, keeping closely in touch with national changes, introducing modular courses in the Science A Levels and broadening the range of A Level courses on offer. The strong tradition of Science teaching was 'immensely' enhanced by the addition of a third storey to the Science block in 1993, with the entire faculty being refurbished. Amongst the outstanding beneficiaries of this were scholars such as John Gregson, who read Biochemistry at University College, Oxford, and David Battley, who read Chemistry at Balliol.

Miller was the first Headmaster to have a flickering screen on his desk, and the computer made analysis of statistics that much easier. His promotion of Dr Christopher Ray to be Director of Studies in 1993 brought a very interesting character to the fore, full

Lilia Abdula (right, Victoria 1991–3) was one of the first beneficiaries of the HMC Eastern European Scheme.

Above right: *Scholars from Eastern Europe: Olga Kljubina and Blanka Vaculikova in 1998.*

Right: *Kateryna Karpenko, Flavia Munteanu and Andrei Balalau in 2013.*

been happy to host a number of students who have fled these hot-houses to prosper and flourish in a less pressured but no less supportive environment. Claire Bush was one of a line of historians to go to St John's College, Cambridge, collecting a tennis Blue *en passant*, just as Annabel Cole would read English at Newnham. Law may be a competitive subject, but that didn't stop Richard Romney, Sam Brooks and Clare Church going to Clare, Christ Church and Selwyn respectively; likewise Medicine, but Richard Perry could combine that with a choral scholarship at Christ Church, while more recently Caroline Reid has fitted in Veterinary Science with a Cambridge rowing Blue at Jesus.

Modern linguists have done well at Oxford, from Nicholas Hindley at Christ Church to Robert Baker at Oriel, Dorothee Hinnah at Trinity to Andrzej Stuart-Thompson at Lincoln. The range is catholic and the way such students continued to grow in the Oxbridge environment, to get good degrees but fit in Blues or wider attainments too, is all heartening. Who should be surprised that Esther Gosling was recently voted President of the JCR at St Hilda's?

It is all a reminder of a few halcyon years when Oxbridge came to Framlingham in the form of the

of ideas and initiatives. Timetabling and teaching arrangements would be reviewed and radically altered over the next few years to the discomfort of some, but the benefit of many. Ray's subsequent rise to be High Master of Manchester Grammar School and Chairman of HMC is evidence of the loss Framlingham sustained with his departure in 1996.

BROAD EXPECTATIONS

Although keen on statistics, James Miller sometimes preferred to measure 'value-added' performance rather than the crude data of most newspaper league tables. *The Sunday Times'* current guide to 'the best schools in East Anglia' (July 2013) lists schools in Cambridge, Norwich, Colchester and Chelmsford, mostly selective day schools and many of them single-sex. Whether their impressive academic statistics make them the 'best' schools is a moot point, and Framlingham has

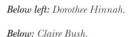

THE BIENNIAL FRAMLINGHAM COLLEGE HISTORY CONFERENCE

Friday 12 March, in the Athlone Hall

Morning session 10.30am to 12.20pm:

'The Feminine Touch: family relations and royal policy in
the reigh on Henry VII' – M.G. Underwood, Esq. (Senior
Archivist, St John's College, Cambridge)

'Making sense of the Reformation: Protestantism from Luther to
Calvin' – Dr R. Rex (University of Cambridge)

Afternoon session 1.45pm to 4pm:

'The impact of Imperialism on Africa, 1880–1945' – Dr R.E.
Robinson (Professor of History of the British Commonwealth,
Balliol College, Oxford)

'The KGB and Soviet History' – Dr Christopher Andrew
(Corpus Christi, Cambridge)

*'Gadzooks! All these great historians are coming to
Framlingham?!'*

Biennial History Conferences of the Miller era. Schools generally have to travel to London to listen to lectures in vast halls, but in 1990 Mark Robinson's father was able to put three distinguished Old Johnians, including Professor Peter Clarke and Dr Peter Linehan, in a car and offer a day of lectures in return for a Fram lunch, a jaunt repeated in 1992. The mutual enjoyment as well as scholarship lightly worn were features of these academic high-points.

David Barker also ran a vibrant Geographical Society through these years, later widening its audience through use of the HPT. Speakers have included university academics, farmers and conservationists, TV weather forecasters and explorers, and most recently, Sir James Paice, M.P. (O.F., 1960–6). Perhaps the most memorable events were an excursion to the Greene King Brewery at Bury St Edmunds courtesy of the Head Brewer, who was a parent, and a presentation by Nick Crane of the BBC *Coast* programme.

Another rather different high point of the 1990s was the stream of Arkwright Scholars pouring out of the TAC. The College won two of these prestigious awards in 1993 (Alex Henney and Archie Gemmill), and this feat was repeated regularly in the years that followed. In 1998 recipient Fergus Kendall's 'Tri-speed recumbent tricycle' won him a string of other awards as well, while in 2000 Craig Hamilton's success would help him secure a place to read Engineering at Cambridge. By 2003 Alex Lyne was able to win Audi's Young Designer of the Year competition, his guitar stand being described by the judges as 'the epitome of Vorsprung durch Technik'.

Right: Fergus Kendall in 1998.

Far right: Alex Lyne in 2003.

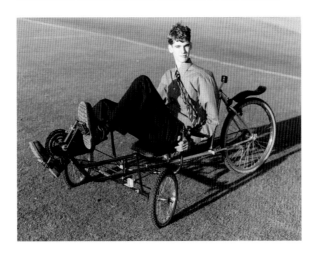

Various forms of public speaking also flourished in the 1990s. For three years in a row Marcus Booth took the College through to the Regional Finals of the Observer Mace Debating Competition, supported in turn by Liz Reece in 1993, Lewis Towns in 1994 and Emma Davies in 1995. Marcus went on to be a force at the St Andrew's University Debating Society, though he is yet to become Prime Minister. Imogen Slaughter, however, has succeeded in becoming Queen Elizabeth (in David Starkey's Tudor TV series): she and Esther Plant won the ESU competition 'Shakespeare on the Platform' in 1993, for their brilliant representation of a scene from *Othello*. However, all this academic activity was, as usual at Framlingham, kept in proportion, and James Miller was very much an all-round schoolmaster, enjoying and encouraging the social, cultural and sporting life of the College.

PAUL'S COURT: THE ST PANCRAS SOLUTION

Bob Morris (Bursar, 1991–2000) recalls the need for the 'transformation of a damp and dark area (which resembled a prison exercise yard called "Tuck-Box" Courtyard) into what is now Paul's Court. A design/cost "beauty parade" was held involving local and London professionals and was won by local architects Hollins, who suggested what quickly became known as the "St Pancras solution". This was opened by Mrs Paul in 1993 and named after her late husband, Roger Paul OBE DL, a former Chairman of Governors (1972–87).'

James Miller writes, 'I was particularly pleased with Paul's Court, not that it was my idea but rather Nick Ward's; I felt from the outset that Fram rather lacked a focal point; Paul's Court solved this in a very imaginative way and also removed a very dreary area'. No doubt these luminaries saw great potential in Paul's Court, but its practical value has since proved remarkable, with everything from match teas to maths competitions, rock nights to charity fund-raisers, pre-dinner drinks to discos and so much more.

By 1994, then, Framlingham was a very different place from the College that James Miller arrived at in 1989. Borrett's had been re-surfaced, pupils' studies were steadily being improved and serious attempts were made to develop facilities for day boys in Ziegele. Paul's Court had been enclosed, vastly enhancing the potential social uses of the main building in and out of term-time. Miller encouraged civilised living, a touch of the classicist about him, and social occasions in the Sixth Form Centre were memorable. These could be formal dinner parties, but Miller also delighted boarding students by allowing them to wear casual clothes after the end of the formal teaching day. The present social facilities for

Top: The School Tuck Shop in 1993: Miss Nekrews helping students to 'work, rest and play'.

Above: A Chamber Orchestra in Paul's Court.

Above: Bob Morris.

Right: 'Tuck-Box Courtyard'.

Studies in the mid-1990s: the irrepressible Tony Ward in Rendlesham.

Doctor Wallace and her Moreau House girls in 1994.

Right: *Head of School Tosin Oguntayo and Mark Ventham on lead vocals at the Leavers' Ball in 1993.*

Below: *Chris Lenton's cartoon at the departure of James Miller, John Maulden and Steve Wright, who was later to become Headmaster of Merchant Taylors', Northwood.*

Sixth Formers in Rose Cottage were created in 1992, an area poised for further development as part of the sesquicentennial programme. Miller even attempted to civilise the Fifth Form (Year 11), though giving them their own centre may have been a step too far, even if student retention improved briefly. The increasing number of girls led to the bold move to convert Moreau into a second boarding house to accommodate them under the redoubtable Doctor Wallace. Leadership courses by Philip le Brocq, championed by Senior Master Hugh Kennon, were mocked by some, but were stimulating to others. It was a dynamic community from which James Miller departed in the summer of 1994. The 'Very Many Thanks' (VMT) that he had so often offered to others had become genuinely mutual.

Reflecting on his time here James Miller has written: 'Fram is fortunate in having some very committed old boys and girls, and I have strong memories of OF functions (and some hair-curling anecdotes of what boys in the school used to get up to at night before the war; probably the less said here, the better). I was lucky too in some very committed and supportive Governors, particularly Pat Howard-Dobson and Jack Dye. I hope that they did not feel too let down when I accepted a job at the Royal Grammar School in Newcastle, a post for which I did not apply and which I first turned down. It must, however, be said that, though I missed Fram, I had 14 very happy and fulfilling years in Newcastle.

'My five years at Fram were hugely enjoyable, if very hard work – a function mainly of the recession. I was left with immense respect for the vast majority of the people with whom I had worked and of the pupils. They taught me a great amount. Their warmth, their enthusiasm, their concern for others, their openness and lack of pretension, their lack of cynicism are characteristics that many schools could learn from.'

'WOMEN, KNOW YOUR LIMITS!'

THE PIONEERING GARRETTS

As the first full academic year was starting at Framlingham in September 1865, Elizabeth Garrett, whose family had been so inextricably linked with the founding of the College and its development thereafter, became the first woman to complete a recognised course of medical training and to achieve a modern legal qualification to practise medicine in Britain. *The Lancet* was quick to commend her on this, albeit in somewhat facetious fashion, under the patronising heading 'Frocks and Gowns', and the establishment remained profoundly suspicious. Such was her pioneering spirit that Elizabeth was to ensure that in future the medical elite contained women as well as men. Her sister, Millicent Fawcett, played a leading role in the Suffrage movement, which won votes for women in 1918 and 1928. Both ladies supported the College financially and each presided at prize-givings in 1899 and 1906. At the celebrations on 10 April 1915 to commemorate the 50th anniversary of the school's opening, the retiring Headmaster, Dr Inskip, warmly thanked the Garrett family in general, and Elizabeth and Millicent in particular, for all the support they had given the College.

THE SPIRIT OF PEMBROKE

In spite of these links with early female emancipation, a biographer of *The Pioneering Garretts* dryly notes, 'Framlingham did not help the cause of education for girls until it became co-educational in 1976' (Jenifer Glynn). Over the first 100 years of the College's existence it was a profoundly male institution, and the occasional appearance of a distinguished lady visitor was like the arrival of someone from another world. However, society was changing in the late 20th century and Laurie Rimmer's bold decision to welcome girls was soon seen as part of an irreversible trend.

Within ten years of their arrival girls had become a fully accepted part of the College, though the pioneering spirit needed for them to flourish is epitomised by Mrs Anne Nesling, Housemistress of Pembroke House (1985–97):

'"Limits? What Limits?" The notion of limits did not feature in either the lexicon or the ethos of the young ladies who joined Framlingham College in Pembroke Day Girl House. "Yes, we can!" was our mantra long before it was adopted by a certain President, and the passing years have confirmed its validity. Taking on board the school motto, along with a healthy respect for a realistic approach, anything was accepted as possible. In the early days when the first females were invited to join such a well-established boys' school, we had to persuade the existing community that it was, indeed, a positive and forward-looking move, with many an adage to spur us on – and none did so more than the one about the need to eat a pudding in order to judge its worth!

'So, what was it like for those pioneering Pembroke girls? Laurie Rimmer's vision was that girls should be able to enter the College and play a full part in the life

Millicent Fawcett (née Garrett) addresses Suffragists in Hyde Park, 1913.

of the school. However, when the new arrivals ventured through the portal they were entering an institution that was male, conservative and very traditional. The innovation led to some considerable disquiet in certain quarters, more than a hint of resentment in others and misconceptions aplenty. Some seemed to be expecting the female pupils to be a cross between the sophisticates from society magazines and the terrors from St Trinian's – no wonder they were apprehensive. Such wariness struck us as rather odd, though, as many of the girls were daughters and granddaughters of Old Framlinghamians and, as relatives of boys then at the school, were hardly an unknown quantity. There was also a view – quickly to be discounted – that a female presence would be all about frills, and doubtless some flouncing to boot, without too much in the way of substance, considerable disruption and probably only a modicum of intellect. A few insinuated that "those girls" would have to be reminded of their place, that there would be limitations to their role, and that their expectations would have to be curtailed as they just would not be able to match the demands that would be made upon them. All that was amusing rather than alarming, given that some aspects of the College at that time were closer to Evelyn Waugh's Llanabba Castle than we could ever have imagined. Still, it did help us to account for and understand some of the resistance we encountered: it was, no doubt, rooted in a suspicion that this new era heralded a dilution of all that was held dear. We kept our counsel and remembered that proverbial pudding.

'The main challenge for the girls was to prove the doubters wrong by becoming fully integrated and successful members of the school community. We had to ask ourselves how our minority could make its mark, and as trailblazers how we could ensure that the interests of the girls were fully promoted and secured for the future. Subtlety was going to be the key. We also had allies. There were those who were quick to spot the girls' work ethic, their enthusiasm and their all-round participation. Also, there was a steadily growing appreciation of the input of the feminine perspective in the school environment and an awareness of the huge potential for the girls to add value. We are enormously grateful to those who did support the girls from the outset and encouraged them to set their sights high, both in and out of the classroom. Another source of approval was from

the majority of boys who were emphatically in favour of the arrival of their female peers!

'From the girls' standpoint it was essential that their presence was seen as part of the evolution of the school. This was not an experiment. The girls were there for the long term so it was crucial that strong foundations were established at the outset. We did not want a feminist charter nor a revolution: we neither expected nor sought special treatment. What we did want was the chance to become an integral part of the school, and our philosophy was simple – let the actions do the talking.

'Along the way we did, of course, have a few skirmishes. There were practical matters to address which led to some tricky negotiations. For example, suitable accommodation had to be provided, facilities for girls' games were required and there was the question of the replacement of the benches in the Dining Hall with more appropriate seating, to name but a few, and it took longer – much longer – for some problems to be dealt with than others. On the whole, though, there was a sympathetic acceptance that some things had to be

Mrs Anne Nesling and Pembroke House, 1994.

Ruth Manly at work sporting her Pembroke House colours.

modified or even changed more radically. Whilst we were dealing with important fundamental issues, there were a few who, with a woeful paucity of insight, thought our time was taken up with a total preoccupation about skirt styles. As well as acquiring academic skills and knowledge it is imperative that young people also acquire values and life skills, such as being aware of the significance of dress codes. Being suitably dressed was one element in the profile of Pembroke girls. Our goal was to engender self-belief by helping the girls to become both erudite and well equipped with all those other accomplishments that would enable them to succeed in their futures. Life skills featured large in the Pembroke curriculum!

'We had to develop tactics for dealing with predictable and unpredictable obstacles, and this was where subtlety came in. Graciousness (and here, perhaps, we do have to admit to just a soupçon of female guile as well) is far more disarming than confrontation – another life skill – but this did not mean that we were not prepared to stand our ground when necessary. The girls were not chaps in skirts. They had their own qualities, attributes and talents and with an unquenchable zest were keen to develop them, thereby adding a new dimension to the school. It was a question of a measured approach. We had to be confident but not overly so, sanguine but not to the point of being unrealistic and, wherever possible, we tried to let results speak for themselves.

'Very soon, and with commendable alacrity, the young ladies began to have an impact in all aspects of College life – in the classroom, music, drama, co-curricular activities, games, CCF, as School Prefects and Head of School. On all fronts they began to be duly recognised. They were hard to ignore. Actions and results were indeed speaking volumes. The girls responded to all the opportunities on offer, their natural abilities were nurtured, their aspirations were supported and they were encouraged in their resolve to become whatever they wanted to be. With an excellent education behind them they were soon off to pursue the gamut of tertiary courses and careers. Among our alumnae are a professional French horn player, a forensic psychologist, graduates in Engineering and Chemistry from Oxford, doctors, a Design and Technology teacher, a vet, English, Law and History graduates from Cambridge, successful businesswomen

and an Army officer commissioned from RMA Sandhurst, to note but a tiny sample. Did someone mention limits? Also, and very importantly, we helped to develop well-balanced and responsible young women who have become wives, mothers, excellent citizens and the best possible recommendation for the school.

'Everyone connected with the College, past, present and future, should be grateful to Laurie Rimmer and the Governors who made that momentous decision to permit girls to pass through the portal. We feel very privileged that we helped to justify their belief that it was the way forward. With a potent mix of pragmatism and idealism the young ladies of Pembroke House won over the sceptics and demonstrated that there are no limits to the achievements attainable at the College. It is very gratifying that the girls are now acknowledged as one of the vital ingredients in the heterogeneous and vibrant community which has established Framlingham College as one of the leading co-educational schools in the region. We are proud to say "Yes, we could! Yes, we did!" That pudding has, indeed, proved its culinary excellence.'

The Pembroke House report written by Jo Ransome and Shireen Cantrell chronicling Anne Nesling's retirement in 1997 clearly conveys the spirit she had engendered over 12 years. The news 'shocked and saddened the House and we're sure that no one was untouched by it … the love that she showed for us, the "Pembroke gels", was huge'. Despite this success some girls still found aspects of College challenging, and Kate Eckford (Pembroke, 1990–5) offers a mixture of memories of her time here: 'One of my set texts while at Framlingham was Dickens's *A Tale of Two Cities*, and the famous first words of this novel go to epitomise what I felt about my time at the College – "It was the best of times, it was the worst of times, it was the age of wisdom, it was the age of foolishness …"

'I can't say that my whole time at Framlingham was the best I ever had. I reserve that for my time at university, where we all had a lot more freedom to do what we wanted, study what we wanted and had mostly lost all the hang-ups about being popular or not being popular. I longed to leave Framlingham and achieve my ambitions and just have a lot more fun than I was having at school where, in many ways, I felt very socially and academically restricted.

'Framlingham was pretty strong at sports and although I was academic I could easily hold my own with some sports. Unfortunately netball wasn't one of those, and during my Lower Sixth I was ousted as Captain of the 2nd netball team, which left me feeling rather bitter, and I decided to give the game up entirely. A friend had decided to do the same and together we embarked on learning squash, with the College bringing in a teacher to help us on our way. I discovered a wonderful new game that I was good at and a whole variety of muscles I never knew existed. My friend and I would battle it out on the squash courts in the winter and in the summer battle it out on the tennis court, and in our last year we both won a cup. I continue to love both sports passionately.

'But tennis wasn't just for outside. There were also games of tennis in my A Level History lessons. I had totally forgotten about this and was glad to have been reminded recently of the scrunched-up pieces of A4 paper being flung from one side of the tiny attic room to the other and being hit, or not, by large, unwieldy textbooks. Tennis was invented in Tudor times, which was what we were studying, so I am sure what we were playing was actually in tune with what we were learning! Aside from the sports pitch and the classroom I also have old photos of some after-school activities. One is from a Scrabble get-together showing a variety of grinning girls and others show us bell-ringing in nearby Sweffling church, a motley crew led by Dr Baird. Maybe this was a strange activity for teenagers trying to be cool to embark on, but it got us out of school and we had a laugh, and I even got an unsuitable boyfriend out of it!

'But not everything was so much fun. There were things like circuit training (that I managed to get out of after the pain of the first time), the annual cross-country run 'Steeps', which was just too horrible for words, the introduction of Saturday morning tests in the Athlone Hall and the general bickering of teenagers. On a more serious note, however, being a day girl in a separate day girls' house in a boarding school wasn't so easy. We mostly felt like outsiders and there weren't that many of us – only six girls in my year by the Upper Sixth. That meant enforced proximity to some people I didn't get on with, and I wasn't always happy with the "grin and bear it" approach.

'With regard to wisdom I certainly enjoyed academic success, attaining four As at A Level and

Pembroke Upper Sixth seated outside The Shack in 1995: Sarah Rutterford, Naomi Horton, Julie Cooper and Kate Eckford.

entry to Cambridge to read History. However, it wasn't an easy path. Being studious in what I felt was a mostly "unstudious" school didn't gain me any favours, nor did being seen as tall, lanky and bespectacled. Later on I had contact lenses, wore my long blonde hair down and could be described instead as tall and slim! In my first year at Cambridge I could go to an "Oscars" party as Ursula Andress and have no qualms in turning up at an Oxfordshire mansion dressed in a bikini with a knife and some shells tied to my waist. But while at Framlingham I always had the reputation for being studious and "square"!

'Still, I loved many of my subjects, History and English in particular. However, when I look back at GCSEs I tend to recall only shivering with fright outside the Chemistry lab as we queued to go in (at the prospect of Chemistry itself rather than Mr Myers Allen) or sitting in Physics not having the foggiest about what was going on. Even GCSE History was a trial I spent with a roomful of boys. At 14 and 15 that was a really dreadful experience. How I ended up being the only girl I'll never know – did the Black Death and the Peasants' Revolt not appeal to females? It would seem not. Either way, I don't think I can forgive any of the girls who chose the other type of history for leaving me in a room of adolescent boys. I won't go into detail about the general chat but I am sure you can imagine.

'However, once I could choose my own subjects at A Level, happier memories of "wisdom" come to mind. At History Society Lochhead, Ferris and I presented a topic on Medieval Witchcraft, seen as quite racy then. More superficially we played the game "who can find a good-looking medieval male?" It wasn't very productive, but it was fun!

'This brings me onto foolishness. Where do I start? My best friend Suzie McEwan and I got up to many japes. One of the best pranks she ever played was while we, the Pembroke Upper Sixth girls, had our study and common room areas in The Shack, the little wooden house on the corner of the playing fields. She covered and wrapped up our entire study in newspaper. The entire study. I think it might have been on one of the last days of school and it looked crazy!

'A lot of our foolish times were in the Upper Sixth when I was much happier and we were ensconced in The Shack. All of us stayed there one night, and we got spooked by some of our boarder friends tapping on windows in a ghostly manner. And we used to chase people out of our garden shouting "Gerrof my land" in a strong Suffolk accent. So, mostly it was good clean fun but of course there was always also the typical teenage trio of boys, cigarettes and alcohol. I have entirely myself to blame for coming up with the idea of producing our own alcohol – toffee vodka to be precise. I think I had read something about making toffee vodka by adding Werther's Originals to vodka so a friend and I got hold of both and experimented. We let our concoction stew for some time in the rotunda, our then common room, and it tasted excellent. I have never lost my taste for flavoured vodka!

'Dickens goes on to write the following in the first sentence of *A Tale of Two Cities*: "it was the season of Light, it was the season of Darkness, it was the spring of hope, it was the winter of despair, we had everything before us, we had nothing before us". When I left Framlingham College I felt without doubt that there was light, hope and that everything was before me. I had survived my five years there, made friends, grown up through my teenage years and experienced so many

things that inevitably I felt that my new life was shining upon me and I was raring to go.'

THE FIRST HEADMISTRESS

Certainly the most spectacular smashing of any remaining glass ceiling came about with the bold appointment of Mrs Gwen Randall in 1994. She arrived in Suffolk from Dauntsey's with husband, David, and teenage daughter, Kate, to become the first female Head of an HMC school (the HMC had yet to become the Headmasters' and Headmistresses' Conference). In the bad old days, they used to say that letting a lady teacher into a boys' school was like taking a powder-puff to creosote a fence, so not surprisingly it took some a little time to get beyond the gender politics of the appointment. It was certainly good for Framlingham to be on the front pages of the national press with Gwen swinging winsomely from the mock-Victorian gas-lights at the front of College. Later the *Daily Telegraph* would provoke a different reaction when, although its correspondent suggested Mrs Randall had great potential as a Head, he also claimed the school she was running was something more genuinely Victorian. The reaction was predictable, with Speech Day that year seeing a formidable counter-blast, after which the *Telegraph* has concentrated on minor issues such as MPs' expenses!

Mrs Randall's challenging disposition was made clear early on with her decision to 'integrate' day students into the boarding houses. This move was not instantly popular, but day students soon fitted into their adopted houses and many were quick to take advantage of the opportunity to flexi-board in familiar surroundings when it suited their purpose. Meanwhile full boarders had the option of weekly boarding, a much more flexible system well-suited to the needs of parents in the modern era. The ending of Ziegele House also freed up space in the centre of College for the significant extension of the Berners Library, as well as the construction of new History, Geography and English classrooms in 1998.

Outside, the removal of the Portakabins where History and Geography had previously been taught allowed for the creation of a light and spacious piazza. This soon became a popular place for students to socialise in summer, though, alas, the proposed water feature never materialised!

Portrait of a Lady: Gwen Randall by John O'Sullivan (Ziegele, 1991–6).

Above: *A-Level historians in the new Ziegele Centre classrooms, 2005.*

Left: *The refurbished and extended Berners Library, overseen and run to good effect by Librarian, Ann Hoole, 1996–2009.*

Far left: *New College uniform in 2000 – out with the old (left) and in with the new (right).*

In the same year Pembroke was opened as a third, but entirely new boarding house for girls, under the leadership of the warm and welcoming Mrs Fiona Read. It was fittingly located at Pembroke Lodge on Pembroke Road where, the Head maintained, 'day and boarding pupils alike enjoy a quality of provision which sets the standard for the other Houses in College. Pembroke House is bright, modern and stylish – like its occupants!'

By this time further enhancements to the College fabric had followed, quite literally, with major changes to the College uniform. In 2000 the green jackets that junior boys used to wear were replaced by smart blue blazers; the junior girls' tartan skirts were universally welcomed; and the sharp suits gave Sixth-Formers the chance to cut a dash.

Substantial improvement was also achieved on the academic front with league tables indicating how much more successful Framlingham students were in the first decade of the 21st century than the seventh decade of the 19th – figures significantly helped by the contribution of increasing numbers of girls.

Right: *Mrs Fiona Read.*

Far right: *Verity Inett in the new Pembroke.*

Above: Girls to the fore celebrating A Level success in 1999, when the College was placed 29th in the Financial Times' *league table of the top boarding schools in England and Wales. This table was based on 'Fees against Examination Results' and no other schools from East Anglia were featured in the top 50. The College enjoyed pride of place among the region's boarding schools again in 2006 in* The Times' *A Level league table. More impressively still that year it was placed 8th in the country in the* Financial Times *'value for money' table.*

Above right: Women at work, 2008.

Right: Deputy Head Academic Clive Norton, with successful GCSE students in 2004.

The rising number of girls also aided significantly in the creation of an increasingly civilised College culture, with studious, high-achieving young ladies beginning to exert an increasingly positive influence on their male counterparts. This was particularly evident in the Sixth Form classroom, where increased numbers of girls were accompanied by an increase in female teaching staff. The classroom dynamic is somewhat rosily recalled by former Head of School Andrzej Stuart-Thompson (Kerrison, 2005–10): 'Under the vast ceiling of Lincoln Library in Oxford, as I sit at my desk musing on Clarice Lispector's self-conscious narrators, I imagine myself washed ashore, like the pilgrim in Luis de Góngora's "Soledad Primera", on an Arcadian island of books. Looking not at my text but out of the window for inspiration, as students sometimes do, I am taken back to my experiences at Framlingham, where my wonderment at the world of knowledge was first awakened. Two years on from leaving the College, I remember the education I received there with profound appreciation and joy, for it was the curiosity for learning fostered in me by my teachers which has given me an important sense of meaning in my life.

'I had teachers who challenged, stretched and supported me every step of my academic career. I have fond memories of each one of them: the teacher whose dedication to ensuring that the whole class reached extraordinary heights meant a thrilling personal GCSE result, the probability of which I could never have calculated; the one who ran to catch up with me after a class, across that courtyard bathed in summer sunlight, to share with me the name of a book, Boethius' *The Consolation of Philosophy*, which minutes previously she was trying to remember for me, simply for the pleasure of reading it; the Head who took the time to tell me about Camus's philosophy in *Le Mythe de Sisyphe* and taught me the worth of struggle, however difficult. I felt privileged to be in such a place of learning.

'The classroom was always an exciting forum for intellectual discourse, each lesson an invitation to discover something new, where it became possible to see the world through the lenses of other languages, cultures and ideas, and everything was masterfully brought to life: the complexities of the first Elizabethan era, Spain on the threshold of its Golden Age, the great exhortations of Cicero to the Roman Senate, Ovid's poetry of transformation, the Pardoner's "saffroned predicacioun", the Faustian dilemma, the beautiful lyricism of the Spanish and French languages. All of these subjects and so many more, taught with the generosity and depth of insight that my teachers showed, have furnished my mind with wonderful images and knowledge, and given me a lifelong love of learning.

'Moreover, I left the College a learner responsible for my own learning, inspired to think critically and creatively. With such a background, how could I fail to be moved to keep seeking new opportunities to educate myself, to acquire dazzling new ways of seeing, and sustain that momentum? And if I could provide a picture of what it was that my teachers helped me to see, in response to the journey I made with them, I would need go no further than to paraphrase a passage from a favourite Spanish poem of mine, in which a band of wedding guests processing through the countryside, seen at a distance, perhaps on the horizon, are revealed to bear a resemblance to waxing and waning moons, or to migrating birds in formation which, like galley-ships, sail across the blue ocean of the sky, penning feathered letters on its surface of diaphanous paper ["Soledad Primera"].'

By the time Andrzej left the College in 2010 Pembroke House had been significantly extended to enable it to house as many pupils as its rivals in Moreau and Victoria. The extension had been opened in 2008 by Sir Richard Dearlove KCMG OBE MA, College Governor and Master of Pembroke College, Cambridge.

Numerical parity enhanced inter-House sporting rivalry for the Douglas Shield and this in turn contributed to success at school level. Girls could participate in an increasingly wide range of activities, taking full advantage of the new fitness suite, extended sports hall and indoor swimming pool opened by Olympic Silver and Commonwealth Gold Medallist Sharron Davies MBE in 2000.

Culturally the refurbishment of the Headmaster Porter Theatre opened by the Earl and Countess

Above: *Pembroke girls enjoying their new common room, 2008.*

Below: *Gwen Randall does the honours.*

Bottom: *Swimming competition in the old outdoor pool in 1995.*

Above: *The new indoor swimming pool.*

Right: *Gwen Randall at the surprise 90th birthday party of Stanley Porter, whose generous legacy made possible the transformation of the Athlone Hall into the Headmaster Porter Theatre.*

Far right: *Senior Deputy Head, Susan Wessels.*

Above: *Floreat Laura! Her first solo album, 2011.*

Above: *Prince Edward and Lord Tollemache lead the Head, Countess of Wessex and Chairman of Governors, Andrew Fane, over to the Headmaster Porter Theatre.*

of Wessex in 2006 was a great stimulus to Music and Drama, areas in which girls also made major contributions. In terms of high achievement in this area Laura Wright's singing career bears witness to endless possibilities: there seem to be no limits on a career which started with winning the BBC Radio 2 Young Chorister competition in 2005 and currently sees her selling large numbers of CDs, as well as collecting a first-class degree from the Royal College of Music.

By the time of Mrs Randall's retirement in 2009 the place of women at Framlingham was unquestioned, and the pioneering aspirations articulated by Anne Nesling had been largely fulfilled. When Paul Taylor took over as Headmaster, he quickly saw the need to appoint Susan Wessels his Senior Deputy Head – no shrinking violet she. Her background as former captain of the South African Olympic hockey team has been a tremendous fillip to girls' sport at the College, but like Norman Borrett before her, she brings a whole range of other qualities to her important role.

Women – No Limits!

Another leading lady in the College, Cath Drummond, Housemistress of Victoria since 2008, gives an up-to-date perspective: 'In 2012, for the first time, all of the teams competing in the Olympic Games have fielded female competitors. Women too have been permitted to participate in the boxing competition. "And that", declared Clare Balding confidently, "means that women have achieved absolute parity." Perhaps she didn't notice that the "escorts" for the teams were all female, all dressed in short skirts and all heavily made-up – as much a decorative feature as the placards they were carrying. The fact that male relay races are traditionally, as the main attraction, "saved" for last, preceded by the "warm-up" female events, probably doesn't bother her too much either.

'And perhaps it shouldn't. It is possible, of course, to be too much on the look-out for potential discrimination and it is indeed laudable that efforts continue to be made to ensure that "parity" is achieved, not just in sport but throughout society. The College is, in this area, ahead of its time – so much so that to be asked to contribute to a chapter for this history specifically devoted to women seems almost superfluous; the women here are an integrated part of the College and not an addendum requiring special notice in order to feel acknowledged. Academically, musically, as members of the CCF, in the Art and DT department, the girls here feel that the opportunities, support and publicity available to them equal those of the boys. There are girls in the accelerated Mathematics sets; the girls who play hockey well play with and against the boys; a female member of the sports staff will be coaching rugby next term. Of course, the College is a reflection of the society in which it exists, and "absolute parity" does not quite operate. The sporting girls will tell you that their kit is less good than that of the boys and their tours less exciting, and there was one occasion when all of the sporting photographs on the school website were of boys. There are sometimes complaints that boys receive bigger food portions. But the photograph issue was remedied within 15 minutes of being reported, and the kitchen staff will give girls more food if they ask for it. In an unequal society – and one in which the inequalities are nowhere so apparent as they are in sport – the College is very much doing its best to treat boys and girls equally.

'Of course, this should be no surprise. The College was the first HMC school to employ a female Head and Susan Wessels is currently responsible for the day-to-day running of the school. Opportunities for female staff are, I think, equal to those afforded to our male counterparts and I certainly haven't encountered a "glass ceiling" here. When one of my (female) colleagues conducted some research into career ambitions, she concluded that female middle managers – as well as men – remain at their current level not because of restrictions imposed by their employer but through their own desire to do what suits their family and lifestyle. Now why women make career choices based on their family might be a feminist issue in itself, but it's not one to lay at the door of the College.

'So I don't think any "limits" are imposed on women – pupils or staff – by the College. Society is, of course, another question, and whilst we have indeed made great strides towards "parity" – "a room of (our) own and five hundred pounds a year" is no longer such an unreachable goal – we are still affected by implicit, if not overt, and in some cases quite intractable, views about what women should and shouldn't be doing. It is rare now to hear, as I did from one Year 11 boy in my first year, that we should be "at home doing the washing up". But that mentality exists – although most men are not brave or foolish enough to voice it openly. We can't escape our society, however, and nothing prevents

Victorious Cambridge Blue, Caroline Reid (back), in 2012 – dynamic and determined. Having competed in the Boat Race again in 2013 and 2014, Caroline was elected President of CUWBC for 2014/15.

The indefatigable Housemistress of Victoria, Cath Drummond, and her Prince Consort!

us. When I had my son, I felt that I had to prove that I could do my job as well as I had done before I became a mother. A colleague – a highly intelligent woman and a respected academic – has commented that she feels an onus to prove that one can be an intelligent woman without being unpleasant. We are doing our jobs with an awareness of what it means to do our jobs as women, and what other people might think it means. Men are just doing their jobs.

'Women do need to continue to fight against discrimination. We would all agree, I think, that some of the practices and rules to which women are subjected in some cultures today, just because they are women, are degrading, humiliating and unacceptable. I didn't teach badly, though, the year I needed to prove that I could be both a teacher and a mother. Perhaps at this level the need to prove ourselves actually makes us do just that. The successful girls the College has seen – we might think of Claire Bush, who took a 1st in History at Cambridge, or Caroline Reid, currently studying Veterinary Medicine at the same university, of Emily Wilford's hockey prowess or Miranda Horvath, highly respected forensic psychologist – are not achieving in spite of the perceived "glass ceiling" but largely because of it. What would we do if we had nothing to prove? And as feminists we should be careful what we wish for; what if nobody was setting us limits we wanted to break? Speaking of which, Mr Sinclair – sports day relays next year: boys first?'

a certain member of the College community from insisting upon referring to me (despite having been introduced to me as the Housemistress of Victoria) as "Rory Drummond's wife".

'As women, then, we remain far more conscious than men about what might be said or thought about

Filles sans frontières – Head Girl Emma Vidler receives her prizes from Richard Sayer (President of the SOF and College Governor) at Speech Day 2013, with Susan Wessels looking on approvingly. Elizabeth Garrett Anderson would also have approved of a Framlingham girl going to Oxford to read Medicine.

8

A COMEDY OF ERRORS

Perhaps down to the 1970s one feels that some elements of high culture triumphed at the College despite rather than because of facilities, but there is no doubt that the past 30 years have vastly widened the opportunities for students interested in music, drama and the visual arts. The fact that these have become serious exam subjects at GCSE and A Level has meant that some students can specialise in them, and advances in technology have changed the ways in which they can be approached. Equally the opportunities to go to concerts, theatre productions and art galleries are legion. It is perhaps fair to say that in these areas the experience of pupils at the College is much richer than in earlier years.

IN QUIRES AND PLACES WHERE THEY SING

Society has grown more secular, and such religion as survives in England and Europe has grown more disparate and individualised. However, the role of chapel in College life remains almost unquestioned, even if the nature of what goes on there has changed greatly. Perhaps the College's original vagueness about being a Church of England school but welcoming Dissenters is actually a strength in modern times, when catholicity in the sense of embracing universality is essential.

This has meant some loss. In the 1960s there were two compulsory services each Sunday, Matins and Evensong, and those services would recognisably follow the 1662 Book of Common Prayer. In one of those services there would be a substantial sermon, often preached by a visiting clergyman. As school numbers

grew, the Chapel could be full and pews, especially near the back of the nave, could be more or less discreetly creaked by the eight boys squeezed into them as a form of protest against the length of the discourse.

The Chapel itself was cruciform in its original shape, with the north wing housing the pipe organ, the altar in the apse at the east end behind the communion rail, and the College Choir with its boy trebles set in rows facing each other. All this was altered with the extension of the building under Rimmer in the 1980s, with the altar moving out of the apse and the Choir seated there facing the main congregation in the nave, now supported by our second electronic organ. Much of the alteration was sensitively done, though the pink roof and upturned chamber pots used as light shades leave much to be desired. OFs gave generously for the chairs in the north transept and, apart from the poor sightlines for a few seats close to the main pillar, the building generally functions well for a school of over 400.

If outsiders wonder at the place of chapel in Framlingham they might wonder more at the nature of the men who have served as Chaplain. The likes of Rupert Kneese were, perhaps inevitably, replaced by gentler men. Vivien Singh served in Porter's last years, and then Rimmer appointed Richard Law in the early 1970s. There were the usual healthy tensions between the Chaplain and the Ordinary, but Richard brought his own form of holiness to the task, while being an officer in the CCF and battling away in the classroom; his wife as singing teacher and three children as pupils could widen his understanding of his flock.

110

The Choir processing into Chapel, 1994.

In 1984 Michael Booker took over: having been Precentor of St Edmundsbury Cathedral and Minor Canon for 15 years, Michael was happy to make Sung Eucharist the central service on most Sundays. In his later years he had much to do at Brandeston after the Reverend Roger Dixon's retirement. Michael's retirement in 1999 after 15 years of devoted service as Chaplain led to two brief tenures, those of Reverends Charles Jefferson and Mark Haworth, after which Mrs Randall seemed to despair of ordained men as she despaired of Bursars. And so Nick Chaplin was appointed to run the finances, while the chaplaincy went to a layman, Steve Waters, a safe pair of hands on the pastoral front and a man willing to be involved in many areas of College life. He has also taken particular care over the memorials on the Chapel walls, adding names omitted to old memorials and overseeing the consecration of new ones to Prince Karadja, along with Sir Patrick Howard-Dobson's coat-of-arms.

Otherwise in the last 20 years, the change in Sabbath observance is perhaps greatest. So many students, if not day students, are weekly boarders, so only rarely are major services held on Sundays. The Music department had to adapt to this, with Choir activities moving chiefly to weekdays, but this has enabled the strong choral tradition to be maintained there. Whether the congregational hymn singing can

continue to match that of earlier times is more open to question, but Framlingham usually finds ways of fixing these things. Many singers claim the foundations of their later success were laid in a chapel choir, and in recent years, Laura Wright's singing at Twickenham rugby and Christina Johnston's starring on the opera stage in Prague are reminders of what willowy oaks can grow from choral acorns.

If then major Sunday services are rare, they are perhaps the more special when they do take place. In the Michaelmas Term, Remembrance Sunday always sees the Chapel filled with College students and the wider Framlingham community, and traditional hymns will get the full treatment, without bombast – students of all nationalities can feel part of such a service of dedication. Liturgical choral works can be performed in chapel, the annual carol service is well supported, and these grand acts of worship are offset by many smaller gatherings.

In opening his great work *Of The Laws of Ecclesiastical Polity* in the 1590s, Richard Hooker wondered whether the Church of England would survive, suggesting, however, that the difficulties it had been able to overcome were evidence of divine protection. Generations of Fram students have hoped their Sunday cricket would end too late for them to attend chapel, or that their exam timing would excuse them from attendance, and yet when all is said and done, would miss it if it were not there. Once in another Somerset rectory due to be sold to the laity, this verse was found:

Above: Laura Wright with members of the England rugby team at Twickenham in 2013.

Below left: The Revd Michael Booker, Chaplain and parent, and his Beetle.

SIR PATRICK HOWARD-DOBSON (RENDLESHAM, 1933–40)

'Sir Pat' was one of our most distinguished OFs. He came to Framlingham after being a chorister at King's College Choir School, Cambridge, and had a superb all-round school career, ending up as Head Prefect. Commissioned into the Queen's Own Hussars in 1941, he saw war service in Burma and Italy, but this was only the prelude to a remarkable rise through the ranks. He became Commandant of the Staff College, Military Secretary and Vice-Chief of the Defence Staff, before retiring as a full general in 1981. Knighted in 1974, he was appointed a Knight Grand Cross of the Order of the Bath in 1979. A man of strong Christian faith, his 'retirement' comprised a plethora of responsibilities including being President of the Royal British Legion. However, he was also an active Governor of the College from 1975 and Chairman from 1987 to 1992. His children and grandchildren came through the College and his son, Peter, is now also a Governor.

Sir Patrick Howard-Dobson (1921–2009) and his armorial bearings in Westminster Abbey.

The Lay Chaplain, Steve Waters, with James Mee, Mrs Gwen Randall and Rabbi Doctor Andrew Goldstein at the Commemoration Service for Prince Constantin Karadja in 2009.

If you see a church that's empty
Tho' its doors are open wide
It is not the Church that's dying
But the people who have died.

One suspects that as long as there are Framlinghamians coming through the front door, they will continue to turn right along the corridor to the Chapel.

MUSIC

John Cooper Green recalls his time as Director of Music at the College: 'When I went to Framlingham in 1980 there was no music school, and the majority of the teaching took place around the Athlone Hall. The main hall was used for class teaching, with the two back rooms, the toilets and foyer for instrumental teaching! Amongst the students was Richard Perry, who had come to the College from St John's College Choir School, Cambridge. Richard had just gained an Associated Board Gold Medal for Grade VI Singing. He was later to gain an alto choral scholarship to Christ Church, Oxford, and then Trinity College, Cambridge, and is now a consultant neurologist at UCLH. The music groups at that time were the Choral Society, Chapel Choir, Barbershop Group, Wind Band and an occasional String Quartet run by Michael Cooke. Andrew Cronin had recently joined the Music staff and was developing the brass and wind bands. He was also a good bass and founded the Barbershop Group (Fram Friseurs) which was continued when he left by Howard Robinson. There was the occasional student taking A Level Music but O Level was not on the syllabus and was taught as an extra after school. This remained so until the introduction of GCSE.

'It was clear that there was a need to develop the instrumental side of music at Framlingham, and so with the backing of the Headmaster, Laurie Rimmer, and the Governors, a Music school was built in 1981 – a catalyst of progress in all aspects of music-making. With the great majority of the students from Brandeston coming to the College, it was decided that we should run the Music department in both schools as one. All the instrumental teachers already taught at both establishments and now the full-time members of the Music department also did the same, which led to joint ventures both instrumentally and chorally. Lawrie Griffiths instigated group violin teaching for the youngest members of the school. A College orchestra could now be formed with support from the local community. Some excellent students began to come through from Brandeston, notably James Millard, later to be Director of Music at Queen's School Chester, Louise Wright, who played horn in the National Youth Orchestra and the violinist Sarah Fulcher.

'The Choral Society began to put on major performances such as Poulenc's *Gloria* and Haydn's *Creation* in the parish church, alongside a concert with the choristers of York Minster, including Herbert Howells's *Take him, Earth, for cherishing*. The introduction of girls throughout the College made a great difference and the Chapel Choir went from strength to strength, and at least once a term went to sing choral evensong in cathedrals such as Norwich, Peterborough, Bury St Edmund's and most

memorably of all in St Paul's. The choir was also much in demand in the area and we regularly sang evensong in Aldeburgh parish church during the festival. The Carol Service became so popular that we began putting on two of them, one for day pupils and the other for boarders, both absolutely packed. A very successful tour of the eastern seaboard states of America in 1989 saw the choir singing in the gardens of the White House, the United Nations building, the Cathedral of St John the Divine in New York and in Framingham, Massachusetts (the town founded by Nicholas Danforth when he left Framlingham in 1634).

'During this period I also introduced the House Singing Competition. With the exception of one or two Houses the standard at first was quite poor, but very soon there was improvement and it became one of the most enjoyable events in the College's calendar, with houses becoming ever more competitive.'

Howard Robinson and a latter-day Barbershop Group in 2004.

Below left: *Victoria House continues the House Singing tradition in 2011.*

Below: *The College Choir that toured the US in 1989.*

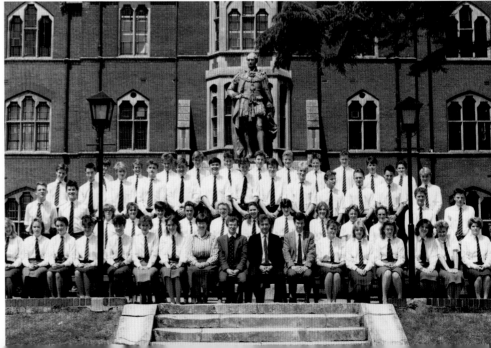

John Legrove at the piano in the Recital Hall.

Above: Seamus Wright on lead vocals, with Charlie Simpson on drums at the Midsummer Evening Concert, 1999, held in the arbour of Pryor House garden.

Above right: Daisy Cooper, Libby Allen, Rob Rogers and Michael Cooke.

Martyn Lane took over as Director of Music in 1992, bringing his own unique style to the post, and with John Legrove continuing as Assistant, classical music flourished. The Choir was reduced in size, the accent being on quality, with Rose Berney as the leading soprano, and other talented musicians included Lisa Cooper (currently Principal Horn of the Danish Aarhus Symphony Orchestra) and Henry Jackman, whose compositional flair would launch him on a career in film score.

In 1995 Rob Rogers brought in a very different style of directorship, more open and accessible, and more eclectic in appeal – one minute Rob could be playing a classical oboe concerto and the next jamming with aspiring rockers. As Charlie Simpson (Stradbroke, 1998–9) of Busted fame puts it: 'Mr Rogers had a beard, wore a trilby and must have been in his 40s; I think he'd taught Jay Kay from Jamiroquai. All the other teachers were much, much older, and more snooty. They wanted me to learn the violin. I wouldn't say he was into the same music as us – but he was a really good bass player and would jam with us. That was the type of guy he was: he wanted to adapt to whatever you wanted to do' (*TES*, 20 April 2012).

Other gifted musicians such as Libby Allen and Daisy Cooper appreciated Rob's classical side. He was much missed after his departure in 2000, but happily has returned in recent years to run Music at Brandeston Hall, where his infectious enthusiasm continues to inspire.

The new Director of Music, Rob Goodrich, soon established himself as a pioneer of ensemble music through his direction of choirs, orchestra, 'windbags' and theatre vocal groups. These fed into major musical productions such as *Jesus Christ Superstar, Les Misérables* and *Fiddler on the Roof.* Annual Cabarets and Midsummer Evening Concerts grew to an unprecedented scale, impressive both for quality and length – few will forget the night the Choir premiered his *Requiem* with Howard Robinson singing the tenor solos … a night when the concert finished just before 11pm! Singing was Rob's major passion and his setting up of entries to the BBC Radio 2 Young Chorister of the Year competition helped launch the careers of Christina Johnston and Laura Wright. Christina is now singing with the Prague State Opera; Laura has carved out a career for herself in both classical and popular music.

Other notable musicians include William and Ollie Poole (a superb Jean Valjean and jazz pianist), Imogen Webb, a lovely cellist, Olivia Castle, Joe Nickson, Rosie Bullen, Emily Higgins and Freya Roy. When John Hutchings joined the College, the ecclesiastical side of choral music was greatly strengthened, helped by his formidable musicianship and brilliant accompaniment on both piano and organ.

Christina Johnston-Myachin performing in Prague Castle.

Chanteuse Chantal Clelland at Cabaret in 2003.

Cellist Imogen Webb at Orford parish church in 2006.

Rob Goodrich with the Chamber Choir in Ely Cathedral in 2005.

Emily Higgins (Victoria, 2007–12) recalls highlights of her musical career at the College: 'A large proportion of my time at the College was spent on stage and in the music rooms. I have very fond memories of all five years of Music at the College. When I first joined, I was thrown in at the deep end as the only Year 9 in Chamber Choir, performing pieces such as Allegri's *Miserere*, my favourite choral piece of all time, which we sang in the Madeleine in Paris. Since then, I must have had hundreds of Mr Hutchings's hilarious Chamber Choir rehearsals, preparing for events such as the Orford scholars' concert, the Advent service in St Michael's, the Ely concert, and the concert in St John's Church in Bury where we performed Fauré's *Requiem*.

'Under the Goodrich Regime, concert performances were almost always well polished and professional, culminating in an entertaining evening of music with many different genres in the programme (despite often being long enough for three separate concerts). I particularly enjoyed being part of Windbags and performing Mr Goodrich's own arrangements of Michael Jackson, the Bee Gees, and Tom Jones to name a few!

'I think it is fair to say that everyone received several doses too many of the renowned "Theatre Vocals" groups (also affectionately known as "Theatre Sluts" among the pupils). Our Year 9 theatre vocals' debut rendition of Britney's "Hit me baby one more time", complete with school ties, pig tails, and nauseating American accents, was an omen of the kind of performances that were to follow in the next few years. However, I remain grateful to Mr Goodrich for all the opportunities to perform in concerts and cabarets, and to sing with my friend Rosie Bullen, with whom I still perform.

Mr Goodrich and colourful songbirds.

'However, the unquestionable high point of my co-curricular involvement at the College was leading Victoria House to a convincing triumph in the House Song and Partsong in Year 13. Even in Year 10 I had been quietly hoping I would be lucky enough to be the House Music Prefect, and our idea for "Candyman" was one Sara Austin and I had even mentioned in Year 11. For the unison we went for Queen's "Don't Stop Me Now". We were lucky that we had not only many musical people in Year 13, such as Alice, Sara and Willie, but also several very promising vocalists in Year 10. It was a very proud moment for me when we won because I knew every girl in the House had enjoyed being up on stage and had given their very best regardless of their musical ability. A similarly gratifying moment was my final Summer Concert in the Chapel, where the Choir, under Mr Rhodes's inspirational leadership, performed a sublime interpretation of Rutter's *Gloria*. The only thing I have to complain about with regard to the Music department is the new addition of the Recording Studios and Music Tech facilities in 2012 – WHY couldn't we get this earlier?!'

Below: Henrike Haltern, leader of the College Orchestra, 2012.

Bottom: Tim Rhodes conducting the Choir in the HPT in 2012.

Where Music Technology will lead in the future is uncertain, but it will surely be accompanied by traditional music-making, which retains its appeal and Tim Rhodes, Director of Music since 2011, is developing all aspects of his rich inheritance.

DRAMA

Until the 1980s Drama was very much an adjunct of the English department, whose members might be deputed to do a school play – in particular Brian Smallcombe took on the mantle of Bob Gillett, producing annual performances such as Tom Stoppard's *Albert's Bridge*, Guy Williams's adaptation of *Oliver Twist* and Shakespeare's *Julius Caesar* in the late 1970s. There were also House plays put on by the pupils – some better than others. However, the arrival of Tony Lawrence on the scene ensured that theatre would come first for many students, and the quality of productions steadily improved.

Housemaster of Rendlesham, Second Master (1993–2011) and, most importantly, Head of Drama, Tony picks up the story: 'Something of a landmark production in 1982 was the performance of the then contemporary *Rock Nativity*, featuring Sarah Bell as Mary and Richard Perry as Joseph, which I directed while still at Brandeston Hall, assisted by Brian Smallcombe. Employing radio microphones and using a full theatre band directed by John Green, the production brought Brandeston and College pupils together onto the same stage and went down a storm with parents. This production was largely responsible for my appointment at the College, initially as a Teacher of English and Head of Drama two years later.

'With a specialist Head of Drama in place and with Theatre Studies being offered as part of the A Level curriculum, the profile of Drama grew considerably. There were two annual school productions; the whole-school production in the autumn term with an alternating programme of Musical/Shakespeare and a lower school/Lower Sixth production in the Summer Term. Early Autumn Term offerings here included *A Midsummer Night's Dream*, *Twelfth Night* and *Measure for Measure*, and the musicals of *West Side Story*, *Smike* and *Annie*, whilst the summer term productions included *Kes*, *The Insect Play*, *The Fire Raisers* and *The Dream of Chief Crazy Horse*. There was also experimentation with theatre in the round; the first full production presented in this style was *Macbeth* in 1987, starring Jane Sims and Mark Young. Later that summer, the pair took the leading roles in a brave and moving production of *A Day in the Death of Joe Egg*.

'From the beginning of the 1990s the demands of public examinations led to there being three full-scale

productions per year. As well as Shakespeare productions, the widening range of musicals included *Cabaret*, *Grease*, *The Beggar's Opera* and *Jesus Christ Superstar*.

'Along with these went a succession of Sixth Form productions and Junior performances, ranging from Chekhov and Brecht to Agatha Christie and John Dighton. For these, the Athlone Hall's ageing light and sound equipment was almost entirely operated by students, who, under the tutelage of heroes such as Nick Mayhew and Isaac Pinnock, developed their skills largely by trial and error and passed them down to younger pupils.

'In the mid-1990s the creation of a new Drama Studio between Pryor House and the Science block gave opportunities for small-scale, intimate performances, including a rather special all-Lower-Sixth, all-female production of *Waiting for Godot*. The Recital Hall was another possible venue, the scene of Jane Sims's production of Strindberg's *Miss Julie*, while performances in the round continued in the Athlone, most memorably in Peter Schaffer's *Equus*. Many students also enjoyed an annual trip to Stratford, watching RSC productions and working with some of the leading theatre practitioners of the time … golden days!

'The complete development and refurbishment of the Athlone Hall into the Headmaster Porter Theatre in 2006 brought significant changes to the nature and performances of plays and musicals, with hugely improved sound and lighting equipment operated by a full-time theatre technician, a role admirably filled by Tom Howard. The balcony and the stage disappeared, replaced by retractable seating and a space which

Above: Imogen Slaughter as Queen Elizabeth I (left) in David Starkey's TV documentary and Jane Sims as Lady Macbeth (right).

offered far greater flexibility. The theatre opened to the public with a production of *Les Misérables* where the live orchestra directed by Rob Goodrich was situated in a completely different part of the building from the actors and the entire production was co-ordinated by means of internal TV monitors and sound loop systems. These improvements mean that almost any kind of performance can be put on to a professional standard and the Hall now plays host to groups as diverse as Framlingham Amateur Dramatic Society and the Cambridge Footlights.'

Among drama students who have made a career in the theatre are Jane Sims (Pembroke, 1983–8), Imogen Slaughter (Victoria, 1992–4), Jo Nuttall (Pembroke, 1992–7) and Martin Bonger (Rendlesham, 1998–2002), all of them inspired by Tony Lawrence. Jane Sims shares her memories of the impact that Drama at the College made on her: 'I have lots. It feels important to say that without my experience of Drama over the five years I was at the College, my work, marriage, life … may all have been very different. In case that's ambiguous, let me clarify. Someone once said to me "Life? It's just one damned thing after another." Well a key "thing" that paved the way to the work, life and the man I love was the time I spent at school – falling in love with theatre.

'Starting at Fram in 1983, I found myself one of only 11 girls in the entire year and the only one who hadn't been to Brandeston. When I arrived, I wasn't used to the culture, the strict uniform, being in a minority,

morning chapel and the difficult maths! They felt alien and a bit scary. What felt equally new – but the opposite of scary – was the level of support and opportunity I experienced. I remember the feeling of welcome when Tony Lawrence invited me to join the cast of *AMND*. It was already cast when I arrived and I was disappointed to have missed the boat. My best friend Jessica Platt marched me to the staff room to ask Tony if there was some way I could be involved. I was sure it was a lost cause till he smiled broadly and said "Of course!" Like magic, *AMND* had an extra fairy (with a made-up name) and my passion for being in productions began.

'Other productions followed and I was always at the auditions: *Oliver!*, *West Side Story*, *Jesus Christ Superstar* … I had chorus roles in all these and remember looking on enviously as Ros Wiley gave her Mary Magdalene and Bobby Scott wowed everyone with her Maria. Truth is I was never a singer, but Tony included us all and I did enjoy those large-cast productions. I can still sense the adrenaline and excitement when we would get changed and go to the Recital Hall for make-up. The group energy and commitment that surrounds all good productions can't be bettered, and that's where I first felt it: bouncing around the Recital Hall, rehearsing lines and waiting to be called to the stage. I was hooked.

'When Sixth Form came around, Tony gave me more opportunities to experience acting and this time it was "serious"! We did *A Day in the Death of Joe Egg* by Peter Nichols. Mark Young, John Annan, Jessica Platt, Vanessa Baker and Fiona Kelsall were all in the production. It's an amazing black comedy about a couple struggling to bring up their daughter Jo, who is brain damaged and requires round-the-clock care. I was fortunate enough to come back for Tony's retirement celebration and do an excerpt – now I'm the right age for the part, with children of my own I have even greater admiration for Tony taking on such a challenging piece with such a young cast. But as usual, he directed a production that allowed us all to shine and my confidence started to really grow. Our sense of responsibility also grew – this play required a lot of line-learning and it was the one thing Tony couldn't do for us. I remember one notable rehearsal (I can still feel the sense of mortification) when he finally lost the plot with our lack of line-learning. We'd never seen him that angry – turns out he can be quite scary! Safe to say, we came back with lines and lesson well learned!

'The moment he asked me to play Lady Macbeth will be with me forever. Have you ever experienced one of those moments when a teacher really sees you – possibly sees more than you can see? Tony is that kind of teacher. I felt this heady mixture of disbelief and elation – not thinking I could do it but feeling delighted to have been asked.

'It all seemed very grown up, and not just the Shakespeare and dark themes. Mark Young was playing Macbeth; one memorable rehearsal Tony directed us to kiss. So we did. His laugh rang out, "No, not like that! Come on guys this is meant to be passionate. You need to kiss properly." Well, I had never kissed anyone, ever – never mind in public or on stage. But we did it. My education was broadening all the time!

'After leaving the College, I went to Bristol University to read English and Drama. This would never have happened had it not been for all the encouragement and support both Tony and the College at large gave me. The spark that started when I donned that fairy costume in Lower Fourth continued to burn. After Bristol, I was welcomed back at the College to help out with English and Drama. Drama and Theatre Studies were now formal subjects and I had a blast teaching Years 9 and 10 and supporting with Sixth Form work and productions. I fell in love with teaching but, despite a strong pull to stay, I left after a year to take an acting job, playing Hermia in *AMND*. Funny how things had gone full circle … and of course Tony came and brought a load of students to see my first professional foray.

'I met my husband on a production a couple of years later and we now have three gorgeous children – who all seem to love treading those boards. Curious to think how those early acting experiences and my years at the College led me here: two words don't quite seem adequate to express my gratitude, but I guess they will have to do: thank you.'

Since 2006 Dorothy Englert has been Head of Drama, bringing her own individual style to a host of productions. Some of these have pushed the boundaries in a way very engaging to adolescents and students have responded with enthusiasm. Amongst junior productions, *Our Day Out* was polished and witty, while seniors have become ever more adventurous. Performing abridged versions of *The Importance of Being Earnest* and *Romeo and Juliet* back to back at the Edinburgh Festival in 2012 was an obvious highlight.

In the 1970s Machin Goodall (Rendlesham, 1975–80) died hilariously in *Journey's End*, a moment where the audience isn't meant to laugh. In the 1980s the Second Master, John Whipp, could review *The Dream of Chief Crazy Horse* thus: 'The plot is repetitive and badly constructed … the dialogue is pretentious, turgid, rhetorical and cliché-ridden … and comments to me afterwards ranged from, "Marvellous!" to "Utterly boring!"' Whatever brickbats can be hurled at more recent productions, they have definitely improved!

Above left: Lady Macbeth (Jane Sims) strengthens Macbeth's (Mark Young) resolve.

Above: Billy Treacy and Lewis Myers-Allen looking Earnest about Edinburgh.

Dorothy Englert, Hugh Edwards and assorted thespians cancan at the Leavers' Ball, 2013.

Left: Will Davies, regional winner of the Audi Young Designer Awards 2004.

Below: Arkwright Scholars 2007 – Hugh Chapman and Nick Thorne.

Five heads are better than one: all five have been heads of department!

ART AND DESIGN

In the 2013 Reith Lectures, Grayson Perry posed the question, 'What is Art?' Egypt has the pyramids, but Framlingham has the 'Design School', more commonly known as the TAC. In this extraordinary piece of 1980s architecture, a host of activities has taken place in the past 30 years. The lower floors have been devoted to woodwork, metalwork, engineering and design; there is a dark room for photographers, and though the old printing shop has disappeared, computers have multiplied at the southern extremity of the building. Upstairs, art takes more traditional forms: painting, sculpting, pottery and textiles. The Lenton cartoon

Miss Suzie Platt sculpting a unicorn, 1992.

shown on p.121 shows the primary movers and shakers in this empire: artists Caroline Mallett and Chris Lenton and Design specialists David Morgan, Stewart Reeve and Martin Brown. From 1988 to 2012 David was Head of Design and Technology, running a formidable department which consistently produced high-quality work, won a succession of national awards and attracted some very able students.

Art and History of Art have also flourished: the upper storey of the pyramid, recently enhanced by the addition of air-conditioning, is well lit and spacious, enabling large classes to undertake a whole range of projects. Generations of Framlinghamians have been proud to take their parents around end-of-year exhibitions, often showing impressive portfolios.

The range of the creative arts at Framlingham is impressive. Many students find their true métier in one or other of the cultural departments, spending many happy hours in an art studio, music school or drama rehearsal. If Munnings came here today he would have got along well with Caroline Mallett and her team, and in all probability wouldn't have prematurely departed for an apprenticeship at Page Brothers, the Norwich lithographers.

Above: *Lucy Hutchings leafing through her portfolio, 2000.*

Right: *Alex Watts by Helena Anthony, 2012.*

Opposite: *Viewing the Royal visit from Rendlesham junior dormitory, 2006.*

Angela Jackson in the darkroom, 2001.

Self-portrait by Victoria Balkwill, 2002.

Magdalena Tuta by Yuri Higashikokubaru, 2012.

Rupert Elmes by Mike Suwannapasri, 2005.

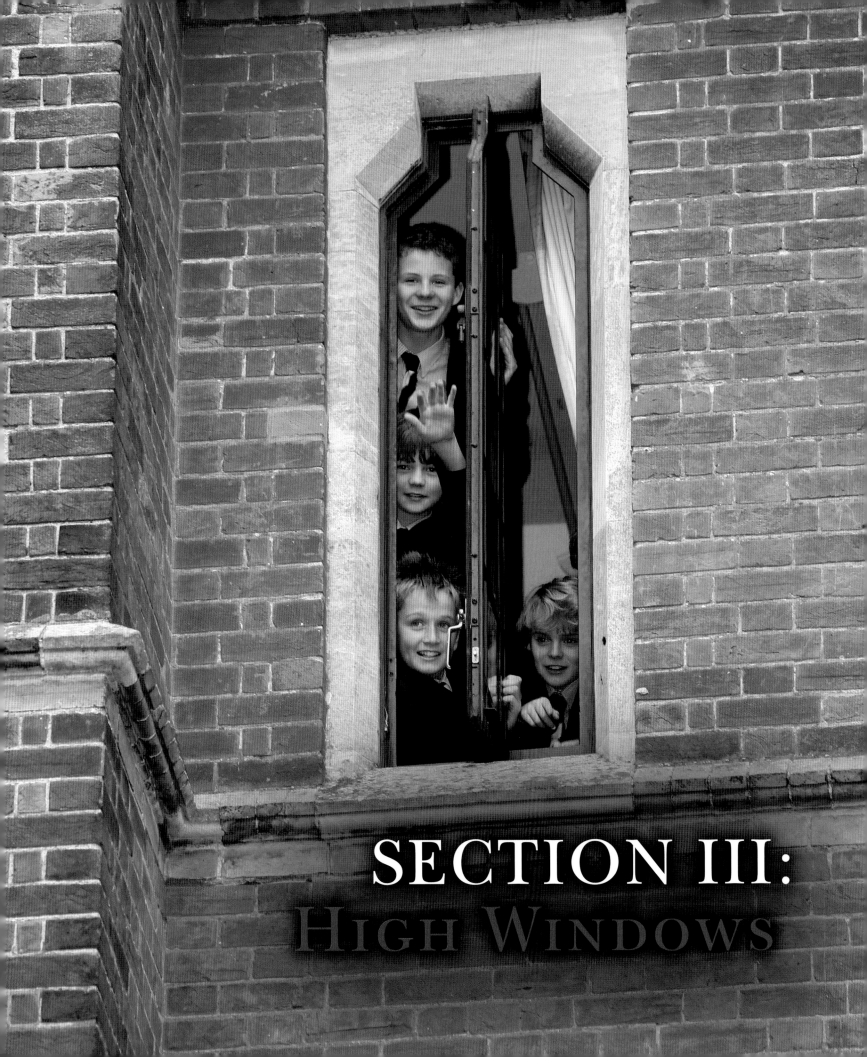

SECTION III:
HIGH WINDOWS

PLAY UP, PLAY UP AND PLAY THE GAME!

'Serious sport has nothing to do with fair play.
It is war minus the shooting.'

– George Orwell

GAMES

As professional sport has become more serious, so have Games. Obviously schools such as Framlingham have always taken Games seriously in one sense – the lovingly detailed reports of soccer matches in 19th-century *Framlinghamian* magazines make this only too clear – and many staff and students remember more about that LBW when the ball did straighten, than they do about the lesson on differential calculus. However, Games have also changed in character over the last 50 years, so that they are barely 'games' at all but contests between sponsored quasi-professional gladiators whistled by quasi-professional umpires.

It was not ever thus. Still, in the 1970s all boys did rugby in the Michaelmas Term. Virtually all staff, however unwilling and unsuited, were drafted into service – there was Section D, Section E and even Section F. (Some of the worst umpires on the circuit were chaplains.) There were House Leagues for those who did not make teams, refereed by staff as unqualified as their charges. Some went out in their macintoshes and ran things from the half-way line, though this was beginning to be frowned upon. Astroturf, of course,

had not been invented, but Lord's was as wonderful a setting for rugby as it remains, and Borrett presided over serious hockey on the easterly half of the Back, while the centre has always been sacred for cricket. Other sports were fitted in – squash and some tennis where players competed for the Youll Cup, while in the summer the Framlingham tournament was held on the Back. In a hot summer, the open-air pool, dug by the boys, continued to offer refreshment to amateur swimmers, and gradually the water cleared with improved filtration. Athletics were fitted in as and how, as was cross-country, especially when snow rendered the grounds unfit (boys spent many an afternoon slogging round Pepper's).

So sport bumbled along at all levels. The long away matches were truly long – it took time for a coach to get to Gresham's or Stortford or Felsted, and lunch was an integral part of proceedings, along with post-match entertainment. If one went with the 1st XI cricket in the days before minibuses, it was a 9am departure for the 11.30 start – junior teams could play several times over! On summer Sundays, the Haymakers under young Johnnie Maulden would try to ensure their matches

Top sportsman, Mark Stacpoole (left), with Joe Jennings, Vicky Carrick and Charlie Hicks, 2001.

lasted long enough to prevent attendance at evening chapel, and away matches might involve gracious acceptance of liquid hospitality at hostelries such as the Easton White Horse. Social cricket involving masters and boys took many forms, but Tuesday evening 20-over games seemed to have been the norm; the side's motto, *in stercore nitimur* ('more elegant in the original than in translation' as Bob Gillett puts it) epitomised the happy approach.

Girls arrived, and that was initially confusing, since they didn't all play rugby, so things moved on. The tracksuit was invented and the shell-suited wonder-boys appeared. Netball came, skirts shortened (or were they 'skorts'?) and the Sports Hall was built, later to be filled with gym equipment, and with an indoor pool attached.

But if Framlingham missed out on the progress of the changing world in the mid-20th century, it did avoid its follies. There were winners and losers, there were team games with intense competition, especially in House matches – often great tests of character. And if the summer exams hadn't gone too well and it had been a long year, Quilibets, so delightfully named, could wrap things up in July and send staff away for their eight weeks with a glow of contentment.

So is it better now? Of course the facilities, the fitness levels, the opportunities for both sexes, the expertise, all have altered immeasurably. Has something been lost? Of course the expertise is less amateur, less quirky. And yet the individuals remain, and some things

do not change: when the first off-drive of summer defeats the despairing extra-cover on the Back, one knows that all is well, that the grass has been cut as well as ever – that comforting hum of the mower, that smell of new-mown grass – ah, time to reach for the Pimms!

College Cricket

'You do well to love cricket,' observed Lord Harris, 'for it is more free from anything sordid, anything dishonourable than any game in the world. To play it keenly, honourably, generously, self-sacrificingly,

Above left: Girls glowing after success at the Rosslyn Park National Rugby Sevens, 1999.

Above: Cricket on the Back, 2005.

Below left: J.D.F. Larter.

Below: A.P. Cowan.

Even as an U14 William Earl (left – with Richard Marston in 1988) had the capacity to compile big scores.

Matt Truman (seated third from right) with the successful U14A cricket XI, 1993.

is a moral lesson in itself and the classroom is God's air and sunshine.' Over the years the College has produced many fine cricketers, most notably David Larter (Rendlesham, 1951–7), who went on to open the bowling for Northamptonshire CCC (666 wickets at 19.53) and play ten Tests for England (37 wickets at 25.43). A more recent fast bowler of note was Ashley Cowan (Garrett, 1987–92), who took the new ball for Essex CCC for many years (284 wickets at 32.86) and toured the West Indies in 1998 with England. While at school he excelled at all sports, but cricket in particular. He played a key role in the 1st XI's significant successes of the early 1990s and as Captain in 1993, despite injury and only being able to bowl off a few paces, took 27 wickets at 12.03 and scored 595 runs at an average of 74.37. He also had the temerity to break the Headmaster's thumb in the staff match!

On the batting front, Herbert Wilson (1899) takes pride of place. In his debut season for Sussex CCC in 1913 he scored 1,352 runs and during his time there amassed over 6,000 runs. He was made Sussex Captain in 1919 and went on to record a career-best 187 against Warwickshire in 1920. The most recent success story, however, is Robert Newton (Rendlesham, 2003–8), who is currently contracted to Northamptonshire CCC. In scoring 102 for Northamptonshire against Leicestershire in the County Championship on 13 September 2010, Rob became the first Old Framlinghamian to score a first-class century in the modern era. The previous closest was Ashley Cowan with a highest score of 94.

Since then Newton has gone on to score many more first-class hundreds. 'I have been fortunate enough to

bat at Cricket HQ at Lord's, Newlands in Cape Town and the WACA in Perth,' he recently wrote, 'and yet the Back at Fram is still one of the best cricket pitches I have ever played on.'

In terms of run scoring feats at the College, Patrick Howard-Dobson (Rendlesham, 1933–40) held the record for the highest aggregate number of runs scored in a season from 1939. This record stood at 996 runs at an average of 54.42 until 1992, when it was eventually broken by William Earl (Rendlesham, 1987–92). William scored 1,084 runs at an average of 83.38, in recognition of which he was awarded the Southern Area *Daily Telegraph* U19 Batting Trophy. Like his older brother before him – Robert Earl (Rendlesham, 1981–6), William captained the 1st XI for two years. In total he scored 2,349 runs for the 1st XI, including six centuries and nine fifties at an average of 44.

Earl's record was superseded by Matthew Truman (Rendlesham, 1992–7) in 1996 when he scored 1,161 runs for the College 1st XI at an average of 72.56, including four centuries and ten fifties. According to Wisden this made Matthew the leading schoolboy run scorer for that calendar year in the United Kingdom. As the following extract reveals, right from the start of his College career, Matthew brought a ferocious intensity of purpose to his cricket: 'Breaking the College record for runs scored in a season will live with me forever. My first taste of really wanting to achieve this was triggered when reading the Framlingham review from the Headmaster, Mr J.F.X. Miller, in the summer before I joined. In the review was a grinning William Earl, who had just smashed the school batting record and had scored numerous centuries, not just small ones either, massive hundreds in a style everyone drooled over. I remember sitting on the steps of the family home and wanting to be that guy.

'The wonder of "The Back", which only the 1st XI were allowed to walk across, gave me huge drive to make the 1st team and play on it; the chance to scream "Get Off The Back" to those who hadn't earned the right to walk on it provided further incentive. Rightly or wrongly, wearing a 1st team jacket in all of the major sports at that time gave me huge pride, and the pleasure of playing on such an incredible cricket pitch will live with me forever. It remains the best wicket I have played on and I have played on a number of the county circuit pitches, and its history needs to be cherished.'

If Matthew Truman remains the record holder for the highest number of runs scored in a season, the most prolific 1st XI run scorer in College history is most certainly Robert Newton (Rendlesham, 2003–8). During this time Robert scored a record-breaking 3,339 runs (947 as a Year 10 at an average of 94.70; ten centuries in all, plus a double century), a figure which would have been even greater if he hadn't regularly had to miss several games a season to turn out for Swardeston CC in the East Anglian Premier League, Northamptonshire CCC or England Schools. Robert remains the only schoolboy to have scored a double century against the MCC – 207 not out on 2 May 2007, a feat followed in 2008 with a similarly destructive innings of 165 not out against the same opposition. Robert's double century was the first to be recorded by a College pupil since H.A. Jones thrashed 208 not out against Woodbridge School in 1895. Robert understandably went on to captain the MCC Schools' side on their tour to India.

There has also been a long-standing tradition of high-calibre cricketers on the 1st XI coaching staff. The early impetus for this was provided by Headmaster Reverend Dr O.D. Inskip, who in 1883 appointed the College's first-ever professional coach, Harry Upton of Surrey CCC. This progress was sustained by Inskip's successor, F.W. Stocks, who had been an Oxford Blue and played county cricket for Leicestershire. Subsequent leading lights included College sporting legend Norman Borrett (Essex CCC, 1937–46), Stuart Westley (Gloucestershire CCC, 1968–76), Peter Hayes (Cambridge University,

1974–7) and 'Suffolk's finest ever bowler' (apologies to G.C. Perkins!), groundsman extraordinaire and cricket professional Colin Rutterford.

David Barker provides an insight into the cricketing ethos at the College in the 1980s: 'As a qualified cricket coach my main task was to instil good technique and an understanding and love of the game amongst the U14s, so that they could progress successfully up through the more senior College teams. Looking back, although not that long ago, it really was a different era in the 1980s; there was a very strong coaching staff with five who had played minor counties cricket and at least three with first-class experience. And incidentally the Common Room had regular Tuesday evening fixtures throughout the Summer Term (which we never lost) and a tour at half-term to the Cambridge area and competition for places during Quilibets' week. Often Saturdays in the Summer Term were the longest day of the week. Fixtures against our rivals in the depths of Norfolk and Essex meant, for the U14s, an 8.30am departure with the 1st XI and a 9.30pm return! The last 20 overs did not start until 6.30pm, even for the U14As. On one Saturday evening immediately after a 7.30pm cricket finish, Peter Hayes and I had to accompany the boys of Stradbroke and Rendlesham to an away fixture of a different kind … a barn dance at St Felix School – such was the nature of the weekend entertainment at this time. But nobody seemed to mind any of this – missing lessons didn't seem to matter and of course it was before the days of computers and electronic games.'

The Hayes–Rutterford coaching partnership nurtured many successful 1st XIs, particularly in the 1990s, when aided by such leading lights as Matthew Rutterford ('a chip off the old block' – 43 wickets at an average of 12.74 in 1990), Earl, Johnny Newton, Cowan, Phillips, Pineo, Elsley (who took a remarkable 53 wickets at an average of 16.20 in 1996), Truman, Hames and Low, the College rarely lost and often reigned supreme in the prestigious Castles Cricket Festival Trophy. Colin also transformed the Back into one of the finest grounds in East Anglia, a standard maintained until 2012 by his brother, Mike Rutterford.

Other 1st XI coaches of note have included Nick Peters, who opened the bowling for Surrey, and former Yorkshire, Sussex and England international Paul Jarvis. However, among the longest-serving coaches of

Below left: Colin Rutterford and young cricketers in 1980.

Below: Robert Newton on his way to his maiden first-class century for Northamptonshire CCC, 2010.

A mixed College XI at Easton CC in 2006.

recent times have been Mark Robinson and Marcus Marvell (minor counties and Middlesex), the latter of whom took over as Master i/c Cricket in 2003, when a renewed enthusiasm for the game became evident.

From something of a low at the turn of the millennium, when summer exam commitments in Years 11, 12 and 13 threatened to destroy the primacy of College cricket altogether, the 1st XI soon re-established its long-standing love for the game and winning culture. Clear signs of a revival were evident in 2002 with the batting heroics of College all-rounder Spencer Veevers-Chorlton, who captured national attention when hitting seven sixes (*sic!*) off an over for Yoxford CC against Mallards. Symptomatic of these happy days was the hugely amusing Sunday fixture played against Easton CC in 2006 to celebrate their centenary. A game against a College XI, featuring both masters and boys (as was the custom in 1906), had marked the opening of this delightful local cricket club and so a return match of a similar ilk seemed appropriate. The *East Anglian Daily Times* (*EADT*) rose to the occasion by publishing a witty report that mirrored the Reverend O.D. Inskip's original account of 1906.

THE WISDEN TABLE FOR OUTSTANDING PERFORMANCES, 2007

	P	W	L	T	D	A	
1st Merchiston Castle School	14	13	1	0	0	5	92.86%
40th Framlingham College	**15**	**9**	**2**	**0**	**4**	**1**	**60.00%**
46th Oakham School	17	10	3	0	4	1	58.82%
57th Eton College	20	11	5	2	2	0	55.00%
58th Kimbolton School	20	11	9	0	0	1	55.00%
73rd Manchester Grammar School	12	6	3	0	3	7	50.00%
75th Royal Grammar School, Newcastle	16	8	3	0	5	1	50.00%
79th Felsted School	17	8	4	0	5	3	47.06%
98th Gresham's School	14	6	2	0	6	3	42.86%
111th Royal Grammar School, Colchester	15	6	6	0	3	5	40.00%
115th Bedford School	13	5	5	0	3	4	38.46%
117th Uppingham School	13	5	7	0	1	2	38.46%
122nd Oundle School	19	7	8	0	4	2	36.84%
124th Culford School	11	4	5	0	2	2	36.36%
133rd Leys School	9	3	2	0	4	1	33.33%
137th Brentwood School	19	6	6	0	7	1	31.58%
142nd Ipswich School	13	4	2	0	7	3	30.77%
148th King's School, Ely	10	3	7	0	0	0	30.00%
150th Tonbridge School	17	5	6	1	5	2	29.41%
158th Norwich School	12	3	5	0	4	1	25.00%
168th Wellington College	15	3	8	0	4	2	20.00%
180th Bishop's Stortford College	7	0	6	0	1	4	0.00%
185th Woodbridge School	10	0	4	0	6	3	0.00%

The 1st XI won the lion's share of its fixtures between 2003 and 2008, a timespan coincidental with the prolific run-scoring of Rob Newton. However, Rob wasn't the only cricketer to excel during this time, when the likes of Stacpoole, Wybar, Davies, Clarke, Pearson and Wright also flourished, along with long-standing opening batting partner Harry Bush, who also went on to enjoy a degree of success in first-class cricket.

In 2007 Wisden published a table ranking the top 185 school 1st XIs by percentage win ratio, but because of its contentious nature this was the only one that ever appeared. The table reproduced on the previous page is a selection showing Framlingham's significant standing at this time.

After a short break Marcus Marvell returned as Head of Cricket in 2011, this time assisted by cricket professional Ben France (Derbyshire, Suffolk and Norfolk CCC). This coincided with another good run of results, with the run-scoring of Robbie Bridgstock in 2011 (589) and 2012 (732) very much to the fore.

College Rugby

Only two former College pupils have achieved full England rugby international recognition: Rear-Admiral Ernest Roberts OBE (OF, 1890–4), who was Captain in 1906 and played six times for England, and Andrew Hancock (OF, 1952–7), who won three international caps and will be forever remembered for his sensational 90-yard run in the 1965 Calcutta Cup: 'I've seen some great tries in Rugby – but Hancock's eclipsed them all' (*Daily Mirror*).

More recent international representative honours have been achieved at Schools' U18 Group by David Macaulay (Rendlesham, 1994–9), who represented Scotland in 1999; Christopher Read (Stradbroke, 1997–2002), who played for England in 2002, and James Hurlock (Rendlesham, 2001–6), who captained England to a clean sweep of victories in the European Championships of 2006. The most recent success, however, is Will Owen (Garrett, 2007–10), who played for England U18s in 2012 and 2013.

Particularly successful 1st XV seasons include: 1994 – when Ben Coulter's team won 15 out of 16 fixtures, including a mini tour of Wales; 1997 – when David

Above left: U14 Captain Diarmid Hurrell et al. – winners of the Suffolk Sevens in 1992, with Steve Wright and long-standing Director of PE and rugby coaching guru, John 'Rocky' Watterson.

Above right: England U18 international Will Owen, 2013.

Left: A.W. Hancock (No. 11) at the England Trials: Twickenham, 1965.

Above: Chris Read breaking from the base of the scrum, with Simon Stacpoole in support, 2001.

Right: David Lambert's 1st XV of 1997, which included David Macaulay (standing third from right).

Lambert's side recorded 12 victories and got through to the London and South-East of England quarter-final of the National *Daily Mail* Rugby Cup; 1998 – when David Macaulay's XV also achieved 12 wins in a season, including a mini tour of Ireland; 2001 – when Chris Read's troops won ten out of 11, and most spectacularly of all, on the back of a rewarding summer tour of South Africa, the undefeated season of 2005. Coached by Director of Sport Richard Curtis, this remains the most successful season in College history, when led by James Hurlock, an irresistible combination of attacking flair and uncompromising defence brought 15 consecutive victories.

In recent years College rugby has become increasingly professionalised, with regular touring, specialist coaches, muscle-building in the fantastic new gym facilities and colourful sponsored kits. Opposition teams have raised their game as well, but Framlingham remains one of the teams to beat on the East Anglian circuit. In 2009, a particularly good year under Charlie Precious's leadership, the 1st XV won nine of their 11 games. James Alvis (Director of Sport, 2006–11) set up much of this and his successor, Simon Sinclair, has since fostered excellent relations with Northampton Saints RFC (for whom he is Head Elite Player Development Group (EPDG) Coach for the Eastern Region) to open up even more opportunities for budding Hancocks.

Right: The undefeated College 1st XV of 2005.

Far right: Victorious England U18 Captain, James Hurlock.

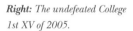

Boys' Hockey

The Borrett tradition of a strong hockey XI has been
well maintained into the modern era. Brian Underwood
took over the running from Norman in 1979 and the
eastern half of the Back continued to be preserved as a
fine grass surface despite the slope. 1983 saw the 1st XI
undefeated under Neil Trowbridge's captaincy in school
matches and on tour in Oosterbeek.

*Opening fixture on Borrett's:
College 0–Suffolk 3. David
Barker tracking back centre stage.*

Former England international David Barker takes
up the story: 'Whilst mainly involved in junior cricket
and hockey coaching for many years, now that my
own representative sport was winding down, I was
asked by Laurie Rimmer to take over the running
of College hockey in 1988 – which I continued until
the 1999/2000 season. By chance this spanned a
period of significant change in school hockey as we
progressed from grass to artificial surfaces, placing us
all, pupils and staff, on a fast learning curve for a totally
different style of play. For most of these years the 1st
XI were Suffolk county champions (as were the U16
and U14 teams) and many individuals were awarded
representative honours. Journeys to various astroturf
pitches across the Eastern Counties seemed to be a
regular feature of cold Sunday mornings in February
for the Divisional rounds but apart from the U16s, on
one occasion, the 1st XI never quite made it to the
National rounds. Having played for the county in the
match against the 1st XI at the opening of Borretts in
1980 (on tarmac!), I was, some ten years later, involved
in the opening fixture of its new astroturf surface, this
time as 1st XI coach – the College played the England
U17 team … and lost! – the push-back was performed
by Christine Janes (née Truman).

'In my last year in charge it was an honour for
the College to be invited to play in the schools match
prior to the 1999 Varsity match at the National Hockey
Centre in Milton Keynes. The occasion marked the 60th
anniversary of NFB's Varsity match and he was also invited

*David Barker and the College 1st
team at Hockey HQ, 1999.*

to present the trophy on that day. The entire College plus Brandeston Hall pupils and staff and some OFs travelled to support the team – who defeated Stowe 1–0.

'Running the hockey in those days involved much more than being 1st XI coach. We ran 11 teams from 1st XI to U14C, each with a regular fixture list and each coached by a member of staff – many of whom needed regular INSET on the latest rules and umpiring skills! We organised reciprocal tours every year at Easter either visiting Oosterbeek HC near Arnhem or arranging a tournament at College for their visit. Hockey was very popular – there were fewer alternative attractions for boarders at the weekend in the Spring Term in those days and all members of the College played a team sport on Saturday. There were enough decent players in the Common Room not only to defeat the College 2nd XI comfortably each year but also to put out a side on Sunday mornings to play each House in turn. It seemed too in those days that each member of staff spent much time with their team rather than being involved in diverse alternative activities – these simply did not exist – no indoor pool, no fitness suite, nor cookery, etc! In addition to games afternoons, cricket and hockey teams would be out practising until dark or evening tea most days after lessons – and when formal second prep was removed, certainly the 1st XI would be out later under floodlights for the 9–10pm slot as well!'

In 2000 boys' hockey was taken over by Jonathan Cuff, a young coach with a less traditional mindset, committed to playing more fixtures – the stats for Ian McLaren's 2003 XI, for instance, read: played 21; won 15; drawn 2; lost 4. From the outset the bar was set alarmingly high and in 2001 and 2002 the 1st XI played against all-International XIs, captained by Jon Slay and described in the *EADT* as 'the strongest hockey teams ever seen in Suffolk', including Dave Matthews, Mark Pearn, Danny Hall and Kwarne Brown; so while the College U18 Suffolk Champions were able to take an unexpected lead, the silky stick-work and superior technique of the 'All Star' players meant that opposition victory was assured by half-time, and the boys were given a taste of something special to aspire to.

Further 'stretch' came in 2004 with participation in the Suffolk Men's Indoor Hockey League, which was duly won with an unblemished set of results against the top adult hockey clubs in the area. This came at the end of a particularly enjoyable season during which the 1st XI achieved a succession of victories by some significant margins, for example: Bishop's Stortford College (14–3), the Leys (11–0) and Sir William Borlase (13–0). This was a fitting end to Captain Mark Stacpoole's four-year run in the side, during which time he had played over 80 games for the 1st XI and scored 84 goals.

However, the most prolific of all was Benedikt König's class of 2005, who won the Governors' Cup for the first time at the St George's Sixes, the Suffolk U18 HA Cup, and were unbeaten at the Bath Festival and on tour to Holland. Their 1st XI playing record is quite remarkable: played 27; won 21; drawn 4; lost 2. Central to this success were the unprecedented goal-scoring feats of Ben König, who, ably supported by Toby Tibbenham, hit the back of the net an incredible 77 times – a College record.

Rob Newton recalls his part in the victory at St George's, Weybridge: 'I had the easiest job in the world scoring tap-ins after our German international, Benny König, seemingly dribbled round the whole of the opposition team … sometimes twice! This was a particularly memorable day. We shocked everyone to beat the home side in the final, not least our coaches Messrs Cuff and Robinson, who had set us the task at the beginning of the day of not finishing bottom of our group! I even managed to bag the winner, a classic finish from all of two feet!'

Will Gallagher, Mark Pearn (Great Britain), Jonnie Harris (College Captain), Danny Hall (Great Britain) and Simon Stacpoole at the 'All Star' festival, 2001.

This was also a period when the U16 squad struck a rich vein of form. They were East of England Indoor Champions in 2005 and in 2006 they were outdoor champions and progressed to the National semi-finals only to lose on strokes to Kent College. In the following year they were East Champions again, but went out in the National quarter-finals.

In the context of something of a purple patch in College hockey across the age groups, 2009 was another spectacularly good year for the 1st XI in which Freddy Whitfield and Ben Gowing led the side to victory in both the Suffolk County Cup and the prestigious St George's Governor's Cup. Their XI a side unbeaten playing record also makes for impressive reading: played 16; won 14; drawn 2 (one of which resulted in defeat on penalty strokes).

The construction of a second floodlit astro on Inskip's in 2011 was a real fillip for College hockey and Tom Brown's over-achieving 1st XI of 2012 were the first to reap the benefits. The exemplary Jon Slay stepped down as Master i/c Hockey at the end of the year and was succeeded by England Boys' U18 assistant coach, Jamie Kingstone. Both men contributed to the Boys' U14 victory in the Nationals in 2014.

Girls' Games

The arrival of girls in 1976 meant that in time Framlingham would build teams in all the major sports, though in the early years sometimes almost everyone in a year group would be in the team and understandably the results did not always look impressive on paper. However, the devoted coaching of Pam Rogers brought the very best out of such squads as were available, so though for a while the boys might allow themselves to feel superior, this has changed massively over the last 30 years, and Mrs Randall's mantra of 'bigger cups for girls' no longer rings so hollow. In hockey, netball and tennis the girls are now regularly very successful at the highest levels.

Girls' Hockey

The combination of a new artificial surface on Borrett's and the prodigious coaching talent of 'astromaniac' Toby Mullins (later to become Headmaster of Seaford College), proved an irresistible combination in the early 1990s. In 1991, 1992 and 1994 the Girls' 1st XI were unbeaten in school matches and in search of competition were forced to resort to playing women's club 1st teams, such as Lowestoft, IES, Copdock and Southend. Kate Whitfield's 1st XI, which included the multi-talented Katie Bull, enjoyed a particularly impressive year in 1991 (played 12: won 11; drawn one). Caroline Donoghue (Victoria, 1990–5) scoring over 100 goals during her 1st team career was another highlight.

From 1995 Girls' Games were run by Kathy Evans (later Mrs Gardens), whose caring and inclusive approach has encouraged many girls to surprise themselves by what they can do, while 1st team standards have been well maintained. The growth in participation encouraged the appointment of more specialist coaches and the chances to excel became greater than ever.

Emily Wilford (Victoria, 2007–12) writes about girls' hockey: 'During my five years at Framlingham, sport was always my favourite pastime, with the weekly games session and matches being the high point of each school week. Throughout the cold winter months and the hot summer days, whatever the weather sport was always the best thing for me.

Left: The imperious Ben König weaves his way through the Oakham defence, 2005.

Below: Pam Rogers in her England hockey kit.

Left: Winners of the prestigious St George's Governor's Cup, 2009.

Above: Master i/c Hockey Jonathan Cuff inspires the successful Girls' 1st XI of 2004.

Above right: The unbeaten Girls' 1st XI, 2008.

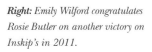

Right: Emily Wilford congratulates Rosie Butler on another victory on Inskip's in 2011.

'In my first few months at Framlingham we were taken on a short U14A hockey tour to Brighton and the South coastline. It was a long bus journey, the start of many, but the tedious journey was never going to dampen our spirits, and much to the delight of Miss Cranmer and Mrs Gregory, we sang our hearts out all the way. It rained for the duration of the tour and was freezing cold, but it provided the team with a great opportunity to really get to know each other and make new friends, as it was still very close to the start of our time at Framlingham. Not only did we get to know each other, but we started to get to know the teachers well with a dance-off on the dance-mat with Miss Cranmer.

'Another tour was to Canada in 2008, which was the real start of my time in the 1st team. We visited Ottawa and Toronto, climbing the CN Tower and visiting Niagara Falls. It wasn't just the trip that was good fun but all the fund-raising involved and the charity show with a dance routine. Obviously before any serious tour there was the circuit-training and fitness that we had to do before departure, which turned out very beneficial as the tour was unbeaten. We returned in September for the 2008 season with high hopes which were realised with the first unbeaten season in years. We were probably so successful since we all got on so well because of the tour, with friends being made across the years like me, Laura Tibbenham, Caroline Reid and Beth Rutterford. The last match of the season against Wymondham College was extremely tense with us just trying to hold them to a draw and not concede. This

season wouldn't have been unbeaten without the work-rate of Caroline Reid, Liz Clymer, Flick Cobbold and the great captaincy of Fiona Stacey.

'In 2010 I became Vice-Captain and we reached the final round before the Nationals and won the St George's Sixes tournament, where Anna de Grave dislocated her knee, but Rosie Butler stepped up and was made player of the tournament. In my final season at school I captained the team to another unbeaten season, where I scored the final of my 131 goals for the school. With an unbeaten tour to Holland it was a great chance to get to know the new Senior Deputy Head, Mrs Wessels, who brought a fresh take to hockey at school. The Holland tour was one of the best trips and the start of many friendships and a great squad. Crucial in this were Rosie Butler and Lucy Dunnett, and together we made up the midfield unit. I spent many hours on hockey pitches and hundreds of hours travelling to matches and tournaments, but I enjoyed it very much and all credit to Mr Slay for making my five

Below: England U21 international, Kitty McWhirter.

Below: England U16 internationals Sophie Hart and Sophie Underwood.

years of hockey at the College a great experience, as not only was he a great coach but also a really decent guy who always wanted every team to do as well as we could.'

In recent years girls' hockey has continued to flourish at all levels under the direction of Jamie Kingstone and Susan Wessels. In 2012 the 1st team lost just one of their regular school fixtures and in 2013, boasting an XI with three England internationals, they won all ten. In all competitions their record reads as follows: played 18; won 15; drawn 3 (one of which resulted in defeat on penalty strokes).

Girls' Netball

At times netball struggled to hold its place as a major game in the 1980s: bad weather could combine with the deteriorating surface of the Moreau Courts to reduce the number of matches to only half a dozen a season, and in 1985 the College VII lost all six of them! Although playing netball and hockey in both the Michaelmas and Lent Terms provided a larger pool of players in these early days, the lack of specialisation and clear focus no doubt had a deleterious effect on results. The arrival of a specialist coach, Denny Jones, however,

Denny Jones with the 1st VII Netball squad, 2011.

Above: Leah Webster with her victorious netballers, 2013.

Above: 1st VI, 1992. *Above right:* Framlingham's 1st IV, who finished third for the second year running at the finals of the National Schools Tennis Competition at Bolton in March 2009.

gave the sport a boost in the 1990s, and teams began to compete in the early rounds of the English National Schools' Netball Tournament. In 2000 the 1st VII recorded an unbeaten season, led by the irrepressible Pippa Knight.

Since then the sport has gone from strength to strength, helped by the Moreau Courts being re-surfaced and floodlit and the Sports Hall being used for 1st team matches. To the ignorant male observer, the girls' enthusiasm for the sport is a great mystery, but real team spirit has been engendered in recent years by Captains such as Esther Gosling and Milly Hopkinson, supported by the enthusiastic coaching of Leah Webster. In 2009 the 1st VII lost only one of their nine matches, and a 16-girl tour of Malta in 2010 returned 'victorious and sun-kissed', all showing how far the sport had come. In 2013 another strong team was unbeaten, with Milly Hopkinson, Lucy Ashby-Hoare and Libby Whitfield sharing the 317 goals scored to set up a goal difference of +173: *floreat pila reticuli!*

Girls' Tennis

Once upon a time girls' tennis was a lady-like plunk-plunk with balls drifting over the net in leisurely parabolas, and boys could threaten to beat girls with a chair tied behind them. Not any more! The power of Pam's drive, 'whizzing them over the net', as Betjeman had it, would inspire Framlingham girls to skim the ball with similar power, and the 1st VI became a serious outfit on the circuit. The

grass courts on Dickson's were a delightful venue for many years before tarmac and astroturf took over, though many lady OFs still compete in the summer tournament on the Back. By the mid-1980s the 1st VI was notching up impressive achievements, such as victory in the Suffolk Schools' U19 Tournament in 1985, led by Nikki King and reaching the third round of the Aberdare Cup under Louise Rogers in 1986. Katie Bull was Captain in the 1992 season, when all senior matches were won along with 1st and 2nd County Tournament titles into the bargain. Katie had the advantage of a grass court at home when the Bull family owned the plot where Pembroke House now stands, and playing with her brother Anthony (very much the star of 1st pair boys' tennis from 1984 to 1989), and the rest of the family no doubt added strength to her play.

The first decade of the new century saw a string of good results, with unbeaten seasons in school matches and further progress in national competitions. Claire Bush, Laura Wright, Tori Aldred, Flick Cobbold, Caroline Reid and Becky Saunders were a formidable combination in 2007/8: the Suffolk U18 Doubles championship was won every year 2002–8, except a blip in 2006, though the 1st IV reached the national finals of the Aberdare Cup that year.

From time to time since, there have been highs such as 2011 when Lydia Green and Amy Hulley were the stars, with Lucy Ashby-Hoare the promising youngster. All this has been orchestrated by Trevor Wright, whose dedication to coaching is worthy of the Rogers tradition, and Kathy Gardens and Esther Gregory have also played major roles.

MINOR GAMES

Not everyone covets the grand stage, and the best symphonies often change from major to minor. Some prefer individual sports, while others find delight in a personal expertise or enthusiasm. The London Olympics of 2012 highlighted a number of such 'minor' sports, and if Beach Volleyball has yet to hit Framlingham, many other sports are practised away from the glare of publicity, often promoted selflessly by staff with a particular bent. David Boatman has inspired many budding Robin Hoods to essay the ancient art of toxophily (archery, to those in the know), Bernard Dyer has inculcated disciplined aggression into many a kick-boxer, while Helen Myers-Allen has introduced aerobics and various active forms of dance. Girls like to go riding, show-jumping, dressage, side-saddle, cross-country hacking – Mrs Randall cornered off a bit of Dickson's for Julie Antz to exercise her horses, while Flick Cobbold often fitted in a chukka or two at weekend polo meets, though perhaps fewer hunt with hounds in post-Blair England. Hunting, shooting and fishing are natural country pursuits, and one remembers Marcus Gladwell angling contentedly on a Sunday though he caught little, while a Chenevix-Trench game pie was a tutor's treat, and a boy who brought a brace of pheasants back to his Housemaster established the right sort of relationship.

Much of this occurs out of school, but on campus people specialise in a host of areas. The old gymnasium

may be long gone, but the fitness suite is there for those addicted to pumping iron and they can build up muscle for all sorts of activities, some leaving ready to row at university. The Sports Hall has seen Gill Knights and Siew-Chiang Lim coach badminton, basketball and volleyball, all favourites for Far Eastern students, but now firmly on the agenda for many natives too. The indoor swimming pool has raised the profile of competitive swimming and, if for most, boys' tennis and athletics come second to the major games, Sports Day on Lord's is always an understated but serious contest in one of the

Above left: Lloyd Upsdell (Rendlesham, 1996–9) – Gold medal Paralympic sprinter.

Above: Verity Smith (Victoria, 2000–2) – England U18 Rounders.

Below: Rounders on the Front in the early 1990s.

Below: Amelia Bevan (Moreau, 2010–15), National Junior Side-Saddle Champion, 2013.

Below right: John Bird (Garrett, 2005–8) – England AAA 800m Champion, 2012.

College's loveliest settings, an inspiration to field and track success. Lord's was also the scene of the first ball bowled in girls' cricket by Nicola Jones at 3.25pm on Wednesday 26 April 1989 – a wide! This activity has waxed and waned since, though the aspiration remains. On the slope up to College is the Golf Course, long overseen by David Morgan from the TAC, and the local courses at Cretingham and Aldeburgh see many good walks spoilt for staff and pupils alike. When Stewart Reeve had had enough of woodwork, he would slip away to the squash courts, a venue for other cruder settling of scores in the bad old days. Down on Pennyfarthing's, Clive Norton and Mark Lavery have whistled many a Sunday Association Football match, while many girls have enjoyed rounders there in summer sunshine. If the seaside or Suffolk rivers beckon, pupils may sail at the hospitable local clubs or further afield – though only Mrs Randall has had to be rescued twice in a day by the RNLI – what a pity John Legrove wasn't on duty that day! In the winter the coast is bleaker, though this doesn't stop cross-country runners from competing even at RHS, while the Christmas holiday skiing may turn into something more serious for some. At times the cross-country has been quite strong, especially when John Bird and Suzie Reid led the way.

So, while some girls aspire to rugby and cricket, as well as hockey, and one suspects these will remain the 'major' games long into the future, there will always be room for the 'minor' activities – the slog round Peppers is rare and there are other ways to the body beautiful and an ever wider range of pursuits. Once there was Alfred Pretty's life-saving in the pond dug by the boys and dwile-flonking in the local villages, but now there is a host of ready-made facilities and equipment waiting for youthful Framlinghamians. Each can follow his or her own star and, after an astronomy session with our own Patrick Moore, Dr Richard Higgins, they may be able to name it too!

Top: Intermediate cross-country runners on Inskip's bank in 1992.

Left: Sailing Internationals – Abigail Stodel (Pembroke, 2003–7) (left); James Bolingbroke (Rendlesham, 2006–11) and Jacob Sallis (Rendlesham, 2004–9) (far left).

Far left: Stuart Jarrold (Rendlesham, 2006–11) – GB U16 Skiing.

Left: Patrick Spraggs (Garrett, 2004–9) – England U18 Golf.

10

HOME AND ABROAD

HOUSE AND HOME

Like many of the great public schools Framlingham's House system is profoundly embedded in the culture of the College and in some ways students' lives are shaped by the Houses in which they live and the friendships formed within them. Making this run smoothly is the truly challenging task undertaken by Housemasters and Housemistresses. In the old days there was no timetable concession and a competent bachelor supported by Prefects could manage a House in his spare time. More recently the demands of parents and a vast amount of social legislation has meant that the job description has changed beyond all recognition and the commitment in time and emotional support has become almost limitless. However, the College has been well served in this regard by many stalwarts. Few Stradbroke boys could forget Clive Thorpe (Housemaster, 1993–2006), so dynamic that he scarcely seemed to need sleep. Before him Ray Liddell was a model of competence, and since then Bernard Dyer has maintained the active tradition, also concurrently fulfilling the role of Head of Modern Languages. Overseeing Rendlesham at the other end of the main building, Tony Lawrence did a long stint, as more recently has Antony Bennett (Housemaster, 2003–14), a counsellor much appreciated by many. Prior to integration David Boatman and Ray Hoole enjoyed many years in Ziegele, proudly wearing their Colman's Mustard ties (though finding controlling the lively day boys wearing at times). Ray, a glutton for punishment, has moved on to the incredibly complex running of exams, while David after a happy stint in Victoria is now Head of Sixth Form. Kerrison has always been different: Tom Stonehouse was an eccentric

character, with a gentlemanly style, and Mark Kendall maintained this tradition in spades, chivvying the most indolent of boys into activity, while Julian Holland has exercised a calmer oversight. Garrett was in good hands under Steve Wright and he was followed by two good men in Myers-Allen and Hobson, both of whose wives did successful stints as Housemistress of Moreau.

In the last 40 years the House Tutor system has grown to become a major part of the school's pastoral care, with resident tutors in all seven Houses living cheek by jowl with their charges, aided by a non-resident team as well. Matron's room is also a source of much more than just clean socks and borrowed ties, and the sensitive direction given by the 'lady on the spot' has often proved invaluable. These House communities gather annually at House dinners in the Dining Hall, where the various entertainments and speakers reflect the different characters of each House and of each generation – it's no surprise that Kerrison in 2002 chose world-class boxer Henry Cooper, whereas Garrett's choice of Dumbledore in 2012 might seem more surprising.

Sir Michael Gambon with Tony Lam and Will Osborne at the Garrett House Dinner, 2012.

Year 9 at Garrett House barbecue, 2004.

141

Perhaps there is an element of competition about these dinners, but certainly House rivalry remains strong in many areas, with House matches keenly contested in every sport from cricket to crabbing; more recently House Dance and Inter-House Quizzes have joined the House Singing as serious competitive fun.

Not all fun is House-based, however, and for many years now the Sixth Form Centre (aka the Subs' Pub) has provided a safe haven for senior pupils to unwind in less formal surroundings and sometimes even to indulge in a rigorously supervised social drink or two. In the early 1990s the Prefects' Club was run by John Watterson in the pre-fabs on the piazza, before being more permanently relocated to the former teachers' digs in Rose Cottage. Here they remained, housing all manner of social activities, from stand-up comedy and rock gigs (Matthew Earley and the Bohanan Boogie Band spring to mind), to discos and theme nights – day students would actually return for these, such was their popularity!

Simon Jowitt recalls a stint as Chairman of the Sixth Form Society, 2003–7: 'The bar was their club and the students took responsibility for every aspect of it. They designed the décor, chose the furnishings, painted the pictures hanging on the walls, organised the music; we never hired in professional discos. The place was decorated with dark moody colours which presented a striking contrast to every other space in the school. I don't suppose the staff and Governors, who occasionally had to use it for meetings, appreciated the style but they were obliging enough to tolerate it. As we subsequently discovered when the law changed, it was almost impossible to attract the vast majority of the Sixth Form to come together and socialise regularly each week without the lure of alcohol. The ability to

serve everybody a drink was certainly what drew in the crowd; however, once they were there, drinking was only a small part of what we were about.

'The main focus of our entertainments was music and dancing. We decided to reject the advice of the ergonomically wise, who pointed out the folly of having the stereo system located in the tiny space around the bar rather than in the generously proportioned main room. When the music started the minority who wanted to watch television or play table football stayed in the main room and everybody else piled into the bar area to create what I can only describe as a nightclub in a sardine tin. The students preferred it that way because it made for a concentrated and intense atmosphere. I liked it because the resulting crush shut down the drinking. Once the dancing began one would have to have been a gifted rugby player to fight one's way through to the bar and an acrobat of sheer genius to retreat from it without spilling your drink. Booze was still for sale but nobody was buying.

'The bar opened at 9pm; at 9.30pm sharp we moved all of the chairs out and cranked up the volume as loud as it would go. That gave everybody a half-hour window of opportunity to get a drink and thereafter it was dancing all the way. On a typical night the joint was heaving: folk were dancing on the tables, the air was humid with sweat and you could see it condensing on the deep red walls. We must have been one of the few Sixth Form bars in the country, indeed perhaps the only one, which found it necessary to post notices prohibiting crowd surfing. If there had been a prize for entertainment mileage per pint I think we would probably have won it. The floor bounced like a trampoline; we routinely fused the lights in the kitchens below. In spite of the assurances of Mick Hart, the Buildings Manager, that the structure could take it,

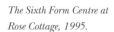

Left: Sweet Suffolk owls at the Victoria House Dinner, 2013.

The Sixth Form Centre at Rose Cottage, 1995.

I confess I was often nervous. I used to stand behind the bar surveying the scene, placing my trust in Victorian joinery, keeping my fingers crossed we would not all end up downstairs in the Catering Office. I knew, however, that for those brief minutes between 9.30pm and closing time at 10.15pm there was nowhere else in the world those present would rather have been.'

Although the House communities and the Sixth Form are very close-knit units, they are also very quick to welcome outsiders: many students join the Sixth Form from other schools or from abroad and by week three nearly all feel at home. Thirty years back a number of the English-Speaking Union (ESU) Scholars spent a Sixth Form year at the College, including John Reiffenstein (Kerrison, 1987–8) and Rebecca Walden (Moreau, 1991–2); since the 1990s young 'gap students' from Australia, New Zealand and South Africa gave and gained a great deal from a year in Suffolk; from 2009 there have been Sixth Form exchanges with leading schools in South Africa: Bishops, Hilton and St Mary's School, Waverley.

Above: Charlie Bullen, cheetah and Gareth Obery.

Right: Suzie Reid on exchange with new friends in South Africa, 2013.

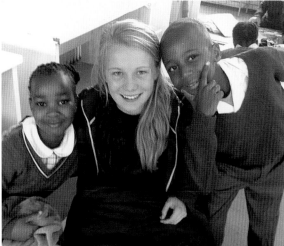

Charlie Bullen (Garrett, 2009–14) recounts his South African experience hosted by his exchange partner, Gareth Obery: 'For just over three months this summer, I was fortunate enough to go to Hilton College in South Africa, about an hour and a half from Durban in Kwa-Zulu Natal, where Gareth goes to school. Before going to Hilton the first thing I had to do was cut off all my long hair as Hilton is a strict all-boys boarding school, completely different from Framlingham. I arrived not knowing or being able to understand anyone with their accents as they use a whole vocabulary of their own slang, but within days I felt at home and surrounded by new mates.

'One of my highlights was definitely the rugby. At the equivalent to Sixth Form age group, teams stretched from 1sts to 8ths and the standard is far higher than in England. The school passion is incredible – for 1st XV rugby matches the whole school chants African war cries and spells 'Hilton' into the stands. Before the game against arch-rivals Michaelhouse, the whole school sang "Oh Boys of Hilton" in the dining room, which was one of the most amazing experiences of my life, sending shivers down my spine. Ten thousand people came to watch, and Hilton won 42–31.

'During the holidays I went on safari and saw hundreds of wild animals, like rhino and elephants. I also got to walk with a cheetah and play with lion cubs – who looked cute but would stalk you and jump up on you from behind. Hilton also had its own nature reserve at the school with giraffe, zebra, wildebeest, warthogs and more, which was awesome.

'Also during the holidays Gareth took me to Mozambique and we got to chill on the beach and enjoy the boiling sea, seeing whales every day! A contrasting experience was visiting the township of Soweto in Johannesburg, and it was moving seeing how much I took for granted. Over the course of my trip I made many friends, especially Gareth, and have many happy memories: it was the most amazing opportunity and I had the time of my life.'

Although one of the advantages of Framlingham is that it is cut off from the wider world, and visiting teams are often bewildered by their last 17 miles on the A1120 (surely the curviest A road in the country!), from time to time Framlinghamians like Charlie suffer from Wanderlust and go out on forays beyond the bounds of Suffolk, whether in military uniform or mufti.

CCF AND THE DUKE OF EDINBURGH'S AWARD

The tradition of a strong CCF continued at the College through into the 1960s under Colonel Podd (described by one cadet as 'a latter-day Captain Mainwaring'), until Squadron Leader Barry Pritchard took over in 1968. Besides the annual CCF camps with their Adventurous Training, from 1971 on students could compete for the new Duke of Edinburgh's Award. To begin with numbers for this were very small (with only two students actually competing), but with activities including map-reading, visiting the elderly and rowing up the Alde, subsequently extended to include stamp-collecting and bell-ringing, numbers steadily began to increase.

The CCF reflects the Armed Forces in having three sections, army, navy and air force, and these groups have gone out and about following their various avocations. Under the guidance of Flt Lts Bob Skitch and Simon Cullum the RAF in particular has taken advantage of chances to fly, and many cadets have achieved flying scholarships over the years. The East Anglian region is particularly blessed with air bases and cadets have been welcomed regularly at RAF Marham, Coltishall, Wattisham, Barnham and Wyton. Gliding at Swanton Morley has also proved very popular and modern flight simulators add to the richness of cadets' experience. The RN section has ebbed and flowed, depending on staff enthusiasm for sailing (in the early 1990s Major Godfrey enjoyed being afloat, while Lt Smallcombe was better at barbecues on dry land), but in good times has been able to take advantage of the Deben, Orford and Aldeburgh, and to make the most of regular visits to Portsmouth and occasional forays

to the Clyde. However, by far the largest section has consistently been the army, for whom Field Days can be challenging: recruits may face terrifying night exercises on Lord's with bangs and flashes orchestrated by Lt Col Myers-Allen, while the Advanced Infantry have regularly been to army bases such as Colchester, where FIBUA (fighting in built-up areas) can be practised. Sometimes Field Day comes a bit early for new recruits and in September 1997 they were put through their paces by enemy agents, 'Thorpedo' and Australian gap-year student G. Buckingham. Summer camps are also an important part of the CCF's year, while on a more ceremonial level, the Biennial Inspection ensures the maintenance of high standards – perhaps these were recognised by the selection of the College on the 150th anniversary of the cadet movement in Great Britain to provide the CCF banner bearer for Remembrance Day at the Royal Albert Hall in 2010. Cadet Edward King represented the 253 Combined Cadet Forces throughout the land.

A number of exceptional and committed cadets gain Army Scholarships, and one of these was Karen Buttenshaw (Victoria, 1988–93), a girl who endeared herself to many throughout her College career, which ended with her being Head of School. Tragically she was killed at the age of only 19 in an accident during an Army Cadet training exercise. James Miller spoke movingly

Above left: On a wing and a prayer: Wheeler, Cullum and Wilkinson at RAF Scampton, 2008.

Above: Field Day, 2000.

at the memorial service held at Brandeston and Karen's memory is kept alive by the annual award of a prize on Speech Day to a pupil with an outstanding school record both in terms of personal achievement and contribution to the College community over five years.

Martin Myers-Allen, Commanding Officer of the College CCF from 1996 to the present, writes on its merger with The Duke of Edinburgh's Award: 'In 1985 Major Hugh Kennon was appointed Contingent Commander and incorporated DofE into CCF recruit training. The scheme blossomed with hundreds of students taking part at the various levels, with the colourful SSI WO2 John Watson BEM a great source of strength up to his retirement in 1995, when WO1 Malcolm Todd BEM took over.

'I was one of Laurie Rimmer's final appointments in 1989, having met him in a bar in London while working as a stockbroker. I became the Awards Officer and Contingent Commander in 1996. CCF numbers peaked in 2006 at 265 cadets and 168 DofE certificates were awarded. Since 2011 Max Taylor has been Awards Officer and over 100 awards continue to be achieved every year. We knew that Hugh Kennon would never really retire and he still enjoys assessing Gold expeditions. Some 2,500 students have been presented with an award since 1971 and they have collectively walked over 150,000 miles in such terrain as the Lake District, Yorkshire and Derbyshire, as well as the Suffolk countryside.

Above: SSI, WO2 John Watson BEM.

Right: WO1 Todd leads the parade in 2002, with David Mallett bearing the standard.

Far right: DofE expedition in Derbyshire in 2008.

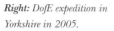

Right: DofE expedition in Yorkshire in 2005.

'In 1995 I persuaded Captain Todd to join me on a new venture I'd come up with late one evening in the Railway Public House described, from scribbles on a beer mat, as "a four-week trekking expedition somewhere in the developing world". Two years later we led nine Gold expeditioners to Bolivia and made a successful ascent of Mount Mururata (5,850 metres). In the CCF Centenary year of 1999, 20 expeditioners went on the arduous Annapurna Trek in Nepal, whilst WO1 Page led a comparatively luxurious expedition to Namibia. "Journeys of Self-Discovery" continued unabated biennially into the 21st century.

'The CCF also continued to hold high-profile parades, notably in 2002 when the Flowerdew VC returned from loan in Canada and in 2006, when the Earl and Countess of Wessex visited the College. The work of Contingent Commanders was recognised when Lt Col Kennon was awarded the MBE, and I was presented with a "Certificate of Recognition for Outstanding Service to The Duke of Edinburgh's Award" (2002) and a "Certificate of Meritorious Service to the CCF" (2011).'

SHOOTING

The College's strong shooting tradition has been maintained into the modern era. WO2 J.W. Meynell joined in the 1950s and served for over 30 years. 'Jack' was legendary in the shooting world, having twice won the Queen's Medal at Bisley, and in 1979 he coached S.G. Craig and J. Hayward-Smith to success in the Cadet Pair Shield. When Malcolm Todd took over, there were also some impressive achievements: for instance in 1997, when the boys came third in the Independent Schools' National Clay Championship (Matthew Hadingham winning the High Gun), the girls were the Ladies National Champions (Rosie Barker winning the Ladies' High Gun); and the following year the boys were National Champions.

Below: Independent Schools' National Clay Champions, 1998.

Below left: Ben Shanson (Stradbroke, 1997–2002).

Below right: Alex 'Sandy' Walker (Rendlesham, 2000–5).

Lt Col Myers-Allen, 2011.

Malcom Todd coached numerous Athelings, of whom seven went on to shoot at international level. In 2001 Ben Shanson and Claire Nall-Cain went on the British Schools' Rifle Association tour of South Africa, where Ben captained the British team, which won 24 medals at the Bloemfontein championships. In 2003 Alex Walker was the youngest-ever member to be selected for the British Cadet Rifle Team, travelling with the Athelings to Canada, where he won the Silver Medal in the District of Columbia championship. Alex later went on to achieve full international honours with Scotland before being selected to represent the senior Great Britain team on their New Zealand tour in 2010.

In 2006 'Toddy' was replaced by WO2 Roy Witham who, after 29 years as a Royal Dragoon Guard, brought extensive cadet training experience to the CCF and the shooting. Success continued, a notable instance being Seb Treacy's captaincy of the 2013 UK Cadets Rifle Shooting Team in Jersey.

Seb Treacy (Garrett, 2009–14) with Les Quinzes trophy in Jersey in 2013.

COLLEGE AND COMMUNITY

One of James Miller's watchwords was 'community', and in recent years this has meant not simply all those that live and work at the College, but people from the town as well. College facilities such as the swimming pool and fitness suites, astroturfs and Headmaster Porter Theatre are regularly used by locals, who are also welcomed at events ranging from chapel services and Framsoc meetings to the more long-standing Framlingham Tennis Tournament, where Christine Janes (née Truman) developed her lawn tennis at the second-oldest tournament in the country before graduating to Wimbledon. Andrew Payn, Director of Operations, has greatly developed other uses of College facilities during school holidays – hairy bikers and brass bands, mingle with sports coaches and international language schools, while others come to get married in the College Chapel and to be photographed with the finest view in Suffolk as backdrop.

Students also go out into the town, not only to taste the 'local' takeaways, but to do their bit for the community. The College has been closely involved with the Framlingham Volunteer Centre over many years, visiting elderly people in their homes, an activity that all parties have found richly rewarding. More recently visits to the old people's home at Mills' Meadow have added a further element to this, and students also host occasional teas and a Christmas lunch in the College Dining Hall.

There are also many links with Sir Robert Hitcham's Primary School. College students used to help entertain children at the After-School Club in St Michael's Rooms, and now there are 'Sport for All' sessions in the College Sports Hall supervised by Year 11 students. Year 12 Modern Linguists also visit the primary school,

The Fram Country Show on the Front, 2012.

where our foreign pupils can give local boys and girls a taste of the real thing. St Michael's Church is also a wonderful venue for the College Choir to sing Evensong occasionally, and the annual Advent Carol Service remains a genuine highlight. A brass group and carol singers are usually let out into the community before Christmas for 'late-night shopping', enhancing the festive atmosphere in the Market Square.

Sometimes the carol singers raise a bit of money for good causes, but some local charities such as the West Villa Project and St Elizabeth Hospice in Ipswich benefit more substantially from regular support. Individual students also take the initiative in promoting national or international charities close to their hearts and give moving addresses in chapel to support their causes. Chapel has long been the focal point for organising charitable works and the current Chaplain, Steve Waters, has maintained the traditions previously fostered by the Reverend Michael Booker. Many OFs continue to serve in challenging parts of the world, a notable case being Dr Mark Twite's part in the mass vaccination of Kosovan refugee children in Macedonia to prevent a cholera epidemic in 1999 – a Cambridge medical education being put to good use indeed.

When it comes to service and generosity of spirit, special tribute must be paid to Jeff Wornham GM (Kerrison, 1990–5), a fireman in the Hertfordshire Fire and Rescue Service. In 2005, having fought through intense heat and dense smoke to save a man from a blazing tower block in Stevenage, Jeff tragically died when returning to the heart of the fire to rescue a woman trapped in an adjacent room. At just 28 years old, Jeff was willing to make the ultimate sacrifice and he was posthumously awarded the George Medal in 2007. Shortly after his death a whole generation of OFs and staff gathered to celebrate Jeff's life, and a Memorial Cricket Match was played on the Back in his honour. Jeff was a talented cricketer and it was apposite that a trophy bearing his name should be awarded annually on Speech Day to the 1st XI's most dashing young cricketer; the first recipient of this beautiful silver trophy was Peter Clarke.

Second Master, Tony Lawrence, lends his support to Comic Relief, c.1995.

Above: *Presentation of a cheque to St Elizabeth Hospice, 2014.*

Right: *Headmaster's Cricket XI v. Old England XI in aid of the East Anglia Air Ambulance, 2010.*

David Barker on the Geography field trip to Paris, 2012.

Clare Church, Julia Sassen, Tom Faulkner and Edwina Reid at the United Nations in Geneva, 1997.

TRIPS AND EXPEDITIONS

Some academic subjects lend themselves more to outward bound projects than others, but most departments can find an excuse sometime in the year to venture into the outside world. Even though geographers rarely look at maps these days, it is

Year 12 Historians with Dr David Starkey, London, 2011.

not surprising that they should be first in the field, as long-standing Head of Geography David Barker writes: 'Whenever I bump into an OF geographer it is inevitably one of the residential field trips that they recall. Landscapes, youth hostels, the weather and incidents that remain in their memory show that all was worthwhile. In particular before the onset of the new modular A Levels, trips during the Easter holidays to Arnside, the Lake District and Malham were particularly memorable. Few Framlinghamians will ever forget the steep treks up to Stickle Tarn in Great Langdale and Castle Rock in Borrowdale – all in pursuit of understanding the effects of glaciation – or climbing the tufa screen of the waterfall at Gordale, the Whitscar caves deep underneath Ingleborough Hill, and the limestone formations at Malham Cove. Latterly, there will be some fond memories of the coastline near Sheringham and perhaps Mr Bean's boat trips to Blakeney Point as well as the spectacular urban geography of the Paris area and travelling on Eurostar. Personal favourites include trips to the Isle of Arran and to the self-catering accommodation in a windmill at Burnham Overy Staithe in Norfolk.'

Art Historians don't fancy the discomforts of the North Norfolk coast, preferring the urban amenities of London, Paris, Florence and Venice, while more locally they can pop to 'Constable Country'. Historians visit a range of castles, from Orford to the Tower of London, though the Steve Wright tradition of going to Bangor

Canada Tour, 2008.

in the Michaelmas half-term has been dropped. The Imperial War Museum at Duxford remains a favourite venue for Year 9, and Sixth Formers enjoy their annual visits to specialist lectures in London.

The Religious Studies Department also takes full advantage of the fine Norman cathedrals of East Anglia, with Ely their usual destination of choice. Students also visit Auschwitz, a sobering and emotionally challenging experience for all. Modern Linguists naturally like to spend time abroad, and French and Spanish trips are slipped into the holidays *de temps en temps!*

From the late 1990s Framlingham featured strongly in the Model United Nations, travelling to The Hague and Geneva; coached by Tom Vignoles, our students regularly made significant contributions. More recently the baton has been passed to Julian Holland, who continues to take students to a wide variety of venues. Tom Vignoles writes: 'The Students' League of Nations in Geneva was a unique opportunity for students to play the role of UN delegates in the Palais des Nations in Geneva, a venue that comes complete with microphones, earpieces and senior Russian

diplomats with utterly unpronounceable surnames. Regularly our students described this event as the absolute highlight of their school careers and on three occasions the resolutions submitted by Framlingham students were so good that they were given the opportunity to lead the debate from the front. Seriously, how many students can say that they have led a debate in two different languages in the Palais des Nations in front of 200+ students and any Russian diplomats who happened to be passing? On one occasion, the Qatari ambassador who was listening at the back was so incensed by the way Qatar had voted in a debate that someone had to quietly point out that it was only a bunch of students engaged in an extended role play!'

Sport has long been a reason to go abroad and such tours are as much cultural experiences as sporting ones, particularly those to far-flung places such as Sri Lanka, Canada, Barbados and South Africa, where the length of time spent allows students to mix with local people. The most long-standing trips, however, are the European ones: hockey players have been welcomed in

Holland for many years, where the exceptional facilities are matched by the extraordinary hospitality that clubs and families offer; Ireland, Wales, France, Malta, Spain and Portugal have also seen Framlinghamians as sporting ambassadors, with a spectacular dinner at the Polo Club in Barcelona at the end of the Los Reyes Tournament in 2010 being especially memorable.

JOURNEYS OF SELF-DISCOVERY

In the first decade of the 21st century Framlingham has built on Martin Myers-Allen's expeditionary legacy. Every two years a number of Sixth Formers volunteer to prepare for, and take part in, expeditions ranging from the rainforests of South America to the Great Wall of China.

Chris Hobson, currently Deputy Head (Pastoral), reports on recent expeditions:

Peru, 2003

'During the summer of 2003 two teams from the College started their expeditions to the Land of the Incas. After the culture shock of Lima on the west coast, acclimatisation training took place in the cold, thin air 700km south in the Inca capital Cusco, trekking to the massive ruined fortress of Sacsayhuaman. The site

Below: Peru, 2003.

Below right: Everest Base Camp.

has three zig-zag ramparts made from stones of up to 300 tons. The next few days were spent visiting equally impressive sites in the Sacred Valley.

'The size of each team then swelled to about 40 individuals with the addition of hired porters, cooks and guides as they started the hike along the stone-paved Inca pathways to Machu Picchu, the enigmatic "Lost City of the Incas". There are few hikes in the world that can offer such a mix of jungle and Sierra. There are so many secluded ruins to explore en route and such stunning mountain views. The most difficult day was the climb over Dead Woman's Pass at 4,200m followed by the descent from Phuyupatamarca to Winaywayna, consisting of 2,339 knee-punishing carved steps.

'Later in the itinerary the teams spent two days whitewater rafting and mountain-biking before heading to Lake Titicaca on the Peruvian plateau at 3,800m to stay with local families on Amantani island. The pace of life slowed dramatically and we were treated to some memorable insights into the traditional lives of the Quechuan people.'

Tibet and Everest Base Camp, 2005

'Trekking to Base Camp Everest is never going to be easy, and this trip proved to be a real test of endurance, as much of it took place at high altitude. Flying into Kathmandu to experience a couple of days in this exciting city, we then made our way through part of Nepal before entering Tibet via the "Friendship Bridge". Our sherpas were terrific, but many of the students experienced problems due to altitude sickness, and at one point we had to drop down to lower altitude

Above: The Borneo squad flanked by Roy Witham and Dr Ruth Noble.

in order to acclimatise sufficiently to move up to Base Camp. Having survived a particularly exhilarating evacuation in an open truck, all members of the groups made it to Base Camp to witness the barren landscape and magnificent views of Mount Everest and to share a once-in-a-lifetime moment together.'

Chile, 2007

'Two groups from the College spent three weeks trekking in Chile and Bolivia, beginning with an exploration session on horseback in the Maipu Valley. Camping proved to be an experience in this region, as temperatures were low, but the views were superb. After an exciting 24-hour coach journey we arrived in the Atacama Desert, one of the driest regions in the world, and spent several days trekking around the magnificent salt flats. For a bit of relaxation we floated in some hot springs and Jack Bullen alarmed us all by almost diving into a boiling geyser. We then spent a couple of days trekking into Bolivia at altitude, but once again some

of the students were beaten by altitude sickness and we were forced to return to lower slopes.'

Nepal and Everest Base Camp, 2009

'The goal of this demanding voyage of self-discovery was to trek all the way to Everest Base Camp (5,357m). After two days in the Thamel district of Kathmandu, during which time we had the chance to visit the monkey temple – the famous Bodinath – and haggle with street traders, we were driven to a small airport to board a light aircraft which was to fly us to Lukla (2,800m). Here we met our trekking team of sherpas and yaks, and had a chance to check our kit and take in some of the breathtaking views, before commencing the 13-day trek to Base Camp. Crossing suspension bridges, camping along the way, we entered the Sagamartha National Park and a trekking village named Namche Bazaar. Our sherpas provided excellent meals to sustain us on the arduous trek and we pushed on past snow-capped mountains and huge waterfalls up to Base Camp, where we all had time to congratulate each other on completing a magnificent adventure, soaking up sights which will remain with us for the rest of our lives.'

Borneo 2011

'Thirty-four Sixth Form students, accompanied by four members of staff, journeyed a total of 14,000 miles to complete two exciting expeditions to the heart of Borneo, encountering the wonderful orangutans of Sepilok, undertaking valuable community projects in a small village on the edge of the Kinabatangan River, which was teeming with wildlife, and completing a four-day trek in the heart of the jungle, sleeping in hammocks along the way.'

China 2013

'In July, an intrepid group of Sixth Formers set off for Beijing to embark upon a three-day cycle trip to the Great Wall. They covered about 50km per day in high temperatures and humidity, and then trekked for 15km along the Great Wall of China, taking in the fascinating scenery along the way. The students adapted to conditions extremely well, and the use of chopsticks at every mealtime became the norm. From the Great Wall, they endured a 19-hour train journey, extended by severe flooding in the area, on to Xian and the sights of the incredible Terracotta Warriors exhibition.'

Right: An Englishman abroad – Chris Hobson and chums on the Great Wall of China.

11

THE FRAMLINGHAM FAMILY: FROM ABBAY TO ZIEGELE

One of the distinctive features of the College is that its numbers are relatively small in comparison with many other great public schools, and this perhaps gives it a level of intimacy that makes the concept of a 'Framlingham family' a reality. At times a degree of isolation in the wilds of Suffolk may intensify this, for better or worse. What is remarkable, however, is the number of families who have continued to send children to Framlingham over many generations, even if not many fathers manage to sire as many as the ten boys that A.J.B. Flowerdew sent to the College in the late 19th century! One exceptional family are the Simpsons and their descendants, including the Rogers and the Smallwoods: George Henry Simpson (OF, 1865–9) was here on the day the College opened and almost 150 years later, his great-great-great-grandson, William Simpson, started in Garrett in 2013.

Since 1949, for many the initiation into the school has come at Brandeston Hall. At first this junior school took children from the age of ten, but this was steadily lowered and now the age of entry is just two-and-a-half. Bob Williams, who was Second Master there from 1971 to 1999, describes the close links between Brandeston and the College: 'On the occasion of the official opening of Brandeston Hall, Dr Montague Rendall uttered the words, "Brandeston Hall is indeed a very part of our Foundation and it would be impossible to think now of Framlingham without it." This moment set in stone the special relationship between Brandeston and the College. However, the links have also been human, with many staff dividing their time between the two sites, especially in the creative arts. Tom Fleming taught woodwork for over 30 years and a succession of Directors of Music and Drama have also spent many hours on the twisting road through Kettleburgh – and occasionally coming to grief, as Tony Lawrence will ruefully recall! Some married partners have also spent much of their working lives, one in each school, including the Podds, the Gilletts, the Robinsons and, in more recent times, the Nortons

Family tradition – Hetta Rogers (Deputy Head of School) in 1999 and William Simpson in 2013.

Leonard Squirrell's evocative watercolour of the front of College, 1947.

For many years Brandeston Hall hosted the Independent Association of Prep Schools (IAPS) orchestral courses. Here at the first in 1972 are (from left) Richard Broad, Headmaster; Arthur Harrison, Chairman of IAPS Orchestra; Benjamin Britten, its first patron; and Robin Wilson, course administrator. Britten had known Framlingham College from the early 1950s, where he would often play squash and enjoy the relaxation of being with 'ordinary public school people'. So much did Britten enjoy the place in fact that he spent much of one weekend in 1953 umpiring a College cricket match with his close friend Peter Pears.

and Myers-Allens. Many OFs have also returned to teach at Brandeston, the longest serving being Michael Baic, Brian Rosen and Simon Cullum.

'Links between the two schools have become especially close in recent decades, with Brandeston pupils being able to take advantage of the ever-increasing facilities at the College, including the indoor swimming pool, superb astroturfs and state-of-the-art Headmaster Porter Theatre. The seamless transition of students up to the College is facilitated by regular familiarisation visits. Sixty-five years on from Brandeston's founding, the feeder school continues to be a major part of the Framlingham family. The annual *Yearbook* recognises the strong emotional bond between Brandeston, the College and the Society of Old Framlinghamians, without whose generosity there would be no junior school at Brandeston Hall.'

Dominic Vipond (Ziegele, 1988–93), whose father Mike was a towering presence at Brandeston for many

years, writes: 'I find it hard to believe that 20 years ago I left Fram, and that my time had finished at a school that never failed to entertain me. I had emerged from the warm cocoon-like existence of Brandeston Hall and was plunged head first into an environment where you had to have your wits about you. My brother, Andrew, had kindly warned me that being the son of a Housemaster at Brandeston was going to make life "fun" for me, and he wasn't wrong, because I spent the best part of that year making sure I was as invisible as possible to boys in older years. I was in Ziegele, so it always felt as if we were on our own and had to prove ourselves to all of the boarding houses. I must admit I loved that and relished the challenges that being in the day house brought, and the times I had in that House were some of the funniest and most enjoyable times I have ever experienced. We were encouraged by David "Boaty" Boatman to create a winning atmosphere, a House spirit if you like, that would ensure Ziegele would compete and perhaps even win the coveted Stock Shield, which was something Ziegele had never done before. Alongside our ambitious Housemaster was Howard "Zowie" Robinson, whose enthusiasm was never rivalled in the Singing competitions, and other staff such as Graham "Growly" Garrett and Graham "Wiggers" Wigley, who brought their sporting chops to the fore when we participated in House matches. Ziegele was affectionately known as "animal house", and any boarder brave or foolish enough to come in during the day would often leave shaking their head in disbelief after observing the daily spate of Birthday Bumps, Highlander or any other game that invariably involved a bin or a locker.

'As I branched out from the carnival atmosphere of Ziegele I realised that Fram had some of the most entertaining staff to ever grace the realms of sleepy Suffolk. I encountered Ian "Bairdy" Baird and his encyclopaedic knowledge of English and waxed lyrical about British history with the humorously frank Michael "Cookie Monster" Cooke. I was lucky enough to also be guided by Tony Lawrence and Steve Wright, who scared the hell out of me at first, but then proved to be mightily adept at somehow ensuring I kept my head above water

in Drama and History and later when we came back to Fram were always the first people to get a round in at the bar. I remain fiercely proud of the fact that four of the ushers at my wedding all played alongside me in the infamous U16 rugby back line under the tuition of John "Rocky" Watterson, who in terms of coaching was before his time in the manner he gave us the freedom to play Barbarian-style rugby. I also even managed to rope in one of my old Fram teachers to play at my wedding, and although he shall remain nameless I am glad he did not revert to type with renditions of "Smoke on the Water" after a few cherry brandies.

'When I meet with the friends I have now had for 30 years or so after a few beers we will always start to talk about Fram and all the things that happened while we were there. It is strange to think that going to a relatively minor public school had such a big impact on all of us and that although we have made many friends at university and in the working world our friendships at Fram have been the oldest and in many ways the strongest we have made.'

Claire Bush (Moreau, 2003–7) gives a boarding girl's perspective: 'When asked where I went to school, the answer, to my surprise, frequently evokes sympathy. Why would your parents banish you to a boarding school? I always laugh at their reaction! What more could a 13-year-old girl wish for than a four-year sleepover? Chatting away to your best friends over Weetos at breakfast, feasting on towers of toast at break-time and settling down with a bowl of popcorn in readiness for the weekly Moreau ritual of *Desperate Housewives*.

'In that environment, it's difficult not to make lifelong friends. Laura Bridgstock, Sam Cherry-Downes and I have gone from sharing a little room on the first floor of Moreau to sharing a (not much larger) flat in North London. You know the best and the worst about each other: your childhood achievements alongside your embarrassing crushes and, in hindsight, questionable decision-making.

'You share some big moments: the standing ovation given by our parents to our performance of *Les Misérables*, the massive group hug after beating arch-rivals Gresham's at the end of an unbeaten netball season and the sound of a whole House-full of girls singing "We are Family" in unison. As well as lifelong friends and lifelong memories, we all picked up lifelong

A moustachioed David Boatman with Ziegele House in 1989. Graham Wigley and Howard Robinson are seated to his left. Both Dominic Vipond and his brother, Andrew, also feature.

debts from our years at Fram. For me it was the dream-team of Robbo and Cookie who together conjured up my interest in history, encouraged me to apply to Cambridge and helped me get a job – whilst all the time amusing me, and the rest of the school, with their dripping sarcasm and tickling innuendo (respectively).

'Another debt that we all owe is to the general ethos of the College which made it possible – and socially acceptable – to run through a short corner and attend a chamber choir rehearsal, all in the same afternoon. We had our pick of sport, music, drama and art – opportunities we can only dream of now. Almost like a family, we celebrated each other's successes, be they rifle-shooting or choral singing. For all these reasons, and more besides, every time a Fram memory pops into my head, it brings a smile to my face!'

The more recently departed Emma Vidler (Moreau, 2008–13) adds to this her own memories: 'Framlingham College – *Ave atque vale*. Although it is not quite a dead brother, these words of Catullus seem a fitting tribute to the school that has given me some of the best years of my life. From a scared, nervous Year 9 it has shaped me into a confident medical undergraduate, thanks to the patience, perseverance and dedication of all the staff.

'Defined by the Headmaster as an unpretentious school, there is something for everyone at Framlingham: you only have to look for it. I loved the fact that there was always a new challenge on the horizon whether academically, a sporting fixture, a House competition or a theme-night costume to plan, and I always found that the more you put into the College the more you could get out of it.

'There are many things about Framlingham I will never forget: Mr Betham's chocolate brownies, the "character building" CCF field weekends, DofE expeditions, and the rivalry between Houses (in particular the House Singing competitions, which are widely regarded as the best nights of the year). Also I will always remember the magnificent view of the Castle from the Science block, often a source of inspiration for me in the middle of double Chemistry at the end of a long Friday afternoon.

'However, it would be rather shallow of me to sum up five years of enjoyment in brownies and idyllic views because it is the soul of the place, stemming from its traditions and the opportunities available that give the

school its character. The friendliness of all the people and the huge variety of activities going on give the place a unique buzz and an atmosphere of genuine warmth, which is what makes it such a lovely place to go to school.'

Framlingham may not be entirely about the Magic Roundabout, but Wendy Zebedee certainly sprang up everywhere from 1999 to 2010: 'Will I ever forget my first day at Framlingham College on 9-9-99? After moving house from West Cumbria two days earlier I was immediately plunged into my new job as receptionist while suffering a heavy cold. One day's help from a gap student and I was "flying solo", grappling with foreign surnames on the telephone! It was a hectic time as I covered the switchboard, fax machine, visitors, some administration, including daily registers and the daily tasks of sorting incoming mail and franking outgoing mail, often all at the same time, it seemed; comfort breaks were a rare treat and some staff were less than helpful. But I was so lucky to find employment there at the very time of my move to be near my elderly mother. Her sister told me I must get a job at the College as her husband, James Inskip's relation, Reverend O.D. Inskip, was a former Headmaster. Also two of my Ransome relations were recent pupils. It seemed to be my destiny when, upon enquiry, it turned out that a new receptionist was needed. How happy I was, too, to learn that I could help exercise and look after the current Headmistress's three horses! Wonderful rides out with pupils in term time and long summer rides, sometimes accompanied, in the holidays to keep the horses fit. Then action pictures taken for the new

Master Chef John Betham at work, 2013.

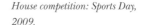

House competition: Sports Day, 2009.

school prospectus but, sadly, by the time it was printed four years after I arrived, the horses had all gone! A few months after I arrived the new swimming pool opened affording us staff free swimming – and then there were all the delicious and varied free meals the College kitchen provided. What a wonderful place of employment, with the most fantastic view. So many visitors arrived in reception quite blown away by that view across the mere to the Castle.

'About two years later it was decided to split the reception and administration duties, so I retreated to the back office as an administrator, dealing with staff and pupils only. I acquired a separate little post room with fax machine, and some time later an excited Clive Norton brought me a second computer that was linked up to mine and a big screen in Paul's Court. We marvelled at the technology that enabled me to type notices in my office and have them appear as if by magic on the Paul's Court screen; then I could jump the arrow back to my original computer to continue with my other work – incredible! It was a bit scary at first knowing everyone in Paul's Court could see my notices appearing even as I typed them!

'In 2005 a pastoral tutor was needed in Victoria House. Out of the four ladies in administration who were asked I was the only one able to take on the extra evening and occasional weekend duties. Having met many of the pupils in my role as administrator I looked forward to seeing what they got up to in a boarding house. It was a real pleasure getting to know the girls, despite the awkwardness of some of them at times. I enjoyed meeting the regular boy visitors, too, and noticing who was with whom! DVD films and pizzas from Zorbas made some weekend duties great fun. I loved the variety of office and pastoral work during this academic year. I remember, too, during these years, the fun I had with the office and teaching staff, including at the Christmas parties.

Wendy Zebedee and girls at Crufts, 2008.

'The following summer a matron for Victoria House was needed at short notice and I was offered the job. I had never considered such a position but was really happy as a pastoral tutor, so I accepted as a last chance to experience a career change before retirement. For my last five years I was a full-time matron, including pastoral tutor duties for the first three of those years. It was lovely to be back in the role of a mother, my own four children having long since flown the nest. But how times had changed since I was a boarder and even since my children were – girls on mobile phones at lights-out times or even watching a film on a laptop computer after lights-out! Perhaps it was increased television and Internet watching that led to their foul language at times – so painful to my ears. Sometimes, too, they had their "favourite" perfume on – cigarette smoke, anathema to my nose. Teenage girls (I had three of my own) can be hard work at times and go through phases of relationship difficulties that can be a challenge to resolve, but each summer brought its sadness, when such lovely young ladies attended the leavers' ball in all their finery and then, often after five years, left my life ... probably forever. There followed in September the challenge of getting to know the new intake and remembering all their names! They soon settled in and joined the excellent House spirit in Victoria. I loved to follow their endeavours and rehearsals for the inter-House competitions.

'On the social side I found the transfer from office staff to domestic staff quite difficult at mealtimes and at the Christmas parties when the separate office and teaching staff party united with those of the domestic, grounds and maintenance staff. My old friends were still there at their customary tables but I now belonged to a different set and I felt as if I was snubbing one group or the other. There was a definite divide between the academic and non-academic staff and straddling the two was difficult and awkward. That apart, my 11 years at the College flew happily by, leaving great memories.'

Claire Barker, mother of three Garrett boys, Patrick (1994–9), Tom (1996–2001) and Ed (2000–5), key figures in the Suffolk Barker mafia, cousins of Brian (1995–2000) and Rosie (Moreau, 1996–8), provides a maternal point of view: 'Write about the College from "a parental perspective", Robbo said. The trouble is, while I am still a parent, I find that perspective has blurred the edges and dulled the pain of those massive cheques (even with scholarships and fraternal discounts); that huge pile of clothes, shoes, sports kit and books assembled every September on the one magical day when everything was clean, named and fitted; the carrier bag of single football boots, crusty sports socks, green whites and assorted tramps' mismatched clothing that returned three months later together with the bill for the following term.

'We visited Fram in 1994 in our search for the right school for our eldest son. With two younger brothers and no sisters, co-education seemed the way forward in a school that mixed academia and sport in a reasonably relaxed manner, with the civilising influence of girls, far enough away for boarding and near enough for coming home for weekends (and also, unfortunately, near enough to rush over with the forgotten gumshield or missing shoe). We liked the Headmaster enormously, felt we were on the same wavelength and signed the boy up almost immediately. The only drawback was no football, but we sorted that out over the next few years. By September the Head was gone, never to be seen again, and the College was in the care of Gwen Randall, the first female Head in the HMC, generating huge amounts of publicity and newspaper articles. "It will be fine," we reassured him, crossing our fingers, and mostly it was, even when she turned up at CCF manoeuvres dressed as a French spy of dubious character, and cricket wasn't as high on her agenda as it should have been.

'We soon discovered that unlike prep school, a parent's most important relationship was with the House Linen Lady first, closely followed by the Housemaster. We were signed up to Garrett House, not just for the next 11 years but for life, really. Today it would be covered by #bleedgreen. We could acknowledge and take pride in the achievements ascribed to the College in general, whether academic, sporting, dramatic or musical, but the House was central and all-encompassing – Stocks Shield, Set Socks, House Singing and even Steeps – for a boy's sense of where his place was – "House, School, Country".

'Preparing for this article all the old term reports were unboxed to re-read and jog the memories of nervous new boys feeling their way, through far-too-relaxed-in-the-face-of-exams, to old-hands-ready-to-leave-for-university-and-the-future. One report said "he has made no secret throughout the year of his lack of interest or ability in art", yet he made a "fried egg hat" that was never forgotten. One was advised to "curb his coruscating wit" by a member of staff who admitted he was the last person qualified to suggest it. One needed "an 8 day week to fit in all his activities and interests – what a good job he has an understanding girlfriend" – no change there then. This was the same son who rang home at the beginning of Year 11 demanding we find him "a new school that wasn't fascist and played football". Over the 45 reports or so the same words recurred – commitment, initiative, reliable, passionate, considerate – words that were echoed in the positions they achieved: two Deputy Heads of school, two Heads of House, School Prefect, House Prefect, two RSMs and a CSM in the CCF, two Gold and one Silver Duke of Edinburgh's Awards as well as sporting achievements for both school and county teams. These reports were more than balanced by the multiple ones that said, "if only he would apply the same intensity to Biology/History/English that he does to sport/Ipswich Town FC/the cast of characters in the Simpsons". We will always have enormous sympathy for the long-suffering staff. Some of them will always remain friends whatever the occasion and wherever we meet; others came and went, leaving no mark. And those interminable Parents' meetings in Paul's Court – inevitably the shortest queue was with the teacher whose report you did not want to hear, clutching a glass of something,

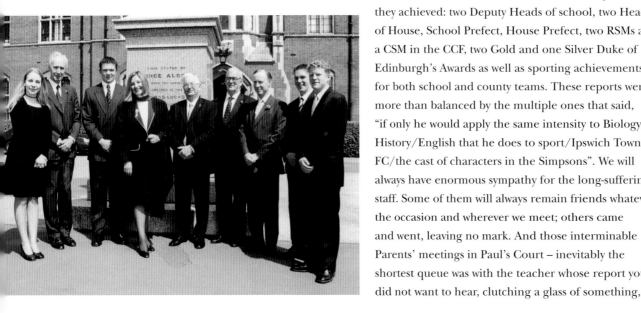

Left: Speech Day, 1999: Mrs Randall with the Chairman of Governors, The Rt. Hon. The Lord Belstead and other dignatories, including Deputy Head of School, Patrick Barker (second from right).

Tom Barker (second from left) on the Peru trip with Mr Myers-Allen in 2003.

Right: Air Vice Marshal Dougherty at the Biennial Inspection, 2010.

knowing those behind you could hear all about your child's shortcomings. Trying to make small talk with other nervous parents one year involved several of us comparing notes on the A Level Business Studies projects we had all completed over the holidays, and on one infamous occasion being persuaded by one son to casually cover our name badges to prove that the sweating, floundering teacher had no idea who he was, and he was right.

'We probably spent more time on touchlines and boundaries than anywhere else in the College, as well as following teams to away matches – rugby at RHS on a winter's afternoon with the fog rolling up the river, hockey at Felsted on their state-of-the-art new astroturf, which froze, and cricket at Ipswich, where I sat with a mother all afternoon until tea when she discovered she was watching the wrong team and someone else's child! The lack of football was remedied by reintroducing House matches, persuading amenable members of staff to referee and presenting a cup for the winners. When this still proved not to be enough, permission was given for training with, and playing for, Framlingham Town FC, which continued for many years and for which we were very grateful.

'We attended plays, House Dinners, Carol Services, Remembrance Day and CCF parades, Sports Days, Fund-raisers and Prize-givings, but mostly passed on the concerts. Then there were the expeditions and

trips – DofE, CCF, United Nations, World Challenge to Annapurna (where multiple bugs came home and left a lasting impression), Venezuela, Peru and Everest – just assembling the kit and rat packs was worthy of an award.

'While we lived every high and suffered through every low – and believe me there were some – hindsight has smoothed the view and fitted the College into the framework of our family life. For our sons it was followed by universities and jobs. Their time at Fram made them "fit for purpose", gave them the solid foundations to build their chosen careers, space to grow, lasting friendships and the support and encouragement to look forward and move upward and to seize their opportunities.'

Air Vice Marshal Simon Dougherty (Garrett, 1962–7), President of the Society of Old Framlinghamians from 2011 and father of James (Garrett, 1988–93), Philip (Garrett, 1990–5) and Clare (Victoria, 1993–8), writes: 'The Society of Old Framlinghamians was founded in 1900 with the purpose of furthering the interests of Framlingham College, of enabling former students to maintain contact with the school and with each other and encouraging links between Old Framlinghamians. The Centenary of the Society was celebrated in due style in 2000. The Society has some 3,500 members of all ages representing a wide range of occupations and professions. Since the College became

co-educational in the 1980s, lady OFs have joined the Society's ranks and play a full part in its activities.

'The Society continues to fulfil its objectives in three ways: firstly, by using money raised through appeals, by way of gift or bequest, or from subscription and investment incomes, the Society helps to ensure that Framlingham College remains a leading British independent school. As a result, each generation benefits from its predecessors, and members ensure that investments are made for future generations. One of the major gifts from the Society was the purchase of Brandeston Hall in 1948 as a living memorial to Old Framlinghamians and former members of staff who made the ultimate sacrifice in the two world wars, and the practice of providing funds for purchase of land adjacent to the College and for various sporting, pastoral and domestic facilities continues. From its earliest inception donations have been used to help with on-going improvements to the College buildings and the provision of sports facilities, and the Society has donated a substantial sum to the 150th Anniversary Appeal. In addition, the Society has endowed a large number of prizes and scholarships for students. A widely applauded innovation was the introduction of Moreau Leaving Scholarships in 2006; annually two scholarships worth £800 per annum for three years are awarded to Year 13 leavers, who in return actively support the Society. This has greatly strengthened the younger element as one of their cohort is responsible for organising at least one "Leaving-Group" event per year.

'Secondly, the Society continues to assist former pupils to maintain contact with the School and each other in a number of ways, including the extensive use of electronic and social media. The Society maintains a comprehensive website, including an electronic directory with contact details of members. News of members and events are published frequently and a huge repository of information about Old Framlinghamians together with access to Society publications and information is provided. The Society of Old Framlinghamians has a Facebook presence and a large LinkedIn group. The last 50 years have seen a massive leap forward, as the Society has maximised its use of modern communications systems.

'By way of printed media, the Society publishes a large section within the annual *Framlingham College Yearbook*, a publication which in itself demonstrates the close "family bonds" between Brandeston Hall, the College and the Society. Here details of all OF activities at home and abroad are recorded, together with up-to-date "intelligence" about members of all generations from all over the world. The Society also publishes a mid-year Newsletter and has been responsible in recent times for the publication of five books: Bob Gillett's *The Second Sixty Years* and *Remembered Days*, Norman Porter's *History of Brandeston Hall*, Richard Sayer's *Master Sportsman* (about Norman Borrett), and John Maulden's *Into the New Millennium*.

'Thirdly, on a more social level, an Annual Dinner is held, alternating yearly between Framlingham College and London. Other regular informal suppers are held in London, Essex, Norfolk,

Below left: The principal founder of the Society in 1900 was Alfred 'Pretty Peerless Prince of Publicity' – (OF, 1870–7) and formidable Second Master (1891–1903).

Below: Bob Gillet, lover of literature, impresario and gentleman schoolmaster.

Steve Wright with Garrett House in 1992, including James and Philip Dougherty, and Mrs Daphne Hall.

Suffolk, Newmarket, the West of England and in the South East, and overseas in Melbourne and Hong Kong. Other gatherings of Old Framlinghamians not organised by the Society frequently occur, often in Suffolk or London. Golf and Shooting Clubs are well supported and teams are entered for a variety of Public Schools Old Boys' and Girls' competitions. In addition there is an Old Framlinghamian Masonic Lodge for members who are, or who wish to become, Freemasons; in 2008 the Lodge celebrated its 60th anniversary and it continues to be incredibly generous to the College. The Society continues to encourage contact between members and the College by supporting Old Framlinghamian teams fielded against the College in cricket, hockey, soccer, netball and golf, and OFs are always welcome at the College. The Constitution of the College requires that seven members of the Board of Governors are Old Framlinghamians and the President of the Society is invited to attend Governors' meetings, a way of enabling OF Governors to contribute directly to the development of the College.

'Over the 114 years of its history, the Society of Old Framlinghamians has evolved with the times, but it continues to pursue its objectives of furthering the interests of Framlingham College, enabling former students to maintain contact with the school and with each other, and encouraging links between Old Framlinghamians. The commitment of Old Framlinghamians to the College and to one another is a source of great pride, and bears comparison with that of any other of our major schools.'

The Governing Body also plays a major role in the life of the College. One of its leading figures over the past 20 years has been Major General J.B. Dye CBE MC DL. He had three grandchildren at the College, Christopher (Rendlesham, 1977–82) and Alastair Pattinson (1980–5), and Guy Morrall (Rendlesham, 1988–90). After his death in 2013 at the age of 93 a well-attended memorial service showed the high esteem and affection in which he was held by many friends from many walks of life. Here is his story in his own words: 'I retired from the army in 1974 and on my return to Suffolk I was cajoled into joining the College Governing Body by General Sir Pat Howard-Dobson – we were already old friends from army days and I was godfather to his son, Simon (OF).

'I was duly elected in 1975 and following the sad death of Ventura Bromage the next year, I became Chairman of the Executive Committee (now the Finances and General Purposes Committee) – it was not a sought-after post and I was elected unanimously! So began 20 years of close involvement with the College until, after some 140 meetings, I handed over to my successor in 1996.

'I realised straight away that to be effective in the appointment it would be essential to have a good working relationship with the Headmaster, Mr Rimmer, who had held the appointment then for five years. Mr Rimmer, of international rugby fame, was king of all he surveyed. The Governing Body were necessary by statute and just tolerated by the Headmaster, but I quickly became aware that in his opinion this new general had little or no part to play in the governance of his College. The army is not without similar problems when taking up a new position. Laurie Rimmer and I took time to get to know each other, sometimes bruising, but it worked and we became close friends. I retain a great admiration for this fine Headmaster and I am still proud of being asked to give the valedictory address at Mr Rimmer's retirement on Speech Day in 1989. I realise now that this period was a learning curve for me, and I was well schooled by the time the new Heads arrived, Mr Miller and then Mrs Randall. With them, I think I probably started at thirty–love.

'Much of significance to the College occurred during Laurie Rimmer's time, in which I was involved. The first was his strong conviction, strongly supported by the Governors, that the College should become an independent school, with all the financial implications of this. The second was the question of co-education. The Headmaster was certain it was the way forward but I told him that many Governors would need to be persuaded. The Headmaster cleverly arranged for all Governors, in pairs, to visit schools which had become co-educational, and also to two girls' schools which had remained single-sex. From our visits we learned what problems there might be in moving to co-education and also what changes would have to be made if girls were admitted. After much discussion the decision was taken to go ahead. It is difficult to imagine now how the College would have fared had it remained with boys only.

'Much of the work of the "F&GPC" is taken up with preserving and improving the fabric of the College, everything from roofs and chimneys to drains. Accommodation for all our pupils has had to be constantly updated and money has also been found for new buildings, most spectacularly in the form of Paul's Court. The transformation of the old Tuck Box Courtyard was strongly supported by the Governors, with £600,000 allocated to the project and, such was the enthusiasm, it was completed in six months. It gave us all great pleasure when Mrs Jean Paul, the widow of Mr Roger Paul, the late Chairman of Governors, opened Paul's Court on 19 November 1993 and named it after her husband.

'The work of the Governing Body is of course to support the Heads of our two schools in every way possible. We have always to remember that it is they who are in the public eye. So much of the success of the College depends on how they are perceived by local schools and the wider world. In this regard, Framlingham has been fortunate in the past and certainly is so now with Mr Paul Taylor and Mr Martin Myers-Allen in charge.

'Theirs is a huge responsibility. As a whole, Framlingham College is an important enterprise in East Suffolk, with an annual turnover of £11 million and with 250 academic and support staff. For them, and for present and future parents and pupils, so much depends on the future success of both schools.

'About this I am entirely confident. It has been a privilege to serve on such a dedicated Governing Body

from whom my confidence stems. I am so glad that my old friend Pat Howard-Dobson called that day, even though his thoughts on my possible involvement were a little wide of the mark.'

Irving Newton was Second Master for many years at Taverham Hall preparatory school in Norfolk, where he continues to teach History and coach cricket. He has directed many pupils towards the College, including his own children, Leanne (Moreau, 2001–6) and Robert (Rendlesham, 2003–8). He writes: 'We faced a dilemma at the end of our daughter's happy time at Taverham Hall because we simply had no idea where she would go to senior school. None of our local day schools appealed so Leanne decided she wanted to board. Nothing wrong

General Dye unveiling the memorial plaque to Laurie Rimmer in 2013.

Lord Tollemache lowers the drawbridge for College Sixth Form Historians in 2008.

with that, but no one in either of our families had ever made that step! Luckily we visited the College and Leanne, having come under the spell of the charismatic Mrs Randall, was soon Framlingham bound.

'We remember seeing Leanne for the first time after starting at the College playing hockey at Wisbech on a cold September afternoon and although unspoken, we had some anxiety about how she was coping. We didn't need to ask because it was obvious from the laughter and banter on the pitch that she had settled in and made new friends. Two years later there was never any doubt that her brother, Robert, would join her, and he was soon flourishing in Rendlesham under the necessary(!) watchful guidance of an impressively patient and calm Antony Bennett.

'It was the sense of community at the College that made us feel we had made the right decision in choosing Framlingham. We were always heartened by the way the pupils enjoyed, supported and shared the successes of others, and also that they were there for each other when things were not going so well. On many occasions we were encouraged by our two to come to the College to watch a play or musical event in which neither was involved but so-and-so was "amazing" in. That pride and joy in what their peers were doing speaks volumes for the spirit of the place and of course it also gave us a chance to see them and share their experiences.

'Somewhere amongst all this, learning has to take place, but you never felt it was all-important or all-consuming. There was always time for other pursuits that would challenge, increase confidence or simply enrich lives. As a result both our two owe Framlingham a great deal. It gave them the skills, the purpose and the belief to strike out into the wider world and be able to assimilate easily into their new environments. Both have returned to Framlingham to seek out old friends and remind staff that they are getting older! Leanne gave a talk on Mary Tudor to the History Society and Rob remains convinced,

albeit tongue-in-cheek, that Messrs Robinson and Marvell will ensure that any new pavilion will bear his name!

'From the point of view of a prep school master, the thing that strikes you first about the College is the sheer beauty of the place. It stands above the pretty market town of Framlingham, with a tranquil mere below it and the commanding presence of the Castle in full view to the east of the River Ore. This superb location is matched by the immaculate presentation of the grounds. In all my 30 years of visiting other schools I have never once come across another institution that is so beautifully presented. Mike Rutterford and his team deserve all the plaudits for their outstanding efforts.

'I have visited the College many times over the years, for tournaments, matches, educational visits and meetings, and on every occasion I and my colleagues have been made most welcome and have come away with a feeling that it is a special place, and I sense that is something the staff at the College appreciate too.

'My favourite place in the College is Paul's Court, an informal meeting place right at the heart of the school where pupils and staff mingle and pass throughout the day. It is amazing how often a quick chat, a cuppa and a piece of cake stretches long into the afternoon in such a convivial place. It is fortunate for me that I can always look forward to a next time, as I return home to North Norfolk.'

12

GRAND DESIGNS

'For each age is a dream that is dying,
Or one that is coming to birth.'

– Arthur O'Shaughnessy

BUILDING FOR THE FUTURE

When the original Crystal Palace burnt down in 1936, Winston Churchill declared, 'this is the end of an age'. However, in 2014 it appears that Chinese billionaire Ni Zhaoxing of the Zhong Rong Group has, with Mayor Boris Johnson's blessing, outlined plans to re-create the Palace on Hyde Park as a £500 million cultural attraction. The new glass house would be 500 metres long and 50 metres high – what would Larkin say? Protesters complain about the loss of beautiful park land and some Londoners may see it as a giant Chinese takeaway, but it is good to know that the spirit of Prince Albert lives. Closer to home we have more practical proposals and the glass extension to the area at the back of Paul's Court will be an exciting addition to celebrate the College's 150th anniversary.

Paul Taylor, current Headmaster, writes on the sesquicentennial building project and its implications: 'The major building project that marks our 150th Anniversary Year is, in part, a reflection and recognition of the changing way in which today's students work, and of the adult world they will be joining. This new building is a two-floor, glass-fronted extension to the back of Paul's Court onto the Piazza. There are four new classrooms – two on each floor. The ground floor

also holds a whole school café and social hub. The first floor sees a new Sixth Form Resource Centre with enhanced Careers and Further Education resources, and a variety of spacious areas for Sixth Form study – with much pupil input into how these are best configured. These developments have enabled us to review and, hopefully, revitalise the use of the Library at the heart of the College. Rather than being essentially a Sixth Form work area, we now hope to make the Library even more central and proactive in the teaching and learning culture here. Valuable space has also been

Computer-generated image of the proposed re-creation of the Crystal Palace.

'A miracle of rare device'. An architect's vision of the rear of the College, 2014.

freed up on the top floor to enhance boarding and day accommodation in Rendlesham and Stradbroke – another major evolution of the original building!

'Allied to this exciting physical development of the site, we are also developing associated aspects of the educational culture of the school. While it is critical that Framlingham remains a school rooted in its local community, it is equally important that it is not parochial. One of the driving forces behind the vision of the new Sixth Form Resource Centre is the desire to prepare students for that fast-changing world of work with an outward-looking perspective, and to this end we are encouraging a culture of enterprise and initiative. They will need strong personal qualities, independence of thought, self-confidence and adaptability, and it is important that we do all we can to ensure that they leave the College excited rather than daunted at the prospect of engaging with the world beyond school.'

QUIS CUSTODIET?

So, even in England, buildings change, as do their uses and the nature of their occupants. A hundred years ago many preparatory schools looked solid enough, and the rectories of Suffolk villages, and on a winter evening one can wonder what will survive. Framlingham College's mock-Gothic building looks so sturdy that it is hard to think of it being toppled and even harder to think it might be returned to being a deer park. In

2014 the little town of Framlingham is threatened with being swamped by a plague of suburban villas eating up the fields which surround it and in the 21st century the College's setting must surely change, though one suspects that what will last longest are the meadows that slope down from Castle and College to the mere. One would have to be a hard-nosed Vandal to destroy that.

Above left: *Paul's Court extension: an interior perspective.*

Below: *Framlingham Castle: 'by far the most magnificent in this county'.*

Julian Tennyson (great-great-grandson of Lord Alfred) puts it best, because most simply, in *Suffolk Scene*, published in 1939 when he was only 26, in the year he would join up for the war that would later kill him. The book ranges all over pre-war Suffolk, but Tennyson writes that 'the Alde is my favourite river' (geographers might like to put an Ore in here) and Framlingham is 'the finest town in east Suffolk' for two reasons: 'firstly, it lies in a strip of country which has all the qualities that are the essence of Suffolk; secondly, it has a castle … by far the most magnificent in this county, but also, as a ruin, nearly the best in all England; if only the hill on which it stands were just a shade higher, then there would be no question about its supremacy'. There stands Framlingham College, 'on an eminence' by Suffolk standards, and there must have been many at times who wished that eminence had been higher. Speakers may wax fulsome on Speech Days and more recently colleagues may play with league tables, academic and otherwise, but Framlingham cannot match the lists of Prime Ministers or Nobel Prize Winners that the best medieval public schools may boast; it cannot rival the sheer quantity of academic brilliance streaming out from the top selective schools; it does not have the cachet nor the snob value attached to Eton or Harrow: and yet the place is chosen and rarely regretted.

Above: A drawing of the multi-functional sports pavillion planned in 1945 and yet to be built.

Below right: David Foreman, College Steward for nearly 50 years, at the Crown Hotel (by W.O. Hutchison).

All are touched by their surroundings. On a clear night you see the moon rising over the Castle, on a misty morning the towers will rise out of the gloom, in sunshine the ripples on the mere welcome you back, laughing like the Lydian waves of Lake Garda that welcomed Catullus home after his long stint in Bithynia. And the bricks and sandstone of the mock-Gothic façade have weathered to become part of the landscape, surely immovable. Custodians of the building come and go, but the turnover is usually slow. Long service can be discovered in almost all departments, a tradition going back to the stewardship of David Foreman and Artie Hall. In the Catering department Bill Nekrews and Nick Gardens did long stints, and after more than a quarter of a century Barry Roberts and Janice Moore are still at work there; Zillah Godfrey, Pauline Everett and Diane Etheridge have been Matrons *par excellence* in Rendlesham, Garrett and Victoria respectively; in Maintenance there have been characters such as Tommy Moyse, Roger Montague, Mick Hart and Dick Jaggard, as well as master-carpenter Keith Bridges, whose oak panelling remains such a prominent feature of the main corridor. In the Cleaning department Mark Rogers marshals his troops with quiet efficiency and good-humour, and in the best tradition of Joyce Burch and Val Leek, they perform miracles to keep the place in pristine condition. Whether clearing up after water from the school baths cascaded through the ceiling of Marian Prebble's office, mopping up the floods that periodically flowed through the Head's House following torrential summer thunderstorms (what a pity that Pryor House had been built over the confluence of a quite brilliant Victorian sewerage system and suffered whenever the single College outlet to the town became overloaded!), or organising temporary sleeping arrangements in the classrooms in the summer holidays to accommodate the thousand members of the YMCA who converged here to celebrate their centenary, these custodians preserve the fabric and good working order of the place with a minimum of fuss. Out of doors the whole campus has been wonderfully tended by generations of long-serving ground staff: in Colin Rutterford's time one remembers Don on his heavy roller and Dennis collecting the flags at close of play, and since then Barry Meadows has preserved the 1st XI square with meticulous care. Fred Cable's immaculately clipped hedges, neatly pollarded trees and the smell of new-mown grass are all part of the ambience of Framlingham.

Long before boys and masters crawl into breakfast, in the cold darkness before the dawn, these men and women are unbolting the great door, and the little army of cleaners and caterers, groundsmen and artisans, set to work to ensure that all is right for the ladies and gentlemen. And remember, there is nothing demeaning about this service: the service is genuine, but these men and women will let you know if something is wrong, and the incomer quickly learns to treat them right. They know the building, what is kept in the lofty towers and the deep Victorian sewers where few venture; as the Psalmist might put it, they know the heights and the depths; the great chimney is theirs, and the absurdly ornamental gables, the mysterious hump outside Victoria House where the artesian well bubbles up; they know the bronzes of the Chapel and every panel of the corridor. From before dawn until after nightfall it is their building: there may be a few security lights and even the odd intrusive camera, but now it is Peter Hein or Roly Scarce you'll meet at night with a torch just checking, and on festive nights that checking will go on into the early hours. There may be revelry, but the flower beds and the sacred turf have their faithful guardians.

Here then is a facility waiting to be used. During the day the support staff multiply, and the Bursar, Nick Chaplin, and Operations Manager, Andrew Payn, will quietly oversee the smooth running of the place. The frail can pop down to the Medical Centre, once the

Sanatorium with its Aeger List, though Sisters such as Linda Allen and Heather Ling were good at seeing through those trying to skive Steeps. Heads could not have functioned without their secretaries – Marian Prebble served four Heads over 31 years, while Ann Cox multi-tasked for Mrs Randall in much the same way as Helen Alcoe cheerfully looks after Mr Taylor. Accountancy was not boring for Helga Andrew, and June Drinkwater and Keith Bridges maintain the feisty tradition there, computer teams handle the ever-developing technology, while the science labs and TAC have their own support staff too. Pastoral care is much talked of in boarding schools now, but at Framlingham the lines are brilliantly blurred, and students can be close to their cleaners and matrons, just as in yesteryear

The chimney still stands, though the Piazza has now been largely subsumed by the new Sixth Form Resource Centre.

Roberta Organ (Head Girl) and Toby Hough (Head of School) with flowers at the Front, 2004.

university men could befriend their bedders and scouts. Perhaps students have too much done for them, but they do have a secure framework to support their working days.

The content of these days is forever subtly changing, but the pattern of breakfast, roll-call, chapel and lessons is still the way most mornings go. Students trudge round with books and laptops, some lessons are better than others, there is a break to socialise, and the essential mobile phone is ever close to hand, while staff retreat to Common Room for an earnest conversation about the sweep of Becket's quiff, the shortness of Samantha's skirt or a manly chat about the rugger. In the afternoon many will get outdoors for active pursuits, and from 5pm onwards some will wend their way home by minibus or parental car, while others settle to prep and the rich and varied menu the evening now offers. It is a simple, stable pattern and it suits most.

Above: Lord Becket's quiff, 2011.

Right: Naomi Rice, with Sophie Springorum and Greg White, 2000.

It suits many teaching staff too, if longevity is anything to go by. Since the 1970s many have served for 20 years and more – the authors included! Fresh-faced youngsters like Tony Lawrence and Martin Myers-Allen have turned into *éminences grises*; after their housemasterships, Smallcombe and Liddell hunted as a pair in the SMT; David Barker and David Boatman have done decades in the Geography department; Ian Baird and Brother Morgan defended Common Room rights for many moons, and Bob Skitch, father of five Framlinghamians, may no longer run the 3rd XV, but continues to oversee university entrance. Other younger fly-by-nights have also made an impact: Ben Edwards and Ricki Smith enlivened the English department and much more; Naomi Rice, Rachel Fowkes and Geraldine Kadera made a glamorous and dynamic trio; Masahiro Kanji and Angélique Horner made friendships throughout the school; young-at-heart men with a Kerrison attachment have been David Ross, Mark Kendall and Charlie Caiger – but each generation will have its own favourites.

True to form, Marcus Booth (Ziegele, 1990–5) offered a late puff of 'wind and guff' to share his predilections: 'Sometime in the balmy summer of 1995, Messrs Booth and Ricki Smith went into verbal battle with Mr Cooke and Emma Davies, in my final debate at the College. It was entitled the "Booth Memorial Debate": I wasn't dead but the debate was a memorial to many an evening debating a wide range of motions with my fellow students under the distinguished chairmanship of Michael Cooke. (Another seasoned debater was Fiona Lochead.) The motion was "This House would rather be English than British". Over ten years ahead of the Scottish referendum on independence, the assembled Framlinghamians plumped fully and squarely for the Union, notwithstanding the strength of arguments on the other side.

'The debating society was just one organisation that I enjoyed taking part in. Whereas historically Heads of School might have been expected to display a certain prowess on the games field, my participation in school sports reached its zenith in the 3rd XV rugby (where I remain certain that Bob Skitch selected me out of charity). However, Matthew Earley and I were founding members of the "Touchline Society". This was not an extended off-games facility; rather it was the preserve of those that made it out week after week to the games field, only to find that they were relegated yet again to numbers 16 and 17 in the pecking order for the rugby side and instead took their place at the side of the pitch on a weekly basis. The Touchline Society was really an in-joke, but one that received the veneer of official approval when the founders mischievously placed a notice into the Headmaster's hands to announce its launch one Assembly.

'My point is serious: a few paragraphs cannot do justice to the rich education that Framlingham offered, a true renaissance experience (and my year group were strong on this). I was a Ziegele boy, but this didn't stop me playing a full part in school life. Clare Montgomery and I were joint Heads of School. I enjoyed Lt Col Kennon's CCF, Tony Lawrence's Drama, Ziegele's House plays and House Singing, "Alleluia!", Mr Suter's general knowledge competitions, cookery (where Crispin Hardy and I were banned for doubling the ingredients), History Society and Latin, and chapel, where Mr Booker kept the Christian flame burning.

'Last but not least, Framlingham allowed each to flourish in accordance with his or her own talents. I cannot fault the academic foundations it gave me in preparing me for a medieval history degree at St Andrew's and for a peripatetic life in politics. I now

The College Clock in the Clock Tower featured at the Great Exhibition of 1851, where it won a gold medal for its makers, Cook and Son of York. Graffiti courtesy of Booth's buddies, wayward Heads of Garrett, Rendlesham, Stradbroke and Ziegele.

sit on the Disciplinary Committee of the Conservative Party and the National Executive of the Society of Conservative Lawyers. I have stood for Parliament. Much of my interest was kindled at school, where I won my first election, being elected onto the School Council in the Fifth Form!'

Leavers gather at Albert in 2011.

'LET THY FATHER-HAND BE SHIELDING
ALL WHO HERE SHALL MEET NO MORE ...'
Labuntur anni, and after one year, two years, five years, or for some Brandestonians up to 15 or 16 years, it is time to leave. The poetry of departures and the end-of-term rituals also move with the times. A colleague at a rival establishment asked a few years back how Framlingham managed these so well, though there have been hiccups here too. There were occasions when the Senior Management and support staff braced themselves for all-nighters and Thorpie's bacon butties were vital sustenance for masters and students alike at 4am. The campus might be re-arranged by those whose Bacchic revels led to errors of judgement, especially sensitive when prize-giving was cruelly the morning after. The recent solution of letting those returning go home before the revelries seems to work much better, and the Upper Sixth's last day is generally a good time for all: parents, staff and the cohort themselves. The evening sun slants across the Castle as drinks are served on the Front, the girls put on their best frocks and formerly louche boys smarten up in dinner jackets. Photo-opportunities abound and there is time to linger before moving through the College to one of Mr Betham's last suppers in the marquee on the Back. There are no speeches, just a good social occasion, the Sixth Form Society's last outing. Once darkness has fallen, fireworks over the Castle are an obligatory interlude, and then the young can dance the night away until their carriages arrive to turn them truly into Old Framlinghamians. Most are eager and ready to leave,

but who on such an occasion does not cast one long and lingering look behind? Edward Fitzgerald lived just down the road at Boulge Hall, and his Victorian recreation of the 12th-century *Rubáiyát of Omar Khayyám* could have been written for such an occasion:

> Ah, Moon of my Delight who know'st no wane,
> The Moon of Heav'n is rising once again:
> How oft hereafter rising shall she look
> Through this same Garden after me – in vain!

BACK TO THE FUTURE

Paul Taylor's arrival from King's Canterbury in 2009 most certainly marked the beginning of a new age, and if there wasn't quite a 'revolution in government', there was most certainly major 'readjustment'. Management structures were formalised, policies consistently applied and the College sailed through an ISI inspection ('excellent') in 2010 and an Ofsted inspection ('outstanding') in 2011. Paul talked about 'reinvigoration of the heart of the College', but the whole institution has received a shot in the arm. Modern communications make it possible for parents, OFs and the wider community to know more about us and to be on campus more often – and Paul's wife, Amanda, plays a major supporting role here. The Headmaster is a great attender, but in the Stocks tradition and with a background in county cricket, he loves nothing better than to take a net on the Back. He knows who's who and how they are doing, something appreciated by pupils, parents and staff alike.

Below right: Surrey CC XI, 1983, with Roger Knight as Captain, but it was Paul Taylor (standing extreme right) who became Headmaster of Framlingham College!

Below: Full moon over Framlingham.

Headmaster Paul Taylor, 2013.

Head of School, Andrzej Stuart-Thompson looks to the future, Speech Day, 2010.

Headmaster Paul Taylor writes: 'It was clear to me when I joined the College that this was a school with a very strong soul, one that had proved its ability to adapt and evolve over time, while retaining the core values of its founding fathers. Framlingham has always been about educating the whole person and the strong culture of pastoral care and the rich co-curricular experience that pupils enjoy remains central to this. Each pupil is individually nurtured and valued for who they are and for what they contribute to the wider school community. Part of this contribution and experience has to be academic, as it was in late Victorian times, but the only true academic measure is achievement relative to each individual child's ability – and on that measure this college can stand shoulder to shoulder with any school in the country. However, alongside the academic attainments of Framlingham pupils, what will really enable most to get on in life will be personal qualities: warmth and courtesy; a positive outlook and willingness to work in a team; honesty and integrity; taking the trouble to present oneself well and to communicate effectively – a sense of humour and a ready smile. These are qualities that have always been associated with Framlinghamians. I hope they will continue to be so and we should never be reticent about promoting them. Moreover, in these uncertain times one needs to look to eternal truths and values: the concept of service; a love of learning; a spiritual awareness based on knowledge, respect and emotional maturity.

'What will the world be like for these ex-alumni? There is an increasing range of options for A Level students, and many may not now go on to university as a matter of course – the Student Loan is no doubt a factor in this. Employers now offer the bright school leaver a genuine and debt-free alternative to university, hoping to attract some of the best students into a combined programme of study and work experience. Some leading companies have even established direct links with specific universities to offer the best of both worlds, offering to pay university tuition fees as part of the package. So what does all this mean for schools? At Framlingham, while we still expect the majority of our students to opt for a university education, we are also keen that this is a properly informed decision and that our pupils are aware that there are valid alternative options. The university world itself is fast-changing. There are now increasingly attractive alternatives in Europe, the US, the Far East and elsewhere, all offering courses taught in English. Our university and careers advice has to become much more sophisticated and we are already responding to this demand. Careers and Further Education already have their own specialist staff, working closer together under the leadership of the Director of Sixth Form, to ensure that our students can make properly informed decisions about their futures.

'So, whither Framlingham? Writing about the future of a school runs the risk of giving a hostage to fortune. These pages are a reminder that a Head is but

a temporary custodian, and is well advised to take into account a school's provenance as a significant factor in formulating any plans for the future. When the next history of the College is written – perhaps at its bi-centenary – I hope it will be reporting on the leading school in East Anglia, known for producing balanced, purposeful and decent young men and women who are well qualified and well prepared for the world that awaits them. There will be another Head sitting at this desk reflecting on all that the College is, and all that it could be, and they will be very lucky. That breath-taking view across the Front to the Castle, mere and church will still be elevating soul and spirit, and the pupils will still inspire through their youthful exuberance and

optimistic outlook on life. Any OF visiting the school will probably be surprised at one or two dramatic physical developments, and will share comments such as, "I wish we had had that in my day", and, "this lot don't know they're born!" However, I also hope that it will be a school that they will still recognise by the "feel" of the place, by its core values and philosophy, by its culture of friendliness and decency, and by its emphasis on the pastoral care that is at the heart of any good school. Those values will have been reassessed and reinterpreted for the challenges of the time, but they will still resonate with those of the founding fathers who so wanted to honour the educational vision of the late Prince Consort.'

AFTERWORD

'The future is dark, the present burdensome: only the past, dead and finished, bears contemplation' – if Professor Sir Geoffrey Elton could not tell the future, his mere epigones should be hesitant to pronounce even on an institution they know so well. In 1964 no one would have foreseen the ladies coming to Framlingham; in 1984 even the most Orwellian would not have envisaged the spread of the computer virus; one wonders how those charged with 'blue-sky' thinking even in the now smoke-free Governors' meetings can see 'the way ahead', Laurie Rimmer's logo for 'the 125th anniversary appeal. Yet the acts of faith of recent years have generally paid off, mainly because they have been enablers and enhancers of continuity. Macaulay pleaded with the House of Lords in 1832 to 'reform, that you may preserve', and the natural conservatism of those who settle in Suffolk has always been so tempered.

The College will continue to evolve, then, and will survive if it sticks to what it does well. Other public schools may claim to be 'the best school of all', and many alternative forms of education will continue to be offered over the coming century. However, one suspects that the personal elements in teaching will remain a great strength here however technology develops, and the setting will continue to draw people. Students will re-discover in each generation the truth set out by Plato and Quintilian, that pleasure should lead them on into further education, and the relationship between tutor and pupil will be at the heart of this. Framlingham can do this as well as anyone, and for a greater range of pupils than many of her rivals. We rejoice in being open and unpretentious – the 19th-century School Song may be open to ridicule in its search for rhymes with Framlingham, but the phrase 'scorning sham' sums up one important element of the school's ethos. The earnest Victorian motto, *Studio sapientia crescit*, encapsulates another. And perhaps for another hundred years, 'the children not yet borne with gladness shall' remember Sir Robert Hitcham and his legacy, Albert and his memorials, and the traditions that placed the College on the eminence on which it still stands.

SELECT BIBLIOGRAPHY

Colin Bateman, *If the Cap Fits*; London, 1993.

John Booth, *Framlingham College. The First Sixty Years*; Ipswich, 1925.

J. D'E. Firth, *Rendall of Winchester*; London, 1954.

Louisa Garrett Anderson, *Elizabeth Garrett Anderson, 1836–1917*; London, 1939.

Leslie Gillett, Framlingham College. The Second Sixty Years, 1992.

Leslie Gillett, *Remembered Days*; Ipswich, 2000.

Jenifer Glynn, *The Pioneering Garretts*; London, 2008.

Christopher Grogan, ed., *Imogen Holst: A Life in Music*; Woodbridge, 2007.

Alexander Hamilton, *Wings of Night: Secret Missions of Group Captain Pickard, DSO and Two Bars, DFC*; London, 1977.

Simon Heffer, *High Minds: The Victorians and the Birth of Modern Britain*; London, 2013.

Jo Manton, *Elizabeth Garrett Anderson*; London, 1965.

Theodore Martin, *The life of His Royal Highness, the Prince Consort*; London, 1879.

John Maulden, *Into the Third Millennium*, 2012.

Sir Alfred Munnings, *An Artist's Life*; London, 1950.

Norman Porter, *A History of Brandeston Hall*; Woodbridge, 2009.

Robert Rhodes James, *Albert Prince Consort*; London, 1983.

Richard Sayer, *Master Sportsman: the story of Norman Borrett*; Suffolk, 2011.

Brian Simon & Ian Bradley, edd., *The Victorian Public School*; Dublin, 1975.

Jules Stewart, *Albert*; London, 2012.

Julian Tennyson, *Suffolk Scene*; Bury St Edmunds, 1939.

Stanley Weintraub, *Uncrowned King: the life of Prince Albert*; New York, 1997.

R.A. Whitehead, *Garrett 200: A Bicentenary History of Garretts of Leiston, 1778–1978*; London, 1978.

A.N. Wilson, *The Victorians*; London, 2007.

Other Sources

College archival materials, including Framlinghamian and Old Framlinghamian magazines, newsletters, prospectuses, appeal brochures, 1864–2014 and Tony Martin's special cache from the bottom of the Otis lift shaft.

John McEwan, ed., *Lambert's Framlingham* (1871–1916); 2000.

E.W. Swanton, 'Great Schools in Sport' in *The Illustrated Sporting and Dramatic News*, November 29th, 1935.

H.J. Smith, 'Collection of Colour Slides of Framlingham, 1959 to 1981'.

Brian Aldiss, 'An introduction to subversion' in the *Sunday Times*, 2nd September, 1990.

David Pitcher, 'All Change for Framlingham'; Bishop's Stortford, 2002.

Society of Old Framlinghamians, 'Their swords are in your keeping', 2005.

Opposite: *College Cadets, 1909 (top image in front of Chapel); Kneese greets the Sawbwa of Mong Mit, 1929 (bottom left); Hague in the classroom, 1950s (bottom right).*

LIST OF HEADMASTERS

HEADS OF FRAMLINGHAM COLLEGE

Rev. A.C. Daymond	1864–1871
Rev. W.W. Bird	1872–1881
Rev. A.H. Scott-White	1881–1886
Rev. Dr. O.D. Inskip	1887–1913
F.W. Stocks	1913–1929
W.H.A. Whitworth	1929–1941
R.W. Kirkman	1941–1955
W.S. Porter	1955–1971
L.I. Rimmer	1971–1989
J.F.X. Miller	1989–1994
Mrs G.M. Randall	1994–2009
P.B. Taylor	2009–

HEADMASTERS OF BRANDESTON HALL

D.D. Kittermaster	1948–1968
R.P. Broad	1968–1974
R.W. Jones	1974–1980
G.P. Newbery	1980–1985
N. Johnson	1985–2000
S. Player	2000–2004
J. Kelsall	2004–2005
N. Woolnough	2005–2007
M. Myers-Allen	2007–

Images of College life, 2013–14.

Opposite, bottom right: *Boys' Under 14 National Hockey Champions, 2014.*

LIST OF SUBSCRIBERS

This book has been made possible through the generosity of the following subscribers

Alix Adams	2004–09	Christopher Cappuccini	1989–94	Clare Dougherty	1988–98
Caroline Adams	2000–05	Sarah J. Carlstroem	2009–14	James Dougherty	1983–93
Ana de Luis Alas	2002– (Staff)	Nick Carlton	1963–70	Philip Dougherty	1985–95
Jonathan Amos	1967–71	David Carr	1967–74	Air Vice-Marshal Simon	
Peter Amsden	1961–8	Adam Carruthers	1990–5	Dougherty	1960–7
Jules Arthur	1979–84	David E. Carter	1953–6	Dring Family	
		Oliver Catford	2012–		
George Peter Brett Bailey	1934–8	James Chapman	1975–84	Sebastian Ebert-Thompson	2011–
Robert Brett Bailey	1959–65	William Chapman	2013–	John W. Edwards	1945–55
Alexander Baines	2010–	John Chater	1992–7	John Ellerby	1967–75
Andrew Baker	1957–66	Cameron Clark	2010–	Bryan Ellis	1950–5
Samuel Baker	2012–	Catherine Elisabeth Clausen		Gordon Ellis	1976–84
David Ballard	1955–62	(née Sholl)		Max Ellis	2010–
Paul Banham	1949–51	Annabel Cody (née Cole)	1988–90	Oscar Ellis	2010–
Tim Bettesworth	1964–7	Bronte Colman	2013–	Brett Emblin	1986–92
Amanda Birch	2010–	Vincent Lagos Colombel	2012–	Chris Essex	1969–75
Fiona Birch	2007–12	Alexander Conway	2012–	Michael J.R. Evans	1945–8
David Bonner	1962–6	Martin Coomber	1959–64		
Antony Boundy	1964–8	George Coulson	2002–	Andrew W. Fane	
Benedict Bournes	2008–	Stuart B. Coulthart	1980–9	**Chairman of Governors**	
William Bournes	2008–13	Anthony H. Cowan FRAeS	1959–64	Tiffany Ferguson	2014–
Phil Bower	1970–4	Louisa Crabtree	2013–	Hugo Field	2011–
Stephen Brice	1981–8	Molly Crabtree	2014–	Harvey Finbow	2012–
Bernard Bridges	1945–54	Pippa Crabtree	2013–	Jeremy Ford	1992–7
John F. Bridges	1957–66	Angus Cundey	1950–4	Jonathan Ford	1958–62
L. David Brook	1936–40			Izaak Frost	2012–14
Sam Brooks	1995–2000	K.H. Dann	1948–50		
Professor Allan Brown	1957–62	Charles Davidson	1999–2004	Gerald A. Garnett	1950–4
Geoffrey Brown	1961–6	Nathan Davidson	1996–2001	Michael A. Geddes	1951–5
George Robin Bensted Brown	1960–4	Hannah Dawson	2011–	Eleanor Gemmill	2007–
Thomas Lindsey Brown	2007–12	Mina Dawson	2013–	Oliver Gemmill	1997–2002
Ian Bryce	1961–5	Alexander Robert Day	2013–	Rebecca Gemmill	1995–2000
Bill Bulstrode	1962–9	Andrew Denham	2011–14	Arthur Getting	2013–
Petronella Burnett-Brown		Robert Denham	2011–14	William Getting	2008–13
Nigel Burnip	1958–65	Richard and Rebecca		Peter Golding	1945–9
Jim Butchart	1951–60	Dening-Smitherman	1987–92	Kevin Gooding	1974–9
Martyn Buttenshaw	1990–5	Hamish Denley	2013–	D.R. Gorham	1958–65
Gordon Campbell		J. Donsworth	1973–95 (Staff)	Tim Gough	1980–5

Laurence Griggs	2005–10	Matthew Ives	1977–82	A.J. Martin	1947–55
Lizzie Griggs	2007–12	Tabitha Ives	2009–12	C.J. Martin	1948–56
Maria T. Grulich				David Mason	1955–9
		Christopher Jary		Brian Mayhew	1946–52
Chris Hall	1964–9	Edward Jary	2013–	Kenneth Mayhew	1929–34
Keith Handley	1947–53	Guy Jenkinson	1971–6	Norman Mayhew	1948–56
Edward Hanlon	1989–94	Peter Johnson	1987–95	Robert John Mayhew	1953–60
Ian Hardaker-Jones	1964–9	Simon Johnson	1987–97	Antony McCord	1976–82
Sophie Hart	2013–	Viacheslav and Christina		Bill McEwen	1970–80
Anthony Hawes	1961–6	Johnston-Myachin	2001–06	Dr Michael A. McGuire	1954–63
John Hayward	1955–8			James Mehta	1967–75
Mark Hedley	1956–65	Hugh and Margaret		Peter Mehta	1961–7
Bruce Henderson	1946–50	Kennon	1973–96 (Staff)	Peter Metcalf	1955–60
Gerald Hendrie	1949–52	John Kersley	1984–7	Colin Micklewright	1954–8
Adam Hendy	1984–9	Adam Key	1986–91	James Miller 1989–94 (Headmaster)	
Emily Higgins	2007–12	Antonia Key	1989–94	Tim Mitchell	1967–77
Katherine Hitchcock	2007–12	Stephan Kummer	1980–1	Andrew Morgan	1986–91
Will Hitchcock	2009–14			Anna Morris (née Holloway)	1989–92
Edmond Ho	1990–5	Nicholas Latter	2011–	Ben Mountford	2011–
Jack Hobbs	2007–	Mattias Lemmens	1996–2000	Christian Muegge	1998–2000
Sophie Hobson	2007–09	Jack Lewis	2012–		
David Hodge	1944–9	Joe Lewis	2012–	Ann Nesling	1984–
J.C. Hodges	1981–90	Robert G. Lintott	1996–2005	(Housemistress and Teacher)	
M.G. Hodges	1952–61	Jason Living	1980–4	Jon Newbery	1979–84
Alexandra Holland	2002–	Bernard van Loon	2013–14	David W.J. Newson	1954–63
Dr R.J. and Mrs S.A. Hoole		David N. Lowe	1966–8	Dr Ruth Noble	2006–
	1996– (Staff)	Derek Lyne	1955–8	(Housemistress Pembroke House)	
Rosalind Houchin	1988–93			Sammy Noori	2005–09
Peter Howard-Dobson	1965–9	Harry Maberly	2010–12	Sam Norton	1982–92
James Howard-Higgins	1985–90	Jasper Maberly	2009–13	Tom Norton	1986–96
Laura Hülsberg	2013–14	James and Veronica Maberly			
Terry Hurlock	1968–73	Joanna Maberly	2012–	Connor O'Leary	2006–11
		Caroline Mallett	1993– (Staff)	Daniel O'Leary	2004–09
David Ibeson	1978–84	Danielle Maran	2000–11	Rebecca O'Leary	2009–14
John Ineson	1943–50	Sarah Maran	2000–	Graham Osborne	1946–52
George Ives	2011–	Michael Marjoram	1942–50	Matt Osborne	1985–90
John Ives	1942–50	Milo Marsh	2014–	Richard Overend	1951–7
Lizzie Ives	1979–84	Professor Neville Marsh	1953–61		

Ian C. Pearson	1970–3	Charles Shallow	2004–09	J.G. Thurlow	1948–56
Nicholas Penny	1957–62	Chris and Rebecca Shaw	1949–56	Dr Malvern Tipping	1973–8
Revd Canon David Pitcher	1944–52	W.F.G. Shaw	1966–72	Bryan Tomalin	1965–8
Robin J.P.D. Podd	1943–55	C.F. Simpson	1965–72	R.L. Trevethick	1945–53
Norman H. Porter	1951–7	Peter Ratcliffe Simpson	1932–40		
M. Powlesland	1940–5	Michael Ratcliffe Simpson	1932–40	Ian S. Vicary	1958–62
Marian Prebble		Charles Peter Smallpeice	1949–56		
1970–2001 (Heads' PA)		Robin Smallwood	1982–6	Toby Waddilove	2012–
Andrew Prewett	1966–73	Brian A. Smith	1954–7	Miles Wade	1971–6
Prince Family		(President SOF 2007–09)		John A. Waugh	1941–8
Luke Pritchard-Barrett	2012–14	Clive Smith	1954–8	Alexandra Emilia Wehmeyer	2013–14
Alfred Pryce	1944–7	Richard Smith	1956–60	Robert Welch	1957–64
		Dr Ann Novello Smyth		Mathew Wells	1995–2001
Dr John Rankin	1947–56	(née Hogarth)	1987–8	Sue Wenn	1999–2013 (Staff)
Dr Jörg Raspe		Chris Sneath	1951–6	Edward Wharton	1980–5
John W. Reader	1978–88	Bertie Southworth	2006–	Bob Williams	1970–2001 (Staff)
Caroline Reid	2004–09	John Southworth	2006–13	Keith Williams	1963–7
Susannah Reid	2009–14	Ron Spencer	1959–64	Robin Williams	1981–91 (Staff)
Peter Risk	1957–60	Tim Spinks	1983–90	Daniel Williman	2010–12
Nigel Robinson	1964–74	Justin Spurrell	1979–82	P.R. Williman	1951–7
Richard Rowe	1965–74	Ivan Stedman	1950–5	Daniel R. Wilson	1987–92
Hannah Rowell	2010–	Barry Stent	1982–7	J.B. Wilson	1957–60
Lucy Rowell	2011–	Revd Canon Simon Stokes	1975–80	J.J. Wilson	1961–5
Col Peter Rowland		Tim Stone	1987–92	P.C. Wilson	1958–62
(late R Signals)	1948–52	Hania Stuart-Thompson		R.J. Wilson	1953–6
J.G. Ruddock-Broyd	1946–52	David R. Summers OAM	1948–56	Chris Woodruff and Kate	
		Jolyon Summers	2013–	Woodruff (née Norton)	1981–91
Ben Sadler	1970–3	Edward Surguy	1977–87	Andrew G. Wright	1948–57
R.J. Sayer	1956–61	Lauren Sutton	2000–05	Hamilton Wright	2013–
S.T. Sayer	1958–63			Susie Wright	2013–
Dr David Seaton	1959–66	H. Patrick Taylor	1943–6	William Wright	2011–

Index

Acknowledgements & Picture Credits

Acknowledgements

Research assistance

Simon Jowitt
Tony Martin
Marcus Marvell
Camilla McCausland
David Pitcher
Norman Porter
Alice Denny Robinson

Secretarial support

Karen Alcock
Helen Alcoe
Suzie Angove
Lynne Sargeant

Picture Credits

Photographs and images contributed by

John Bridges
David Brook
Martin Brown
Bill Bulstrode
Simon Cullum
Andrew Currie
Charlotte Gower
Richard Higgins
Tom Huggins
Jon Hutchings
Chris Keeble
Tony Martin
Prof. Neville Marsh
Dr. M.A. McGuire
David Medler
Peter Metcalf
David Pitcher
Norman Porter
James Ruddock-Broyd
H.J. Smith
Simon Stacpoole
Philip Summers
Max Taylor

Channel 4
The East Anglian Daily Times
Franklin Ellis Architects
RFU Archive
The Long Shop Museum, Leiston
Zhongrong Group

Framlingham School Song.

Written by
G. J. WILLANS, B.A. (O.F.)

Composed by
R. S. BARNICOTT, Mus. B.